C000310916

THE WAY OF THE
PRACTICAL MYSTIC

Other titles by Henry Thomas Hamblin,
currently published by The Hamblin Vision

THE MESSAGE OF A FLOWER

THE LITTLE BOOK OF RIGHT THINKING

SIMPLE TALKS ON SCIENCE OF THOUGHT

HIS WISDOM GUIDING

THE HAMBLIN BOOK OF ÐAILY READINGS

WITHIN YOU IS THE POWER

THE POWER OF THOUGHT

MY SEARCH FOR TRUTH (AUTOBIOGRAPHY)

THE STORY OF MY LIFE (AUTOBIOGRAPHY)

LIFE WITHOUT STRAIN

DIVINE ADJUSTMENT

THE OPEN DOOR

THE LORD'S PRAYER (INTERPRETATION)

DAILY MEDITATIONS

GOD'S SUSTAINING GRACE

THE ANTIDOTE FOR WORRY

GOD OUR CENTRE AND SOURCE

THE LIFE OF THE SPIRIT

HENRY THOMAS HAMBLIN

THE WAY OF THE
PRACTICAL
MYSTIC

The Hamblin
Spiritual Course

POLAIR PUBLISHING · LONDON

First published in book form, September 2004
by Polair Publishing, P O Box 34886, London W8 6YR
www.polairpublishing.co.uk

British Library Cataloguing-in-Publication Data
A catalogue record for this book is available from the British
Library

ISBN 0-9545389-5-1

Set in 11 on 13.5 pt Baskerville
and printed and bound in Great Britain
by Cambridge University Press

CONTENTS

FOREWORD

In a newspaper article published in the summer of 2004, Henry Thomas Hamblin ('HTH'), the Sussex mystic and thinker, appears with the following words issuing from his lips: 'Who would think I'd still inspire decades from now?'. Who indeed would have realized, least of all Hamblin himself, that his ideas would have a lasting influence from their prodigious outflowing in the 1920s right down to the twenty-first century. The reason for their continuing influence and wide appeal is not difficult to understand. It lies in the fact that they embody eternal truths expressed with rare simplicity and directness.

The essence of Hamblin's ideas lay in his certitude that if we change our thoughts to coincide with the Ideas in the Divine Mind, then the transformation of the inner life will flow out into the outer life and make it infinitely happier and more fruitful in every way.

Early in the twentieth century, Hamblin's ideas were considered revolutionary, at the cutting edge of the so-called 'new thought' movement, but in reality those ideas are timeless, beyond all conceptions of 'old' and 'new'. When asked where his knowledge came from, HTH said he depended upon the Bible and *Pilgrim's Progress*, but he also said: 'It is true that I know some things which I have never learned from books or people, but how I learned them I do not know. I simply know them, and always have known them. Increase of knowledge seems to be due to a recalling to memory of things which I have known eternally—at least, that is how it seems to me.'*

* Editor's note to a letter dated August 16, 1934.

In the minds of many, Hamblin is associated with 'positive thinking'. While it is true that this kind of thinking was part of his work, to reduce it to no more than that would be to do it a gross injustice. Hamblin was essentially a spiritual warrior and practical mystic. His work was essentially a message of love, not as a sentimental feeling but as the living of an intensely practical and useful life. We have only to look at his life to realize that he achieved this on several levels. He was a thoughtful husband and father of three children; despite a poor education, he educated himself and became a successful ophthalmic optician with a thriving business in the West End of London. However, after escalating conflict between that part of him which was businessman and the part which was mystic and lover of the countryside, he retired from his business life and moved to Bosham in West Sussex, where he joined the Army and later the Royal Flying Corps. After the death of his son, Dick, at the age of 10, in 1918, Hamblin entered almost a second incarnation as prolific thinker and writer. He wrote a number of books and articles and in October 1921 he launched a magazine, 'The Science of Thought Review', which continues, to this day, as 'New Vision'. Finally, we come to the subject of the present book, the spiritual Course he wrote which helped thousands all over the world, and we hope will help to illuminate the Way for thousands more.

The Story behind this book and the Hamblin Spiritual Course

Although today he is much better known by the books he wrote, many of them intentionally brief and pocket-sized, Hamblin tended to see a comprehensive Course as the best way to help his readers unfold their inner powers:

'It is an interesting fact that most people make more progress through the medium of a course of lessons than through a lot of undisciplined reading. Many seekers of Truth read book after book, but make little or no progress. They are like a person who eats enormously of a great variety of foodstuffs, in the hope that he will derive the right kind of nourishment, but who only succeeds in producing a bad attack of indigestion. The same person, if supplied with a small meal of properly selected foods, would be able to digest what he ate, and thus be nourished and strengthened.'*

So, prompted by the perfect World of Reality which he so clearly envisioned, it was in the summer of 1920 that Hamblin launched a spiritual Course under the umbrella of The Science of Thought Institute. He was inspired by a desire to present to the spiritual seeker one idea of Truth at a time rather than the desultory reading of numerous books. Hamblin was keen to unite the heart with the head and the will, and therefore his aim was to move away from what he termed 'head knowledge alone' to putting that knowledge into practice. It was then, he said, that 'we learn in quite a different way. In an interior way we really *know*.'

As we have already noted, HTH, as we will hereafter call him, was a practical mystic. After the Course was produced, he decided that although it was eminently practical, helping people to become happier and healthier, it simply wasn't 'spiritual enough'. He also decided that it was 'too advanced for many people'. With the urge to scrap the Course and start again came the act, and before too many days had passed the Course was recalled, committed to Mother Earth and burned in the garden. The fire was said to have burned for days. From a worldly point of view, this was indeed folly, but Hamblin was a self-confessed 'whole-hogger' who did nothing by half measures. After a good deal of time had passed, from the ashes of that fire arose a new phoenix, a Course of twenty-six lessons. Each lesson in the Course was accompanied by an inspiring letter, acting as further guidance for the seeker. In the years that followed many students availed themselves of the precious wisdom of the Course and their lives were enriched by it.

* The words are from HTH's pamphlet, *Some Thoughts on Thought*.

Launching of the Course in the Twenty-First Century

In the years that have passed since HT Hamblin's death, the original Course and accompanying letters have been stowed in boxes at Bosham House. This is where they have remained until now. Probably the most precious asset of the Trust, what to do with them has been the subject of a great deal of discussion and quiet reflection. One thing became very clear to all concerned, the Course was no good sitting in boxes! In this Age of Aquarius it seems timely that the eternal truths contained in the Course be re-released in their pristine state, yet carefully scrutinized to reflect the needs of the present age. HTH's grandson, John Delafield, always aware of this tremendous Work, and his mother, Joan Ackroyd (Hamblin's daughter), kindly gave their permission for the Course to be re-released. The question was: in what form should it be released? It was Dr Mark Sleep who then had the vision of a book being compiled and published comprising all the lessons of the Course. It was subsequently decided that the helpful letters accompanying the Course should also be included. In this way, and for the first time, the public would have access to the teachings of a truly great soul. From there, the book has received its final editing from Colum Hayward.

If you are seeking to enter into a closer, more loving relationship with the Divine, this book is undoubtedly for you. It is pre-eminently a Coursebook for all those who aspire to be practical mystics.

All royalties from the book are kindly being donated by John and Joan to The Hamblin Trust.

We send it out into the world in love and gratitude.

ELIZABETH MEDLER

PUBLISHER'S NOTE

ALL WE KNOW externally about the Spiritual Course that HTH finally devised, and which is reproduced in this book, is that it 'took a very long time to write'. However, we do know that the Course it replaced, which Hamblin destroyed, dates from 1920. Nor is it entirely clear how often subscribers received their lessons, but as there are twenty-six of them, it seems likely that they were sent out either weekly or fortnightly. (Actually, there are twenty-seven, but Lesson XVIIa seems to have been intended as an 'extra' and the originals were, as here, numbered to XXVI.) The package was quite a substantial one each time, HTH obviously being most keen to guide his reader as far as possible in the use of the material. First in importance, but last in order, was the lesson itself. What greeted the subscriber first was a letter, often of about the same length as the lesson itself, apparently written after it. To this was appended, for the bulk of the course, notes of instruction in HTH's form of meditation. As if the long letter were inadequate introduction to the lesson, there was (from the second lesson onwards) a short letter, too, which formed a cover page to the lesson itself. Lastly, there were other regular contributions, which extend over periods of the course: a set of thoughts on divine supply at one stage and a set of notes on deeper spiritual experience at a later one, for instance. This arrangement has been preserved in this volume, the only alteration being that each opening letter now bears the new chapter title, 'Week One', etc.

The present, twenty-first century, edition of the Course was seen through labour and birth by one of Hamblin's sometime Trustees, Dr Mark C. W. Sleep. Mark's vision effectively got the whole project off the ground and great thanks are due to him. He arranged the material into thirty-two new lessons, drawing on his own experience and also upon material by HTH's close friend, the famous writer on 'the Infinite Way', Joel S. Goldsmith. Ultimately, we have chosen to go back to Hamblin's original course without any material by others, but including virtually all of the ancillary material, which the earlier arrangement did not. In this edition, therefore, virtually all of the lessons appear intact. The letters which accompanied them (indeed all the ancillary material) were more prone to be topical and to contain thoughts and ideas which have less contemporary resonance today. Therefore, where cuts have been made (and they are not substantial), in over ninety per cent of cases they have come from the letters and accompanying notes. One or two deleted passages were for teachers. Omitted text has sometimes been summarised in italics.

The use of 'Week One', 'Week Two' and so on is not part of HTH's own titling. Some sort of chapter system was required to bind together the parts of each lesson, and in view of the fact there were twenty-six, some allusion to weeks seemed sensible. Readers should not for one moment feel that they have just one week to devote to each lesson, but should take as long over each as they like. The term 'week' is a token only.

Editing has been kept to a minimum, but has been infrequently necessary. Punctuation has been modernized, the occasional archaism has been updated, and a very few alterations have been made to improve the flow. We should like to have made the text non-gender-specific, but this was not the norm in HTH's time, and to do so would have meant substantial alteration. We hope that every reader will take HTH's 'he' and 'man' in the inclusive sense we are sure he intended (see p. 292 for confirmation of this); a few such expressions have been changed. It was also HTH's habit to capitalize anything remotely connected with the Godhead. This is part of his style, but it was also a way of distinguishing ideal qualities from human attributes. Most significantly among these, 'Spirit' normally implies the Di-

vine Spirit. Lastly, HTH was seriously fond of backing up his writing with biblical quotations. In his day, most were probably familiar
to his readers. Today, it seems better to include references to them
where they can be identified; but so as not to break the text up we
have created a simple list by page, at the back of the book.

HTH carefully signed off each letter, typically with a phrase
such as 'Your fellow-sharer in the Infinite Love'. Where these
salutations become repetitious, we have reduced them, but where
they are individual, they are irresisitible.

Terms used in the book

In view of the title we have given the book (the original Course
bore no other identifying title), it may be surprising for the reader
to encounter a slight hostility on HTH's part to the word 'mystical'. This is because he was the sworn enemy of a sloppy passivity, which he felt took the individual nowhere. With the term
'Practical' attached to it, 'Mysticism' seems a perfectly fair description of what HTH offers, although 'Positive' might be another word to convey what is special about HTH's mysticism.
Certainly, it is true to say that the whole Course is a prolonged
meditation on the practice of the mystical path.

This takes us to a second word to consider, 'meditation'. There
is much in the Course about meditation, but HTH's technique
is not one of emptying the mind or concentrating on the breath
according to the Eastern practice. The book itself explains what
HTH means by meditation (in particular, see the special notes
on meditation in Week Four); it is a deep focusing on a particular
subject, or upon an idea of God.

HTH was the originator of what he called 'Science of
Thought' teaching. Where this term occurs, his whole pattern
of teaching is implied. More terms which are part of HTH's
'method' are dwelt with in the text: denials and affirmations,
and what he describes as 'treatments' (processes or intercessions).

His use of the terms 'subconscious' and 'superconscious' is

distinctly not that of the modern psychologist, and the second
term is particularly well clarified by a remark in Letter XXIV,
'We possess a higher or spiritual mind; and we also possess a
higher or spiritual consciousness'. Even his subconscious is not
the traditional subconscious, but rather a 'background' mind,
which can work out problems for us while we sleep, be used to
develop right habits, and so on. However intuitive, it is still a
lower or 'animal' mind, as Letter VI and Lesson VI indicate.

Another special term used by HTH which may be known to
students of the esoteric but not to more mainstream readers, is 'the
Cosmic Christ'. This is explained at some length on page 23.

HTH has a concept of 'sin' which occasionally embraces conventional sin, but which is more regularly seen as 'acting out of
harmony with Divine Law' in any way, even holding negative
attitudes or refusing to allow growth to come from a situation.
Letter VII is the best place to acquire a better understanding of
HTH's concept.

An Encouragement to Would-be Users

HTH is a serious teacher, and this book demands constant application. At times our teacher seems to demand a Christianity
few would claim to aim at today. What he offers is, ultimately,
totally worthwhile, because the experience in which it is rooted
is so genuine. HTH periodically lets slip how completely he writes
out of the fires of personal experience, not out of mere cerebra-
tion. For instance, Lesson XVI indicates how the threefold path
of realization he there offers was discovered through blood and
tears. HTH's personal commitment comes through progressively;
by the end, to use a Sufi term, it is clear he is a 'God-intoxicated
Man'. At the conclusion, the student, along with HTH, 'descends
from the mountaintop from which he has viewed the promised
land and returns to live his new life amongst the busy haunts of
men'. This is the teaching of the great Bodhisattva Vow in Bud-
dhism.

GENERAL ADVICE
BEFORE STARTING THE COURSE

Hamblin begins his letter of general advice with a greeting which will become familiar as the Course progresses, 'Dear Fellow-Student of Truth', and asks his readers: 'Will you please make a careful note of all that applies to your particular case, and put the rest on the shelf of your mind, so to speak, as later, it may come in useful?' He continues:

IT IS NOT the amount of study that one does that leads to a realization of Truth, and to the Divine Union; indeed, the less study, in an intellectual sense, that is done, the better. Do not look upon this Course as an intellectual study at all, but as a meditation upon Truth, whose object is the awakening of an inward spiritual awareness within the Soul. Truth can never be apprehended by or through the intellect. Truth transcends the intellect, and, when we understand or realize Truth, we know in our very soul that which the greatest intellect can never grasp. As our Lord said, 'These things are hidden from the wise and prudent, and are revealed unto babes'.

Therefore, while taking the Course, do not study the lessons, in the ordinary sense of the word, as you would a textbook of science; for, if you do, you will never enter into Truth. Also do not expect to find in the Course some magic secret, for you will find none. Instead, realize that what is required is that an inward spiritual faculty, lying dormant in your soul, has to be aroused, and when it is awakened, Truth will be apparent in all things, and everything will be made plain. Further, realize that neither study nor the Course can, of itself, arouse this ability of the soul to know God and Truth by direct knowing, but that it is entirely the work of the Spirit of Truth. Of ourselves we can do nothing, it is the Spirit Who doeth all things. It is Spirit Who has led you to this teaching and aroused your interest in our books and pamphlets. Now, therefore, believe and realize, as you read the lessons, doing as nearly as possible what they recommend you to do, and meditating upon the simple truths which they expound, that the Spirit is going to open the eyes of your soul. Of yourself you can do nothing. Therefore pray that the Spirit of Truth may reveal Truth directly to your soul, instead of through your intellect, and *believe* that your prayer is already answered.

Among many words of guidance about what to avoid in following a spiritual path, Hamblin speaks with clarity about the use and abuse of emotion:

Learn to see the difference between true feeling and emotionalism. You will find that these Lessons will purify the emotions and deepen true feeling. This is not repression, but transmutation. Also, avoid ecstasies. I am aware that some of the greatest saints have enjoyed them, but against this, we have to remember we are not yet saints, and that to ordinary people ecstasy and depression are extremes. These Lessons will help you to achieve balance.

Also, avoid longing for the next world and the next life. This leads to a state of utter helplessness, incapacity, inefficiency and deterioration of character.

Also, avoid all impractical mysticism. As we shall see later, interest in practical affairs and work and service is of the utmost importance in spiritual development.

Also, avoid spending too much time in subjective reflection and practices. It is necessary to spend almost the whole of our time in work and service in order to maintain *balance*.

Also, avoid trying to see visions, to see strange things, or hear voices. *Be normal.*

ENTERING THE SILENCE

In this opening letter, Hamblin also defines what he means by 'the Silence' and shows that his teaching is based above all upon an awareness of the indwelling Christ. In the following passage, he shows how his word 'Christ' relates to 'God' and to 'Jesus', and gives some help.

In Science of Thought teaching, entering the Silence is no mystical performance, neither is it the cultivation of a state either of trance or semi-trance. It is the very antithesis of the state of negative passivity. To allow oneself to sink down into a passive, negative state, inhibiting all thought, and waiting for whatever influence may come along, is to be most severely condemned. By sinking down into relaxed passivity, you simply contact lower planes, but by raising yourself up to your highest conception of Light, Good, Love, Wholeness, etc., you make contact with the Christ-Plane, from which all healing and spiritual power proceed.

When we relax in the Silence, we become negative to the world and positive towards God. An alert receptivity is actually highly positive.

Entering the Silence is simply following our Lord's instructions with regard to prayer. Jesus tells us when we pray to retire into our inner chamber, and shut the door of the mind upon everything except God, and then to commune with our Father in secret. We have to shut the door upon the cares and enticements of the world, and the external life, and find the presence of God. We also have to keep the doors shut against all lower influences, and this is done automatically if we *raise* our thoughts and consciousness to our highest conception of God and Perfection, namely Perfect Spiritual Man, our Saviour and Lord.

HTH consistently uses the name 'Jesus' for the man and 'Christ' for the embodiment of God. In Lesson I, he will explain the term 'the Cosmic Christ'.

Christ is God—God manifest. He is the Divine *Logos*, God's Perfect Idea. He is the stem of the Tree from which all that is grows. He is the true Vine, of which all true followers are the branches. We draw our life and nourishment from Him. A branch of the True Vine is *in* the Vine, rooted into and joined with the stem; yet the Vine is in the branch. Its sap and nourishment are the life of the branch. Therefore, we live and move and have our being in Christ, and Christ lives in us and is the hope of our glory. To the regenerated soul, Christ is *all in all.*

Therefore, in this Course, when we speak of God and the Infinite, we speak of Christ, for Christ is God made *understandable* to man. Christ is God made manifest in Love, Perfection, Beauty, and Wholeness. Our Lord also reveals to us in His Purity and Perfection, in His Perfect Divinity and complete and faultless manhood, God's idea concerning us. In Jesus Christ we see *what we have ultimately to be.*

The only One to Whom we can surrender our will is Christ, or the Father through Christ. Our will is given to us so that we may exercise it. In one sense it is our protection. We have to be masters and to resign our wills to no-one but Christ. Take notice that Christ does not appear as an outside entity. Do not surrender your will to anyone but Christ, Who is your highest conception of love, wisdom, purity, perfection, wholeness, harmony, self-sacrifice and all the highest virtues and qualities; and is also the Spirit that raised up Jesus.

If you maintain a wise balance, keeping your spiritual life awake by prayer and contact with your Divine Source, at the same time living a very practical, busy life of service, and also maintaining a very positive attitude towards everything but God and His Christ, you cannot fail to make progress along perfectly safe and sound lines.

Service is a key concept in Hamblin's vision of practical mysticism, a technique he calls 'the Science of Thought'.

The great secret underlying spiritual development is giving and receiving. Not only must the student of the Divine Mysteries learn to commune daily with the Infinite, thus becoming filled with Divine Power, but he or she must express this Power in work, service, and living. There is probably nothing more harmful than to receive spiritual power and not to express it in service to life and the world. It is utterly destructive to the spiritual life and also to the health and nervous system.

All who seek Divine Union and to know the Truth that sets men and women free must express the power they receive in some form of service. Those who retire selfishly into their shell and cease to take an interest in their fellows, thinking that by continual study or research they can find the Truth, are always grievously disappointed.

Science of Thought is a gospel of work and service. First obtain the Power, then express it daily in better work, more loving service and in tasks more perfectly performed. Take an interest in life, then life will take an interest in you. Be practical, not a dreamer. Avoid, at all costs, daydreaming and wishing. Learn to pay attention to exterior affairs. Learn the art of observation.

Let me repeat, *be practical*. It is impossible to be well and happy or to advance in the spiritual life without service and work and practical contact with the external world. We know that the external world is not real or lasting, in an absolute sense, but it is real enough to our present consciousness. This life has been given us for experience, therefore we must get all the experience possible out of life, and be as practical and helpful as we know how to be. Strive, therefore, to become more capable, practical and efficient, in order that you may serve better.

Above all, avoid being self-centred. Lose yourself in service to others. This is no counsel of perfection: it is not only possible, but is the basis of all true progress, success, happiness and health. By loving our neighbours as our own self and by serving others, we make true advancement possible—but not otherwise.

With regard to service, it is useless for us to wait for our true niche in life: we must make a start with the material now at our command. We must be faithful in small things before we can be found worthy of being entrusted with greater and more important service. Many people complain that their lives are not a success; they never can be, simply because they do not serve faithfully in their present position, nor make use of the material that they now possess.

It is always possible to serve. If some people who are now idle would take a small pair of shears and cut the grass on the grave of an unknown and forgotten person, plant some flowers, and say over it a few prayers, they would know the joy of service—and, for once, obey the spiritual law that demands, from each one of us, the giving of the best we have, without hope of reward.

Therefore, perform your daily tasks better than is demanded of you. Give something for which you cannot be paid, and make all your work an offering of love to humankind, life and the world. By so doing, you come into harmony with spiritual law, and inevitably you will be promoted to greater things, in course of time.

Finally, Hamblin offers some crucial words of encouragement and ends his preliminary words with another of his characteristic salutations:

Keep on. Persevere. Do not backslide. Do not allow anything to prevent you from communing daily with the Infinite. If you persevere and make contact daily with your spiritual Source, you will become filled with Divine Power; then if you express this Power in service, in love, in work, in tasks more perfectly performed, in greater ability, effort, striving and efficiency, you will go from strength to strength and from victory to victory. If, on the contrary, you allow lethargy, or the cares and duties of the external life, or its pleasures and excitements, to prevent you from making this daily contact, you cut yourself off from your Divine Supply. Your spiritual life, in consequence, becomes stifled and dead. When once you get out of the habit of communing with the Infinite, it is not easy to make another start. Therefore, never in any circumstances allow anything to prevent your daily communion with the One Source of all Life and Power.

Desiring greatly that you may derive benefit from the lessons,
I am, Yours in the Truth,
For Science of Thought Institute,
HENRY THOMAS HAMBLIN, Founder.

WEEK ONE:
THE SILENCE

Dear Comrade on the Path,

The term 'Cosmic Christ' used in this lesson means Universal Christ. Christ is the Divine Logos, or Word, or Thought, or Idea, the second person of the Triune Godhead of the theologians. Christ is the only-begotten Son, the Divine Archetypal Man, and, being God, is omnipresent. He indwells us and draws us upward to Himself, until we are led to say, like the great apostle Paul, 'Not I, but Christ liveth in me'.* When the time is ripe, the soul of man yields to the influence of the Spirit, its outer

---

*In an Appendix to the main Lesson in Week One, HTH gave a further explanation of his term 'the Cosmic Christ', there defining it as:

'The Divine Logos, or Word. There is unmanifest Deity—Father (the transcendent side, or aspect, of God, which is ever beyond us). There is the manifest Word or Idea, the only-begotten Son of the Father. This is the Divine Logos—the universal perfect expression of God, or perfect God in creative expression (this is the understanding side, or aspect, of God: it is also the love aspect). Jesus Christ is a special manifestation of the Divine Logos. He is the Light of the World Who came to dwell with men and women, 'but His own received Him not'. Christ dwells in us by His Spirit. Christ is Omnipresent Spirit, and we are in Him and He is in us, and because Christ is with the Father, so also are we, because we are in Christ and Christ is in us.

'The Holy Spirit proceeds from the Father and the Son, and is another aspect of Deity. The Holy Spirit may be likened to the Divine breath, quickening in us eternal life; or the Divine Presence which is always with us. We can, therefore, speak of God, of Christ (of the Logos), of the Father, of Spirit. They all refer to various aspects of the One God, all equally powerful, perfect and wonderful.'

husks are melted, and, after sincere repentance and much humbling of heart, the life of the Spirit displaces the life of the flesh. This change is mystically described as the second birth, or the birth of the Christ within the soul. After this change, man is a new creature, desiring the things of the Spirit, rather than those of the flesh. We use the word Cosmic, or Universal, because Christ, or the Divine Word or Logos, is not confined only to the life and person of Jesus. This was His manifestation on this planet, but, we believe, the whole universe is Christ's. He is the Lord of all.

Entering the Silence is really finding the Christ within. It is also entering, in a very special sense, the Divine Presence. By doing this continually we gradually become changed, until it is always 'Not I but Christ', and 'Christ is All and in All', in very truth.

With regard to posture when entering the Silence, experience has taught me that some students, but only some, can enter the Silence better and more effectually by reclining comfortably. The great thing is to be very *still*, and then to *know*. Others get better results by sitting up perfectly straight. A good thing to do is, every day, to practise sitting very still, or reclining, without moving a muscle, yet with all muscles and nerves relaxed. When this is being done the breathing should not be restricted, but allowed to be slow and deep. I do not, however, advocate special breathing with a view to spiritual development. It has certain dangers and is unnecessary.

The words suggested in Lesson I as a centre upon which the thoughts should focus may suit some students, but not all. Such should use a different thought—one that suits them, and which calls up a pleasurable emotion. A 'joy' or 'happiness' thought may suit them better. Also some students, when young, may have had the Bible forced on them. Some may even have had to learn passages in the Bible as a punishment! To such, certain Biblical texts may call up entirely the wrong kind of emotion, bringing to the mind a train of undesirable thoughts—which, of course, is the very thing we desire to avoid. Such should make up a sentence of their own, couched in a different phraseology, so as to avoid awakening the old thoughts, emotions and antagonisms, or choose a text that suggests restfulness to their mind.

To many (and I must include myself in this category, for further light and revelation do but reveal to me greater heights, depths and possibilities in what is termed 'Our Lord's Prayer'), there is no better introduction to the Silence than the words 'Our Father which art in Heaven'. Jesus tells us to avoid repeating set prayers and, instead, to enter the closet, or Silence: to shut the door of the senses upon the external life, and to commune with 'Our Father' in secret. If we do this, our Lord tells us, our Father, Who seeth and heareth in the secret place, or Silence (and Who alone can be heard or 'contacted' in the Silence) will recompense us.

To start entering the Silence with these words ('Our Father which art in Heaven') on our lips and in our hearts is to bring us into such an attitude of mind and soul as will ensure an instant contact with Heaven itself. I say Heaven advisedly, for that with which we make contact is not the spirit world of the Spiritualist, for this is merely Sheol, the place of departed spirits, or the Astral Plane, as Theosophists term it. When we retire from the senses and commune with 'Our Father', we enter the Silence, or Heaven, the Presence of God. It is not 'Our Father which art in Sheol, or the Astral Plane', with whom we are taught to commune in secret, but 'Our Father which art in Heaven'. As soon as we are in communion with 'Our Father' we are in heavenly places. It is only by the Christ in us that we can do this. Without Him we can do nothing. He is the Way, the Truth and the Life: we all come to the Father through Him. One in whom the Christ has not yet been born cannot enter the presence of God. One, however, who has been spiritually awakened, born again of the Spirit and in whom the Christ dwells, is able, through the indwelling One, to enter the secret place and commune with 'Our Father which art in Heaven'. Christ, too, is in us and also in heavenly places. He is with the Father and in us, simultaneously, and is the connecting link between God and man.

This, to me, explains the text about Christ being at the right hand of God the Father, interceding on our behalf. Christ in us, born in us from above: Christ at the right hand of God the Father. Christ is omnipresent Spirit. Here we have the elements of possible unity. Later on there is the union of the Redeemer and the redeemed. Then we become one in consciousness with the Divine Archetypal Man, and see everything through His eyes and with His understanding. Then we see things as they are and not as they falsely appear.

To contemplate the Cosmos through the Divine Archetype is to see it in its everlasting perfection and beauty.

'Contemplate through Me (the archetype)', said the Pymander, 'the Cosmos now subject to thy vision; regard carefully its beauty, a Body in pure perfection, though one than which there is none more ancient, in the prime of life, and ever young, nay, rather in ever fuller and yet fuller prime'. (*The Divine Pymander of Hermes Trismegistus*)

From the foregoing, it will be seen that 'entering the Silence' is not an occult performance but is simply prayer as taught by our Lord Jesus Christ.

HTH next touches on the typical mystical distinction between things that are outside of ourselves and what is inward. He begins with an answer in parable form from the New Testament.

In one sense, external things are of but little importance. Everything relating to the Kingdom is a paradox, and this is no exception. While it is true that external things may have but little importance, it is equally true that they have some. Inversely, while it is true that eternal things are of sole importance, it is yet true that external things are of importance also. External things are of very great importance, in one sense, and in their proper place. Behind every material thing is a spiritual meaning, and every material experience is a test or training by which we are prepared for the Kingdom of Heaven; that is, to live in it permanently. According to the way we live 'here' and develop our 'talents', so shall we live 'there'. Not on the Astral Plane, or in Sheol, but in Heaven, which is the permanent abode of Sons of God—i.e., regenerated mortals, those raised from corruption into incorruption by the new birth of the Spirit, and built up in faith and character by the Spirit of Truth into the full stature of Christ.

Therefore, external things have their value, and a very high value it is, when looked at from the right point of view. But when we approach the Divine Presence and deal with the Eternal Verities, everything else shrinks into insignificance. Then the things which seem so alarmingly important to the natural man or woman-worldly ambitions, social position, material success, other people's opinion, and so on—are found to be of no importance at all.

Here HTH brings in a tool which he will describe further in coming lessons—the use of affirmations and also what he refers to as 'denials'. He at once gives us an example of the latter.

One method which some use of entering the Silence is to make use of denials and affirmations until the outer voices are hushed, and the Divine Presence only is realized. This may be helpful to beginners, and can be done in this way: *'No child of God is hindered by external things. Each child of God, because of his spiritual nature, has no difficulty in keeping his attention directed to spiritual things.'*

The above impersonal wording is suggested because it is possible with some that even affirming themselves to be children of God may suggest a sense of separateness. To such, the words 'because I am one with Thee' may be more helpful than the words 'because I am a child of God'. We can never be separated, in actuality, from our Divine Source, although, in consciousness, we may be separated by sin, ignorance, and wrong beliefs. Actually, however, we are always in a state of oneness. Unity is the Divine Reality. Separation is merely a temporary experience, in consciousness only.

Do not, on any account, allow yourself to go to sleep any night without sending your love and blessing to all humankind and to all Nature as well. Let your benediction rest upon all. This is of great importance.

Lesson I is exceedingly important. Its teaching has to be followed during the whole of the Course and the other lessons tacked on to it, so to speak. Let no student think that all that he or she has to do is to follow it for a week or a fortnight, and then to let it alone. Let the student not think either that it can be mastered in a week, or a fortnight, or even a year. Even the most advanced teacher is always learning to enter the Silence more perfectly, and to practise more thoroughly the Presence of God.

No-one who is afraid to do so should attempt to enter the Silence. It should be an act of love, like a child seeking its mother's arms. No-one should try to enter the Silence who has not forgiven all who have wronged him, or whom he or she dislikes. No-one should try to enter the Silence who does not believe strongly in the Omnipresence of Good and that Good is vastly more powerful than evil.

We all have to learn, at some time or other, to be still and to rest in the Truth: to give up all effort and striving, even praying, or 'treating', and just to let God's Perfect Order manifest itself. Of ourselves we can do nothing. We have simply to allow the Spirit to do all things for us. We have simply to stand on one side, so to speak, and let the inherent Divine Perfection appear. After a certain stage, we can make no progress if we strive and make effort. We have to learn to let go—to let God do the work, in His own way, instead of trying to do everything ourselves. Yet all the time outward activities continue, and, in our daily work, we become more speedy, alert, practical and efficient.

The stage that we have to reach is a continual sense of oneness with God. When we realize our oneness with the Divine Spirit—with the *One*—effort and strain become things of the past. *Oneness, Wholeness, Completeness* make effort and striving unnecessary. We are able to accomplish more, without effort or fatigue, for we allow the Divine Order to manifest in our life, instead of the disorder of human effort.

Truth declares that God is the only Creator, or the Supreme Being Who is the Source of All; and that all His creations are perfect. At once, mortal mind enquires, 'How then the imperfection that I see about me: imperfections in nature, in man, in humanity'! This can be explained in many ways, but none of them is either complete or satisfactory. This proves that the things of the Spirit can only be spiritually discerned, and that the great problems of life cannot be intellectually solved. It is possible, however, to be spiritually illumined and to know, deep down in the soul, the glorious truth that all is well and that not one thing in all God's Universe has gone awry.

Until this stage of illumination is reached, however, it is helpful to remember that by close metaphysical reasoning we are brought to the logical conclusion that not only is there no imperfection in reality, but that imperfection does not even exist, in itself. There is only one Fountain of Life, which is perfect and pure. This Life is not only perfect and pure, but is also infinite. Therefore, there can be no other. God is One, Whole, Complete, Infinite—there can be nothing else.

The more deeply we think, the clearer it becomes that we can be sure of nothing external to ourselves. That is to say, the world as we know it is found not to be what it seems, and what it really is we know not. We can, however, be sure of one thing, and that is consciousness. We possess consciousness, and upon this the impressions which constitute life impinge. It is because our present consciousness is limited, and because we are not seeing with the eyes of Christ, that we see evil and imperfection. So long as we are tied down to our ordinary consciousness we are apparently surrounded by evil and imperfection; but when we experience a flash of extended or expanded consciousness we realize, in a way such as cannot be described or even spoken of, but which each student can experience for himself, or herself, that there is nothing wrong with the universe in reality, but that all is well—gloriously, indescribably, divinely well.

Therefore keep this thought ever in your mind: *All is well, All is perfect,* beyond the fog of mortal misimagining. Constantly raise your thoughts above 'the fog', and make contact with the Divine Reality.

The Universe of Perfection is God's idea—is what He thinks it is. The universe of imperfection is what humanity mis-thinks, or mis-imagines it to be. By thinking in harmony with God, by endeavouring to see things as He sees them, and by bringing our erring imagination into captivity to the All-Wise Imagination, we do our part towards realizing the Truth. Of ourselves, however, we can do nothing. We have to do our little part, but it is the Spirit of Truth Who alone can bring us into complete realization of Truth.

One other Point, and I really am finished. Let all your approach to God be one of praise and thanksgiving. Gratitude, love, adoration, reverence, deep gratitude, devotion: these are the open sesame to the great Heart of God. God's Heart does not change but the suppliant becomes fit to enter, by reason of his praise, love and thanksgiving.

Not only should we Praise God continually for the many blessings in our lives that are manifest, but also those which we do not appear to possess, but which we know are ours in reality (or in Spirit). In Spirit we possess all things: therefore, let us praise God for them continually. Also let us praise God for all our circumstances and experiences, no matter how unpleasant they may be. They are the very best possible for us at the time, and our lives could not be really successful without them. Let us, therefore, thank God, with a really grateful heart, for all our unpleasant and painful circumstances. By so doing we learn to think and act in such a way as to bring into manifestation a more harmonious environment.

Let the words: *'I thank Thee and praise Thee, Father'* be continually on your lips.

And now, beloved, may 'the peace of God, which passeth all understanding, keep your hearts and minds through Christ Jesus'.

Your fellow-sharer in the Infinite Love,

HENRY THOMAS HAMBLIN

THOUGHTS ON DIVINE SUPPLY

The object of these 'thoughts' is to help the student to develop 'the abundance consciousness'. One who attains to this consciousness is raised above poverty, lack and financial worry; also he or she is delivered from the power of competition and the love of money. It cuts at the very root of acquisitiveness, love of possessions, and all the evils which greed and covetousness produce in so many lives. To find the imperishable riches of the Infinite Mind is to be delivered from all the fears, longings, disappointments and enticements which make a hideous nightmare of the lives of those who are yet in bondage, either to poverty or the love of money and possessions.

Thought 1
Poverty, lack, misery are all created by the human mind or mortal creative imaginative power. They are not things outside ourselves, of which we are the victims. The first step towards freedom is to realize and acknowledge that the cause of our troubles is within ourselves.

There is only one life, and this is the life of God manifesting in each one of us. The life-force which manifests in the form of health, abundance, happiness, and joy, is the same life-force which manifests in the form of disease, sickness, poverty, misery, and wretchedness. The reason why one person may manifest all that is good, and another one all that is negative and what we call evil is that in the former case the one universal life-force is allowed to manifest in a normal manner, and in the latter case it is diverted into the wrong channel.

Carry this thought strongly in your mind, that God's perfect life can only manifest in the form of abundance and freedom from all financial difficulty, if unimpeded or undiverted by mortal error and mis-imagining.

Make use of some such affirmation as the following:

'I will no longer limit the Infinite Life, but will express it in beauty and abundance and fullness of joy'.

LESSON I

THE SILENCE

In writing this Course, I assume that you have read my little books. The object of this Course is not to provide you with a vast amount of reading matter; instead I desire to guide you, in as few words as possible, along the Path which leads to the truest success and happiness (liberation and joy). It is not by much reading that progress is made: it is through meditation that we find God.

Life consists of cause and effect. That which takes place in the Unseen is 'cause': the visible life of the senses is 'effect'. People in the West spend, as a rule, the whole of their waking hours in the objective life of the senses, entirely neglecting that greater life which is invisible. Life can be truly successful only when a certain part of the waking existence is spent in the Unseen, Eternal, or Reality.

Mind is creative, and you can, by retiring from the circumference of your life, find your true centre, thus touching the secret source of Divine Power. What you affirm (i.e., declare to be true) and realize in the secret place within, where the Infinite One abides in fullness, will later become manifest in your outward life.

The practice of entering the Silence is the highest form of prayer. The highest form of prayer does not consist of supplications. We are not beggars, or we need not be, for all things are ours, and our prayers are answered even before we can voice them. Real prayer is finding God in a very true sense. It is the inner communion of spirit: it is the merging of the individual into the Universal: it is the losing of the finite in the Infinite: it is finding and entering into a state of perfect peace.

Prayer is of various grades. There is the prayer of the uninitiated, which consists of begging God for something. There is the prayer of the more advanced, who simply states his or her requests as in the model prayer given by Jesus. This was given not as a formula to be repeated at the end of a begging petition, but as a model upon which we should build our prayers. It consists of a series of requests from the Infinite. It does not beg or whine: it asks no favours: it simply requests that which, in the Infinite love of God our Father, already belongs to us. It invokes the action of an infinitely just law. 'Forgive us our trespasses as we forgive those who trespass against us'. Beyond this again is the prayer of those who have advanced farther along the Path. This highest form of prayer is the withdrawal from the life of the senses and the apprehension of the Presence of God. When this Presence is recognized as a retreat, the soul realizes intuitively, by direct knowing, that it possesses all things. 'All things are yours', cried the Apostle Paul, 'for ye are Christ's (the Indwelling Cosmic Christ) and Christ is God's'. When we enter the Silence, we find the perfect Christ and through this union we become one with God Himself. We have then no need to plead or beg, for all things are ours.

It is not possible to attain to this stage all at once, but it is the goal towards which the teaching of these lessons is directed. All affirmations, denials, and meditations contained in these lessons are designed to lead you to this higher state of consciousness and realization.

Any prayer is better than no prayer at all, and all prayer is good, because it is a turning to God the Author of all life and Power. While it is true that contemplation and realization are the highest forms of prayer, yet when we are in trouble it is often helpful to cry unto the Lord, and to ask for deliverance. At such times we should cast ourselves in utter surrender and abandon upon God, taking one of His precious promises as the basis of our prayer. One that has been helpful to me personally in times of stress has been the fifteenth verse of the Ninety-First Psalm, which is as follows: 'He shall call upon Me, and I will answer him: I will be with him in trouble: I will deliver him, and honour him. With long life will I satisfy him, and shew him My salvation'.

If we keep on casting ourselves upon God, the one Power and the only Deliverer, claiming this promise as our authority, so to speak, then no matter how great our trouble may be, after a time a sense of realization and peace comes to us, and then we know that all is well. God knows, therefore all must be well. Then we can rejoice in God according to the Scriptures: 'Delight thyself also in the Lord; and He shall give thee the desires of thine heart'. When we delight and praise God in this way, we open our consciousness to receive the good that God is anxious we should enjoy.

The first thing is to set aside a certain time (a few minutes at first will be sufficient), both night and morning, for meditation in the Unseen, and for entering the Silence. If this is not at first possible, it will become so if you persistently make the best possible use of any fractions of time that are available. If you do the very best you can, while remaining faithful to duties and responsibilities, the invisible Laws and Divine Forces will so arrange your life and control circumstances that you will, in time have all the leisure for the silence and meditation that you need.

Some teachers advocate sitting in the same chair, in the same room, and in the same position, day after day. This is not necessary in all cases. I myself have sometimes found it more helpful to walk about in my garden than to be caged in a room, but I feel sure that no matter what my circumstances or surroundings might be, I could still find the Presence of God. The principal thing is to find a spot where you are least likely to be disturbed.

When you have done this, let the body become comfortably relaxed, and all nervous tension given up. Let the muscles be supple and loose. Let there be no clenching of the hands or screwing up of the nerves. Now proceed to retire from the life of the senses. Withdraw from the circumference and reach to the centre. Cease to think about business, sport, family cares, finances and all physical activities. These, although they appear to be very important, are merely ripples on the surface: the reality is deep down. One untrained in thought-control will find it difficult to ignore the external life of the senses. That trouble at the office, that forthcoming social function, that fear or that worry, will persistently come into your mind and lead your thoughts away from the Supreme Reality. Some teachers recommend the inhibition of all thought. This is possible to the few, but quite beyond the ordinary individual. A much simpler and more effective method is to concentrate upon one thought, and, as others arrive, dismiss them and return to the central thought of your meditation. For instance, you might take this thought: *'Thou wilt keep him in perfect peace, whose mind is stayed on Thee'*, or any other text that appeals to you, such as: *'Be still and know that I am God'*, *'The Lord is my Shepherd, I shall not want'*, or, *'Come unto Me and I will give you rest'*. Repeat it quietly, insisting that your mind should concentrate upon the thought of God's Peace.

As soon as you begin, a thought connected with the outer life will intrude, demanding attention. Immediately dismiss it, quietly but firmly, returning again to repeating the sentence and trying to realize its truth. This struggle for concentration may appear to be quite hopeless at first, but is not so in reality. If you continue the effort, you will gradually improve until the day will dawn when you can enter into the secret place, and nothing will have power to disturb you. We are told that students of yoga, at one stage of their initiation, have to acquire the power to concentrate entirely upon the Divine Bliss for one hour and a quarter. This will doubtless seem incredible to you, although it is not so impossible as it appears, but to enter into God's Peace and Consciousness for even a few minutes only is a great achievement for a Western mind. To make this a daily practice is to work a complete transformation of life. It will help you in your concentration if you realize that the apparent importance of external things is largely illusory. They appear to be very real and important, but are not so in reality. When you enter the Silence, you leave the finite and enter the realm of the Infinite: you leave the unreal and approach the One Reality: you pass from the temporal into the Eternal: of what importance then are external things? Apprehend this thought of the unimportance of external things compared with the Great Eternal Reality, and you will find it possible to enter the Silence. External duties are important in one sense and must be attended to faithfully; but when we contemplate the Eternal they become as nothing in comparison.

When you have reached a state of quietness, peace and joy in God, you have entered the Secret Place of the Most High. You have entered that place which is described in the Ninety-First Psalm as the Shadow of the Almighty, or the covering and sheltering Wings of God. Nothing more is needed, actually, than this. We may think that we must pray for this thing or that thing, or for this person or that person; but, if we have really reached this state of quietness and peace with God, then no such prayers are needed. Abiding in God in this way gradually heals the whole life. We should forget all our troubles and cares and, also, the troubles of all who are in our hearts, and whom we desire to help; and just rest in God and in a realization of Divine Love.

Do not be disappointed if you cannot reach this stage *now*. The purpose of the whole of this Course is to put you in the right road towards attainment to this great thing.

The object of all prayer and 'treatments', is to reach this state of rest and peace, in which we know that all is well. When we pray or 'treat' for another, then we bear their burden as well as our own, and have to work through the darkness until we reach the same realization and sense of rest and peace. Our sole aim is to find God, and the rest and peace that are found in the Silence, which is the Presence of God.

Denials, affirmations, meditations, are all necessary in order to clear away the fog of error, to still the conscious mind, and bring one into a realization of Truth and quiet rest in the Presence and Love of God.

Every effort to find the Peace of God, although it may be unsuccessful, or only partially successful, makes it easier for the next attempt. It is a matter for practice and perseverance. One cannot become an adept in a week or a few weeks, but one can derive benefit from the teaching at all stages of one's unfoldment.

The term 'the Silence' is perhaps liable to be misunderstood. What is often termed 'entering the Silence' is merely the cultivation of passivity. Instead of allowing ourselves to sink down into a state of passivity, we should reach up to God, until we reach His Presence and feel His Power. By concentrating upon an affirmative text of Scripture, this becomes possible. At first we may be able to make no progress: our mind may seem in a whirl, but if we keep on concentrating upon our text, calmly and firmly affirming it, then gradually the outer or surface mind becomes stilled, and a sense of awareness is awakened, so that we realize, in a measure, the truth that stands behind, or lies underneath, the text upon which we are concentrating.

*

In conclusion, let me impress upon you that all that you do in connection with this Course should be done calmly, peacefully, restfully, and without strain or anxiousness. You do not have to do the works, it is the Father. *He doeth the works.* All that you have to do is to speak the word, declare the Truth, affirm what is true of Reality, and then Truth by its own power will manifest itself.

I pray that this teaching may be greatly blessed in your experience, and that each lesson may come to you just at the right moment, bringing to you just the message you need at the time.

Do not fail to conclude your work in the Unseen by sending forth your blessing to everybody. Turn to the East with its countries and peoples, and being in touch, say, 'Dear People, I love you. I send out my love to you in all its fullness. Peace be unto you and blessedness and knowledge of the Truth'. Then turn to the West and proceed as before; also, in turn, to the North and South. Then include the Universe and all God's marvellous Creation, and say: 'Dear Suns and Moons and planets and space, ye who show forth the Glory of the Infinite One: dear earth and sky and sea and all creatures great and small: dear flowers and trees and soft winds and gentle dew, I love you all, I love you. Peace be unto you. We are all one with each other and with the Father Who is the one Source of all. Together we form one complete whole'.

WEEK TWO:
FAITH

Letter II begins with a common question from students, which is why, 'if they think only good thoughts, should they not lead lives of perfect happiness and peace?'. It leads to a discussion of what it means to be a 'right thinker', Hamblin's term for those who follow the 'Science of Thought'. He responds:

THIS RAISES a great question, which, unless it be answered satisfactorily, may cause much confusion, perplexity and doubt.

First of all, however, let it be said, the trouble may be due to an attempt to force matters. Affirmations may be used with such fervour as to arouse the antagonism of the subconscious mind, thus producing the reverse effect of that which is desired. It may also be due to the change in the individual being all on the surface. The subconscious may still go on thinking, in a pessimistic and hopeless manner, producing all manner of disease and negative conditions. This state is due to too much work on the surface in the form of making use of statements of Truth, and too little meditation in the 'quiet'. It can be corrected by making a habit of quiet, restful waiting upon God. Again it may be they are not right thinkers at all, and that their thoughts are far from being in harmony with Truth. Right thinking implies thinking every thought in harmony with Truth and thinking only those thoughts which are, in an absolute sense, true. In other words, it means thinking from the standpoint of the Universal Mind, or as God thinks. Very few ever even approximate to this. People write to me at times and say that right thinking has not done much for them. They have followed it for years but they are no better. They have read every modern book, almost, that has been written on the subject, and have sat under various teachers, but still they are no better. The reason is that they have never even begun to become right thinkers. It is obvious, from their letters, that they literally wallow in a sea of morbid thoughts, and habitually allow their thoughts to dwell upon negative or undesirable things, yet they claim to be right thinkers. The remedy for this state of things is obvious. Again, it may be due to anxious effort. The student may have the idea that by strenuous thinking, wide reading and painful study, he can find the Truth. There is no greater error. Better read nothing at all than too much. Truth can only be found by waiting quietly upon God.

It may also be that the student is not meeting life in the right spirit. He or she may look upon right thinking as a form of mind power by which he or she can dominate circumstances and alter his or her objective life. One who does this is bound to suffer, for as soon as he has suppressed one form of disharmony, another one, worse than before, appears. Such a one can gain freedom from trouble only by surrendering to the Divine Will, and co-operating with life instead of opposing it. Again, it is possible that the student may be running away from life's experiences. Those who do this find trouble, difficulty and suffering meeting them at every hand. Trouble of this kind disappears if life's experiences are faced and met in the right spirit.

Granted however that the students first referred to are genuine and are proceeding in a correct manner, the reason may be as follows:

There are two classes of Right Thinkers. There are those who merely want to improve this life; who desire better health and circumstances, who wish for more harmony, and who want to live a godly life, to do their duty and to be good citizens, but who have no impelling desire to brave the heights of spiritual attainment. On the other hand, there are those who are on the Path, although they may not yet be aware of it. Theirs is the steep and sharp ascent to God. These are the adventurous souls who are prepared to brave anything, endure anything, and risk everything, if only they might find God and effect union with Him. Such attain to God-consciousness in this life, and do not, so I believe, pass at death to Sheol, but go direct to Heaven, the Presence of God, to form part of the Christ Kingdom in the Heavens. The former—those who follow the slower ascent to God, need have no fear for the future. Their journey is much slower, but they arrive ultimately. They form the rank and file of God's great army; the others are the vanguard, the pioneers, the leaders.

By saying that those who follow the slower path need have no fear, we mean that although these souls do not attain to Divine Union in this life, their progress Godwards still continues. The Spirit still carries on Its perfect work. As the inspired Whittier says: 'I only know I cannot drift Beyond His love and care.'

Every soul is dear to the heart of God, and infinite wisdom and love guide it and minister to it all the way.

It follows, naturally, that the path of the rank and file is much easier than that of the pioneer. When the ordinary individual ceases to produce disharmony through wrong thinking and faults of character, his or her life becomes much more harmonious and truly successful. He or she has dark times of bereavement and sorrow, but many spells of happiness. He or she enjoys the latter and forgets, partially, at any rate, the former. He or she trusts God, serves his or her day and generation, and fills his or her part in the scheme of things, but has no ambition to scale the heights. Such a one is content with the lowlands and quiet pastures.

The pioneer, the real Comrade of the Path, the one who aspires to tread the same Path that has been trodden by our Lord, and also by a handful gathered out of each generation of men, is an entirely different type. He or she dares all in order to gain all—God. His or her path (The Path) is a steep one. Compared with the ordinary path, it is mountaineering contrasted with walking over rolling downs. It is steep because the student has to change, in character, so quickly. Also his or her next stop is al-

ways a big step forward and upward, therefore the tests that must
be applied in order to judge of his or her fitness and prove his or
her worth must be correspondingly severe.

But it is well worth while.

There is also another reason why one person may have a
much more difficult life than another. Such a person may be, in
the ordinary way, destined to live a troublous life of change and
ups and downs. The turbulent experiences which this person
has to meet are the best thing, for him or her. This person's life,
difficult as it is, gives him or her just the experience that he or
she needs for the highest unfoldment. Another person would not
be helped by the same experiences, and has, perhaps, to live a
quieter life. Both can be successful in their respective fields. Both
can be greatly helped by right thinking. Both can learn the greatest
possible amount from their respective lives. And, in spite of the
dissimilarity of their lives, it may be that both may attain to the
Divine Union.

It is human to think that a difficult or troublous life is 'evil'
and a comparatively easy one 'good', yet there is, probably, no
greater error. Some can only develop by meeting difficulty—
they go to pieces, and deteriorate, as soon as life becomes smooth
and easy. Others, of a different type, make the best progress by
living a quiet life of contemplation combined with good works.
Each gets the experiences that are best for his or her individual
needs. There is no such thing as evil, or 'malefic', or 'afflicted'
aspects or influence. All life is good, and what we have to do is to
find the good beneath the apparent evil.

Of course a great deal of the trouble and disharmony of life
is due to meeting it in the wrong spirit, by wrong thinking, by
rebelling against life instead of co-operating with it. When we
bring our thoughts, wills, and lives into harmony with the Divine, all these self-created troubles flee away.

There are three dangers, especially, to be avoided at this point.
One is the entertaining of any thought of superiority. If we think
that we are more advanced than other people and better than

they, we are bolting the door of progress in our own faces. We are *not* better than they, and it is the greatest of errors, or follies, to think or imagine, that we are. The fact that we may be a little further forward than another is not due to any virtue of our own. Also, the one who is in a lowly stage of unfoldment is just as good and perfect, in a Cosmic sense, according to his stage, as the most advanced. A tadpole is perfect, *as a tadpole*, although it may, from the point of view of a frog, be inferior. We must always be willing to be the least of all, and to acknowledge that the lowest is equal to ourselves. There must be no love of adulation, or desire that others should think we are something great.

Because others may be engaged in selfish strivings for wealth, or because they may be seeking happiness through sensation, and because we do not seek for either, we must not assume that we are any better or more unselfish than they. We are not. Our selfishness has merely taken a fresh turn. We are prosecuting the same search—for rest for our souls in God. The only difference is that we have learnt through experience that possessing 'things' can never help us in our quest, but can only hinder, and that the same applies to sensation. We, in the mercy and grace of God, know more—that is the only difference.

Spiritual pride is at once the most insidious and the most destructive of all vices. It is capable of bringing an aspiring saint down to the lowest rung of the ladder, more easily than any other. The 'saintly' person who holds up his or her hands in righteous horror at the sins of the flesh is in far more danger of falling into hell, and deeply too, than is the gross sinner. Let us all beware of spiritual pride and self-righteousness.

The second sin, or error, against which we are warned, is twofold. (a) We must not think because we have received a certain measure of Truth that it is final and that henceforward we know everything. Actually, the more advanced we become, the more we find there is for us to know. (b) We must not think that because we know some of the Truth that our way of looking at things, or our approach to Truth, is the only right one. One way may suit one person, and a different way may suit another. God has appointed many ways unto Himself, yet in essence they are one. God sees the oneness and unity, and we see the diversity, apparent contradiction and multiplicity. Therefore, let us instead of fault-finding and criticism, give to all our benediction and love.

The third error which keeps us out of the Kingdom of God is seeking for results. In other words, seeking God for the sake of the loaves and fishes (health, wealth and love) instead of seeking the Kingdom first. Those who are obsessed with the idea of getting results never make any progress in the spiritual life. Our Lord does not say: 'Seek ye first for healthy abundance and human loves, and then the Kingdom of God shall be added unto you'. What He does say is: 'Seek ye first the Kingdom of God and His righteousness, and all these things (the necessary things of life) shall be added unto you'. In going through this Course again, with the aid of these letters, results must be looked upon as quite secondary and as merely outward indications that inward spiritual changes are taking place, or have taken place.

What is required of us is that we seek God with a whole heart and a single eye. There must be no double-dealing with God. We must have one object only, and this to find Him and be united with Him. Actually, we have no need at all to seek for the loaves and fishes, for it is impossible for us to lack any good thing, if we put God first and seek Him until we find Him, and live daily and hourly in the Divine Presence.

Students have written from time to time to say that they have done this or that, or followed one teaching or another, and yet they are no better. 'I have done all this or that until I am tired; I have been treated by famous healers, yet I am no better, or my circumstances remain as difficult as ever'. Just so. They have been trying to get results, instead of seeking God, or His Kingdom, with their whole heart. What I have told them has been to reverse their mental attitude altogether, and to look upon their 'affliction' as a necessary (in their particular case) spiritual experience, which must be co-operated with, instead of being opposed and treated against. Those who have followed this advice have had a wonderful spiritual unfoldment, in which God has been revealed to them as the All in All. All the time during which they were treating against their troubles and to get results, they were fighting against the leading of the Spirit.

These dear people were 'in the Path' and were not aware of the fact. There is a difference between those who are, strictly speaking, in the Path and those who are not. The former must look upon difficult experiences as special lessons, or tests, having for their object the student's spiritual unfoldment and initiation into the Divine Mysteries. They must therefore look upon them as valuable experiences which must be co-operated with instead of being opposed. In any case, if the sole object is to find God and Truth, no experience will be opposed, because the student will know that his or her circumstances are always the best for him at the time, and that their object is to help him or her on the spiritual journey.

Tests are applied to each pilgrim in the Path, not only to prove his or her worth and fitness for higher service and further revelation, but also in order to increase his or her faith. The great soul is the one who is great both in love and faith. Trouble, difficulty, temptation, all increase our faith. Even if we fail, it is revealed to us that if we had exercised more faith, we could have conquered instead of failing ignominiously. Faith grows through use. By continually calling upon God, by making use of Him, and trusting Him, we find that our prayers are answered, according to our faith. This gives us confidence and increases our faith. It is by 'trying' God and by 'proving' Him, and by ever seeking to live in the Divine Presence, that faith is nurtured and brought to full growth. Later on, faith gives place to full and absolute certainty—but this, at present, is a far cry.

What we have to exercise is the faith that refuses to be shaken even though God may seem to have forsaken us. God does not forsake us really—He only hides his face, in order that we may develop the faith that can never fail. No matter whether prayers are answered or not, nor whether God's Presence is so near us as to be felt, or apparently far away, still will we have faith in Him, in His love and wisdom, and in our oneness with Him.

Our beloved Lord stands at the threshold of the Life Eternal, saying: 'Enter ye in at the strait gate because strait is the gate and narrow is the way which leadeth unto life, and few there be who find it'. Listen also to the great apostle: 'Wherefore ... let us lay aside every weight and the sin which doth so easily beset us and run with patience the race that is set before us, looking unto Jesus the author and finisher of our faith'.

Yours in patient service,

HENRY THOMAS HAMBLIN

GENERAL INSTRUCTIONS

Remember that your only enemy is self. Also that you do not have to fight, so much as to hold yourself in the right attitude, so that the Spirit can work through you. 'Not I, but Christ'. 'You do not have to fight: you do not have to struggle: you have only to *know*.'

Do not omit to send out your love every night to all your fellow creatures, human and sub-human, and to all nature. Praise, bless and glorify God. Adore Him, thank Him and worship Him, for He is the Supreme One, Who transcends all thought and philosophic conception. Again I say, Love your fellows: send them your love and benediction, especially those who seek to hurt you.

By loving and adoring God, and by loving and blessing your fellows, you will bring so much joy into your soul there will not be room enough to contain it.

Above all, cultivate quietness and restfulness. 'In returning and rest shall ye be saved: in quietness and confidence shall be your strength.' 'They that wait upon the Lord shall renew their strength.' 'Rest in the Lord: wait patiently for Him and He shall give thee thy heart's desires.' The Kingdom cannot be taken by storm, but can be found by quiet, persistent seeking. Not in the storm or earthquake, but the still small voice.

Beneath, or behind, the turmoil of life is to be found a quiet

Resting Place. This point of contact between the soul and its Spiritual Source is still, calm, reposeful. It is a state of balance, poise, harmony, repose, stillness. It is not stagnation or inactivity, for in Spirit everything *is*, and there is a state of perfect wholeness, completeness, oneness. Therefore, there is no effort, no strain, nothing to be accomplished.

By entering the Silence, you leave a state of becoming, and enter into this realm of *is-ness*. By resting in this quiet place you renew your strength. It is perhaps better for some people to learn first to contact this still place, or Silence, in a satisfactory manner, before attempting to meditate upon any particular quality of Divine Character that they wish to incorporate with their own character. On the other hand, there are those who are helped by their desire for a certain thing. They are wise who seek for Divine Wisdom rather than for any earthly thing.

In early stages we need to incite ourselves to action, by making use of statements of Truth, audibly uttered. In later stages you will be able to rest in the Truth and to *know* the Truth, rather than to affirm that which you believe to be true. The latter leads up to the former. Our object is not to employ any magical use of words. It may be that wonders can be worked by this means but we are not sure they are of the Spirit. We use statements of Truth merely in order to convince ourselves of Truth, to cast out thoughts of error, and to realize Truth. When we realize, or become conscious of Truth, we can rest in It, until It permeates our whole consciousness. Words should not, in the writer's opinion, be used as a magical incantation.

At all times you should expand your mind and enlarge your thoughts. The Divine Life is Infinite, in beauty, power and extent. We limit its expression by our thoughts. All things are ours, really. 'The whole Universe is given to you for a garden of delight', says Edward Carpenter, and it is gloriously true. 'All the Divine Forces hasten to minister to our eternal joy', declares the same writer, with equal truth. We limit these glorious possibilities by the puny, narrow and parochial nature of our thoughts and ideas. By expanding our minds and thinking larger, more beautiful, more glorious, finer, broader, loftier, and deeper thoughts, we allow more of the Divine Splendour to appear.

By thinking always from the standpoint of God's eternal perfection, everlasting being, the wholeness of His perfect Life, the infinite nature of His bounty, the inherent good in our fellows, the essential goodness of life, the joy with which the real Universe is saturated: by thinking only thoughts of expansion, beauty, uplift, of things as they really are, in God's Archetypal Idea: by refusing to acknowledge lack, limitation, or apparent barriers, and by thinking only in a wider, deeper and richer manner; by all these we appropriate more of the Truth, thus bringing more Perfection into manifestation.

Putting the same truth in other words: if we think larger thoughts, dwell upon higher and richer ideas of life, and expand the boundaries of our mind, the Spirit Who ever works on our behalf will bring greater things into manifestation.

LESSON II

Dear Fellow Student of Truth,

Without faith it is impossible either to climb the Path of Attainment or achieve success in the affairs of life. No-one can climb the steep ascent to God-consciousness who does not live by faith, neither can success in the battle of life be won by one who doubts and fears.

If you will only believe that God is Omnipresent Good and that God is All: if you will realize that nothing but good can come into your life: if you will stick to this belief through thick and thin, constantly affirming its truth, in spite of the false evidence of the senses, you will become more than a conqueror in the strife: you will demonstrate the power of faith and enter into a higher, richer, and fuller life, of freedom, liberation, and victory. Only exercise faith and you can never fail.

This lesson explains what faith is: it also tells you how to increase it.

Affirming for you a life of faith and victory,

I am, Yours in Truth and Service.

HENRY THOMAS HAMBLIN

SPECIAL THOUGHTS ON DIVINE SUPPLY

Thought II

The idea that Life wants us to suffer poverty is an entirely mistaken one. Life (God) desires to express through us ever-increasing perfection, wholeness and beauty. Poverty is not a sign of godliness. So far from Life desiring that we should lack and suffer poverty and restriction of means, the truth of the matter is that Life is far more anxious to express abundance in our lives than we are willing that it should do so. Always life is trying to manifest abundance, prosperity and beauty in our lives, but we will not let it. At every moment it is seeking us, seeking us, seeking us; yet we turn it away. In our ignorance we transform the Power which produced this beautiful universe and this abundant earth into lack and disorder. Yet, in spite of our rebuffs, abundance still seeks to manifest in our lives.

The old mortal idea that we have to seek abundance must be changed. So long as we think in this way we drive our good away. The old mortal error must be reversed into Truth. Instead of having to seek and chase after abundance, we have to realize that it is seeking us. Not only so, but we must think, speak, act and live in the light of this glorious truth.

If you examine your thoughts and your speech, you may find that you have been living in a thought atmosphere of error: that you have been thinking, living and speaking from the standpoint of separateness from abundance, of its elusive nature, and as something that can be won, or possessed, only with the greatest difficulty. Remember it is those who believe, and have a subconscious conviction, that abundance is seeking them, who always 'fall on their feet', and who continually prosper, no matter how hard times may be; while it is those who believe that prosperity is not for them, and who look upon it as something very difficult to obtain, and as something that is always seeking to elude their grasp, and escape from them, who are forever in difficulty, 'fighting' adversity, failure, hard times, poverty and distress.

Therefore, reverse all this error and wrong thought and say continually, not with anxiety and fearfulness, but with restful confidence and joy:

Abundance is seeking me, I will no longer keep it away.'

LESSON II

FAITH

The path on which you have entered is not an easy one. Nothing worth having can ever be obtained without effort. It is necessary to climb a hill before we can enjoy the view from the summit. The upward Path, upon which you are travelling, is the ancient Path of Attainment, made sacred, but not one whit easier, by the feet of countless thousands who have passed before you and climbed the steep ascent to God. All the world's saints, prophets, seers and saviours have passed this way, and have met and overcome the same difficulties which you will encounter.

The starting-out on the great adventure is generally accompanied by much joy and uplift. Everything is seen through rose-tinted glasses. There is a great spiritual quickening and awakening, and the old life with its passions and temptations seems very far away. But, after a time, difficulties arise and mists of uncertainty gather round the Path. The trouble may be new, but, as a rule, is an intensification of the old. If ill-health has been your difficulty, then you may feel worse instead of better. If

precarious finances have tried you, they may appear to become
more involved. If passion or anger or irritability has been your
bane, then it may become more violent. If this proves to be the
case with you, be not dismayed: all who have 'attained' have
shared this experience. They have overcome and so can you, for
the same Omnipotent Power which made them more than conquerors is also yours. This experience is not evil, although it may
appear to be so: it is simply the test of your apprenticeship. Without these tests we could never progress: therefore they cannot be
evil, but are instead the steps by which we rise to higher stages.
The dark hour of the soul precedes the most glorious in-burst of
light. Extremes always meet, and the worse the position apparently grows, the nearer you are to your deliverance.

The times of refreshment and spiritual uplift and happiness
and joy are far greater than the dark times, but I should be a
poor teacher if I did not warn you against that which lies before
you. Remember, however, that these times are not evil: they are
merely good in disguise. You have only to stand fast, and you will
come through victoriously.

During the early stages of our journey, we have to rely entirely upon faith. We have no visible proof that we shall ever
reach a higher and richer life: we have to trust the Invisible. Faith
is of two kinds: that based on intuition, and that founded upon
knowledge and experience. The latter is impossible without the
former, and is the outcome of the former. All true religion is
based upon an intuitive awareness of, and longing after, God.
Man is not religious because he has his sacred scriptures; on the
contrary, he has his sacred scriptures because he is deeply and
fundamentally religious. It is upon this God-given, delicate sense
of intuition that faith depends. Faith comes not from without,
but from within. No evidence of the senses will ever produce
faith, for the evidence of the senses can at any time be proved to
be false and illusory. It is only *within* that one can become conscious of God and be sure that one is an immortal being. 'The
Kingdom of God cometh not with observation; neither shall they

say, Lo here! or Lo there! for, behold, the Kingdom of God is within you'. It was intuition which attracted my writings to you. It was intuition that made you take up this Course. It is upon intuition that you must rely until the time comes when you will be able to demonstrate the truth of that in which you have believed. When you have demonstrated the working of the Law, 'First in the Unseen and then in the Seen', your faith will be strengthened, and you will be able to say, without any doubt or misgiving, 'I know in whom I have believed'. It is easy to believe and have faith, or to think that you have faith, when things go smoothly, but when the sky becomes dark and the path arduous, and the evidence of the senses makes all further progress appear to be impossible, it is difficult. Yet, in spite of this, you have only to stand firm in order to win a glorious victory. It is during these periods that you need to spend more time than ever in the Unseen. When you find yourself right up against a wall and further progress seems impossible, then is the time to retire into the Unseen and rejoice in the freedom and liberation of the Infinite. Do not think, however, that while things are running smoothly, you can afford to neglect entering the Silence; for, if you do, you will find it impossible, when the testing-time comes, to find God.

To enter the Silence and to find God in the Unseen is an art that comes by practice. It cannot be taken up and laid down at will: it must be practised constantly and regularly. The strength and constancy of your faith depend largely upon the amount of time that you spend in the Unseen. It is there that your faith is born; it is there that your faith is nourished and strengthened. After communion with the Divine One within your own soul, you are able to face, in your outer life, what may look like certain defeat, because your faith tells you that the Infinite will find some way out of the difficulty. If you are strong in faith, you will be able to overcome insuperable difficulties, and achieve the apparently impossible. Jesus said to the two blind men: 'According to your faith be it unto you', and immediately their eyes were opened. He inspired their faith, and you, by looking within and finding the Indwelling Christ, will find your faith inspired and strengthened, so that you can overcome all the difficulties of your path. Armed with a great faith, you can never be defeated. You may be checked for a time: you may apparently be hindered, *but you can never fail.*

'Faith', said St Paul, 'Is the substance of things hoped for; the evidence of things not seen.' We affirm what we know to be the truth about Man, the child of God, although it may be the very opposite of that state of affairs that may be surrounding us at the time. What we affirm we cling to by faith, and never let go because we know that it is Truth—the truth about man as a child of God, as he is in Christ. We know that man, as a child of God, and as he is in Christ, is perfect: that he can never lack any good thing, that he can never be sick or diseased; that he can never be touched by any forces of disorder. Serene, calm, unafraid, beautiful, whole, complete, he stands in Christ, manifesting His infinite perfection. This is the truth about man as he really is, as he is, a child of God, hid with Christ in God.

We exercise faith by affirming the truth about God as Love, Wisdom, Joy, Peace, and the Author of all Good, and the truth about ourself (or man) as a child of God, reflecting in Christ the harmony, beauty and perfection and wholeness of the Divine, and then hanging on, through thick and thin, to the truth that we have declared. We affirm and declare what we believe to be the Truth, yet we can perhaps see no evidence of it in outward circumstances. Then it is that we understand what St Paul meant when he defined faith as the 'evidence of things not seen'. The Truth we have declared is 'the things not seen', but by our faith they are in time brought into manifestation.

When we affirm the Truth about Man, as being beautiful, serene, whole, harmonious; whose life is filled with every good and blessing, we do not have to fight against anything. We use denials merely to get wrong ideas and concepts out of our mind and consciousness, which would otherwise prevent us from realizing the Truth. But we do not have to fight or work against anything, 'for it is your Father's good pleasure to give you the Kingdom'. God wants us to manifest and enjoy all the good that He has designed for us. When the Prodigal Son returned home, he asked to be made one of his Father's hired servants. But his Father showered every possible rich gift upon him. The Father wants to treat us in the same way, and does do so according to our faith. We have to hang on to God and Truth, by faith: then Truth, by its own power and life, brings good and health, and harmony, and abundance in place of the negative ills that have hitherto manifested; and also the serenity and poise, moral strength and character that each one of us desires to display. Whenever we affirm or declare Truth, we come into harmony with all the Divine forces, so that all the Powers of Good and Divine Order are behind us, pushing us forward to a more abundant and glorious life of overcoming, victory, grace, and power.

Daily Routine

Enter the Silence both night and morning. You will possibly have difficulty in concentrating your thoughts. If so, do not say, 'I cannot concentrate', or 'My power of concentration is weak', for this will tend to make it worse. Rather, realize that the Infinite Mind is in you, that you are part of the Great One Mind of God. The wave is a wave and not an ocean: it has its identity and individuality, yet it is a part of the great ocean. So, also, are you part of the Universal Mind. You will find it helpful to say: 'Man can never experience any difficulty in directing attention to his Spiritual Source, for he is attracted by Divine Love and is ruled and governed in Love'.

Also, after retiring at night, just as you are falling asleep, you can repeat over quietly and restfully the same words.

The realization that Love is drawing you will make it easy for you to concentrate.

WEEK THREE:
INFINITE POWER

LESSON III contains several very great truths, in fact the greatest truths that can ever come to man. In the Lesson they are treated superficially and briefly, but the time has now arrived for these great truths to be emphasized and explained more fully.

The Infinite Power of God is within the individual through his oneness with the one Source of all Life and. Power. Man has no real power apart from oneness: he possesses no power until he realizes and acknowledges his oneness with God. It is very necessary that we realize that the Power of which we speak is not the power of the human personality, but the Divine Spark, the Christ, or Divinity within the soul. Personality implies separation—hence weakness, fatigue, exhaustion and nervous breakdown. Oneness implies strength—effortless accomplishment, boundless power. We are linked up to the Source of all Power, but only as we acknowledge our oneness with the One Power. We have continually to purge from our mind the error of separateness and at all times to affirm our oneness with our Divine Source. Of ourselves we can do nothing, no matter how much we may strive. But when we realize our oneness with the ONE we can accomplish the apparently impossible, without either effort or strain. One who realizes his oneness with the One Source of all Power, if called upon to do so, could govern the world without a shadow of care.

There is only one Power. Another great error that we have to expunge from the mind is that the one fountain of Life can give forth a stream that is at once pure and polluted. There is only one fountain; and this fountain, being perfect, can give forth only that which is pure and perfect. The one fountain gives forth the pure essence of Providential Power, or Life-Force (Creative). It cannot give forth an evil or polluted stream, and it certainly cannot give forth a mixture of good and evil.

This pure Providential Power, or Life, is the substance out of which each one creates his individual life. That is, to a very great extent. Our life is not altogether in our own hands. For instance, the impulse which sent us on this wonderful, adventurous journey through time and space came not from ourselves, but from the Will of the Supreme Being. A great thought, this! We are each one a thought–idea of the Infinite Mind, and are passing through time and space, projected by the Divine Will, which is inspired by infinite Wisdom and Love. There can be nothing wrong, or really evil, about a life that has its origin in the Divine Will inspired by Infinite Wisdom and, Love. We know that the main events and experiences of life are arranged for us in the Infinite Wisdom and Love of the Divine Mind.

But if the outline, or skeleton, of our life is foreordained, as some declare, it is left to us to fill in the details. Our life is perfect as it is arranged in the Divine Mind, and it rests with us as to whether we live it in a high vibration or a low one, upon a lofty plane or a debased one, positively or negatively, with courage and faith, or in doubt and fear.

While we have to admit that the big events in our life are foreordained, just as our being alive at all here is foreordained, yet we literally create our life and circumstances by the way we meet each day's experiences. We have the power to divert the Life-Force into different channels. For instance, if a person speaks roughly to us, we can either retaliate, or give 'the soft answer that turneth away wrath'. What a difference an apparently trivial thing such as this makes to our life! If we are faced with difficulty and danger we can either play the hero or run away. If we are faced with a choice of luxury and probably happiness for ourselves, at the expense of others, or involving the sacrifice of principle, we can either follow the path of ease, luxury, self-indulgence and probable (or problematical, rather) happiness, or the stern path of duty and apparent self-renunciation. What tremendous issues hang upon this choice being wisely made! If the former path is taken, great is the sorrow, suffering and remorse. If the latter path is chosen, great is the joy, peace and happiness that is experienced. Both paths, in the mercy and love of God, may lead to the same destination—the former through suffering, remorse, repentance and tears, and the latter through self-discipline and the overcoming of self and sense desire.

We have it then in our power either to live 'a hell of a life', or one of tranquillity and joy. We can turn the Divine Power into the wrong channel and make a wilderness to live in, in wretchedness and woe; or we can take the same Power and make of it a veritable heaven. Actually, of course, God's real universe is forever perfect, but we can only interpret it, owing to our limited consciousness, in terms of matter, according to our beliefs, thoughts, words and deeds. We do not, in actual fact, change the real universe in any way. It remains perfect always. What we do change is our consciousness. This metaphysical aspect of the subject, however, cannot be dealt with at this juncture. The changing of the one Good Power into seeming evil, by our own thoughts, actions, etc., is a good way of presenting the Truth at this stage. The point is that there is only one Life which is perfect, and it becomes good or evil to us according to our mental attitude, our actions and what we think about it. If we think that Life is evil, or if we fear that it may be evil, it will most probably appear to manifest in evil form. Whereas if we believe it to be good, and are quite sure in our hearts that it can only bring good to us, we find that good only manifests in our life, body and circumstances.

Life, then, is almost entirely what we like to make of it.

If, however, there is only one Power which is good, how comes temptation? The answer is that temptation is not evil in actuality. It is part of God's perfect Plan. Temptation is beautifully arranged so that we are never over-tempted. We can always conquer through the Christ Power within us. Temptation, in one sense, is good, in that it proves us and makes us strong. We could never gain strength, attain wisdom or make any progress in the Spiritual Life if we were not tempted in every possible way.

The above is of course the philosophic point of view. To the one tempted, temptation is either good or evil according to whether he or she overcomes or gives in to it. If he or she overcomes, he or she is greatly strengthened and encouraged. He or she is better in every way for the temptation—therefore to him or her it is good. One, however, who is overtaken in sin and falls from his high estate, is in a pitiable condition. To him, temptation is evil—simply because he has given in to it and it has debased him to the dust. Sin is the cause of suffering and pain, great is the distress and misery of one who has attempted much, and has attained to great heights, yet gives in to temptation.

The more advanced we become, the more subtle and searching are the tests to which we are subjected. I confess that I am lost in admiration at the cleverness and subtlety of the tests which are applied to us. There is no evading them; they search us out even in our holiest moments. These severe tests are of course necessary. We could never attain to higher things, nor learn wisdom, nor become fit to bear greater responsibility, if we were not searched, tested, tried in this way.

*

It is sometimes said that God and His manifestation are one. This is not Pantheism. Pantheism is the doctrine that God is the Universe and the Universe is God. It teaches the immanence of God in everything and there it stops.

The truth is that God is both immanent and transcendent. The life in a bird or a caterpillar is God's life, but it is not His transcendent life, which is eternal. Immortality comes to the soul through the birth of the Christ within the soul. While God and His manifestation are, in a sense, one, He is also distinct, for He is transcendent. While He is one with that which passes away, He is, in another sense, not so, because He, the Eternal, can only be one with that which endures. God is all there is, in the sense that nothing can come from any other source, because there is no other source; yet in another sense, God transcends all and is above all.

By the new birth, we come into oneness with the Eternal Life of God. We become one with Him in a special and mystical sense. Old things pass away and all things become new. We realize our immortality. We know that our life is eternal, because we are one with the eternal I AM THAT I AM. It is through the Christ within that we become conscious of this at-one-ment.

The object of all tests, trials and temptations is to make us stronger. The object is not to destroy us, or to break us, but to *make* us.

We have the Divine Power within us to remain steadfast and 'unmovable'. The more we realize that temptation is both good and necessary and that it is the Divine Plan that we should conquer, and that the power of the personality is useless and the Power of the Indwelling Christ is always sufficient, the easier it is for us to overcome, becoming much stronger and better through the experience.

The affirmation, 'I live my life in the Infinite, and the Infinite is in me', may of course be rendered, 'I live daily and hourly in the Presence of God, and this same Divine Radiance is in me'. Imagine yourself living in the glow of the Divine Radiance, and see this same Radiance filling your whole body full of Light.

The important thing is to spend a time, each night and morning, in making contact with your Divine Source (entering the Silence), in realizing and meditating upon the Truth, and in quietly and restfully affirming that that it is manifesting in your life now, and then during the day meeting every difficulty with an affirmation of Truth, so that no suggestions of evil can find a lodging place in your mind. Also in making contact with your Divine Source, in praise and thanksgiving, continually. In course of time you will be able to make contact continually and live constantly, and consciously, in the Presence of God.

The Calm Peace of the Secret Place abide in you,

Yours in the Great Fellowship,

HENRY THOMAS HAMBLIN

GENERAL INSTRUCTIONS

Later on, I shall explain the system of meditation which I use myself, but in the meantime will you continue your usual routine, but more restfully and quietly? While it is of the greatest importance that we reverse our thoughts through the day, bringing them all into captivity to Christ; also that we meet all suggestions of adversity, and all appearances of evil, with affirmations of Truth, yet by far the greatest impression is made upon our inner mind and thought-life by quiet meditation, in the Silence, upon Divine things. When you have learnt really to enter the quiet place you can make a practice of taking a thought in with you. By this means, you can build up any desired quality—or rather, the Divine Perfection, which already *is*, is revealed in, or reflected into you, and into your life.

To practise thought control, thought reversal, etc., and to employ the use of statements of Truth, without meditation in the quiet place, night and morning, is like trying to grow a crop by raking the ground instead of digging it. Raking the ground is good, but only after digging has taken place. The effectiveness of the raking depends on the thoroughness of the digging. Meditation in the quiet place gets down to the very subsoil of our being, and changes us 'deep down' where ordinary methods fail.

A mistake we are all liable to make is in thinking we can change ourselves by willpower, determination, and willed suggestion. Experience has taught me that it is only by waiting upon God that we can become changed. By entering the Presence— the quiet place—we open ourselves to the regenerative influences of the Spirit. When engaged in the activities of life this deeper, inner part of us is closed up, so to speak, and cannot be influenced to the same extent. However, just as in gardening raking the ground is necessary in addition to digging, so also, are thought-control, thought-reversal and the use of statements of Truth necessary for the cultivation of a truly spiritual mind. The latter, however, become much easier through our calm meditation in the quiet place.

What thoughts, then, shall be meditated upon in the Silence? This will all be explained in later letters but, at this stage, there is one main thought which may be dwelt upon. *'There is only Good. One pure fountain from which all life proceeds.'*

Carry this idea into the quiet place, and even if your meditations are not yet perfect, you will be richly blessed. Later on, I hope to give you some hints on how to meditate upon this truth and others also.

LESSON III

Dear Fellow Student of Truth,

Lying dormant within you is a Power which can never fail, for it is the Power of the Infinite. It can raise you to heights of attainment undreamed of by the uninitiated. It can make you master of your fate, captain of your soul. This Power is Divine: it is the Power of the Indwelling One, the Cosmic Christ, the Logos or God's Perfect Idea: it can never fail. But you must trust in it, you must call upon it; and if you do, it will awaken and manifest in your life in the form of health, happiness, nobility and character, truest success and highest service to mankind.

There is no height to which you cannot climb: there is no difficulty which you cannot overcome, if you have faith in this Divine Power within you, and call it to your aid.

Arise! shine! for thy Light has come.

Yours in Service and Truth,

HENRY THOMAS HAMBLIN

SPECIAL THOUGHTS ON DIVINE SUPPLY

Thought III

Do not think that there is anything good in life that you cannot, may not, or should not have.

All things are yours, if you will only accept them.

Life desires to pour out its richest blessings upon you. Divine Wisdom does not want you to love money, to be acquisitive, to trample on your fellow men, to hoard up wealth, or to fill your life with the useless 'junk' which deluded people think will bring happiness. What Wisdom desires for you is an abundance of all the good things that are necessary for *your highest wellbeing.* Can you possibly desire anything better than this?

The idea that God does not want us to have a sufficiency of good things in life is an error that is deeply embedded in the inner mind of the majority of people, and is the cause of more poverty, distress, financial care and worry than all other causes put together. This idea was deeply embedded in my own mind. I was early taught to look upon abundance or easy circumstances as not only something as utterly beyond my reach as the moon, but also as something that is wicked and ungodly. This error, which was a libel on God's character, kept me in poverty for years, but when I cast it out, cultivating a more abundant and prosperous consciousness, my circumstances changed so rapidly for the better, it became quite embarrassing.

Get this new thought (it is new to most people) into your mind and consciousness: the thought that, so far from a wise abundance and prosperity being wicked or against God's will, it is, most emphatically, God's will and the desire of the whole universe, that you should have an abundance of good things and never be stinted or restricted any more.

Sing with a glad heart continually,

'All that the Father hath is mine'.

'Infinite abundance is richly provided for all the Sons of men'.

What an insult to God to beg and pray for things when all the time all things have been given to us out of the infinite abundance, and are already ours!

LESSON III

THE POWER

Within each one of us is Infinite Power. This Power does not belong to the finite or false personality or to the 'self', but to our real, spiritual, Higher Self, or Indwelling Christ. This real Self, or Indwelling Spirit, is covered up by the illusions of the sense-life, and by selfishness, fear and hate: it is obscured by beliefs in weakness, separateness and impotence: but when we unfold the wrappings and find the Kingdom within, we enter a life of almost boundless power.

There is only one real Power in the Universe and It is good. There are not two powers, one of good and one of evil: there is only the One. In a steam-engine there is only one power, but the driver can use that power to go either forward or backward. He can also obey the signals and drive his train to safety, or he can drive his train to destruction; yet there is only the one power and this is good. In like manner, the Power within man is good, but man can so misuse It that It produces apparent evil, and this evil is simply a painful effect, remedial in its action, designed to bring man back to God, the Infinite Good.

(In one sense, of course, the Power is neither good nor evil, it is that out of which things both good and evil are formed. It is like electricity, which is neither good nor evil, itself, but can be made to serve good or evil ends by the use to which man puts it. But we need not go into this aspect of the subject. What we have to remember is that the intention of life is good and that Love is behind all.)

Those, however, who know not the Christ within, who recog-

nize no Divine Power, and who are not established, in thought
and consciousness, in the Good, are subject to negative influences and forces, generally called evil powers. These forces, influences or powers are, however, negative. They can exist only
where Christ is absent in consciousness. But you, by establishing
yourself in the All Good, by relying entirely on Christ, by realizing and acknowledging that you of yourself are weak and helpless, but that the Power of Christ in you is all-powerful, by
directing all your thoughts Christwards, to the good, the beautiful and the true: by so doing, you are freed from the power or
forces of evil, or negation of Good, so that they cannot touch
you in any way. The love of sin and the power of habit gradually
die away as your thoughts, desires, aspirations and love become
more completely centred in Christ, Who is both your risen Lord
and your Indwelling One. 'Christ', said St Paul, 'is within you,
and is the hope of your glory'. The point that I want to bring
home is this: That Christ is the Substance and Reality and is All-
Powerful. By abiding in Him, and by His life in you, you are
established in Eternal Good. The powers of evil (so-called) are a
negation and are not real, permanent or omnipotent and cannot affect you, because you live in Christ. They are a negative
absence of the Real. They are a negation. By living the truly
Spiritual Life, you are not only delivered from all negative powers and forces, so that you realize that for you there is no evil, but
the lower part of your nature is also transmuted into the higher,
the material into the spiritual, the fleshly desire into the Heavenly, until at last you become, through the grace of God, entirely
changed, and actually, and not merely potentially, a child of God.
'Beloved', said St John, 'now are we the sons of God'. He had
attained and had learnt the great secret.

There is therefore no evil or malevolent purpose in the Divine
Scheme, for all God's purposes are kindly and full of love and
His plan is perfect. There is only God (Infinite Good). All is well.

The mystically-termed 'devil' and 'prince of this world', re-
spectively, work through the subconscious mind with its impulse

and the illusions of the senses. Yet these, too, in one sense, are good; for the former supplies us with that downward pull, by the overcoming of which we become strong, and the latter shields us from the blinding Truth until the time comes when our eyes are strong enough, and pure enough, to behold It. All is well.

The power within man, then, is good, for it is the Power of Christ and there is none other. It is boundless and inexhaustible, for it is God's Power and He is omnipotent. There is no weakness in God: He is the Almighty Power, and those who trust in this Power, and make us of it, *can never fail.* You, O brother, O sister of mine, you can never fail, for the Power of the Infinite is within you. The higher you aspire, the more this Power will manifest in your life.

Within each one of us is the Indwelling One, and He has come that we might have life and that we might have it more abundantly. We can have this abundant life by realizing this wondrous Power within and by calling it into expression. How this can be done will be explained in future lessons: for the present, we will use some helpful affirmations which will impress the truths we have learnt upon our consciousness.

'*I live and have my being in Christ, and Christ liveth in me.*'

'*There is only One Power, the Power of Christ, and this Power is in me.*'

'*This Power is not my own, yet it lives in me.*'

'*I have no Power of my own. It is the Power of Christ in me.*'

'*Realizing my own weakness, I depend entirely upon Thee.*'

Let us meditate upon the Infinite Power. There is One Power in the Universe and this is God. It is the Divine Spirit in motion. It fills all space. All the Universe is a manifestation of the One Power. Suns, moons and planets are maintained in their places and follow their appointed path, sustained and energized by this One Power. This Infinite Power is in me. It has no limit, except the limit I place upon it by my finite viewpoint and doubt and fear. This Power is spiritual. There is no real power that is not spiritual. *Thy power, O Christ, is in me.* It is not my own, it is Thine, but it dwells in me. This power can never fail. It never tires: It never fails. The more I trust It and rely upon It, the greater will become my achievements, the more easily shall I overcome my difficulties. The greater my faith in Thy Power which is within me, the greater will the demonstration be, for Thy Power is Infinite. Therefore I would trust Thy Power (the Power that is not my own but which is within me) more and more. There is no limit to my upward climb if I trust in, and rely upon, Thee.

O Infinite Power of God, manifest Thou in my life, in health and strength, happiness and joy and highest service to all mankind. May this Power, within me, bring forth all the fruits of the Spirit, that I may mount up to the heart of God. O gracious Indwelling One, Who art the Source of all power, I yield myself to Thee: I desire to become transformed into Thy image of the perfect Idea, the Likeness of God: I desire to conform my life to Thy Will and Purpose. The Infinite Love has said that I shall one day be perfect even as my Heavenly Father is perfect; therefore let Thy infinite Power abound so that I climb the steep ascent to God.

*

In the next lesson, we start out on the great quest. In the meantime, make use of the affirmations; spend as much time as possible in the Silence, both night and morning; and get in touch with your Divine Centre. Abstain from fault-finding and imputing wrong or unworthy motives to others. Give others the credit for being as sincere and well-intentioned as yourself. Try to see the Christ in others. Speak of others only to help and bless. Find no fault with anything in God's Universe. Affirm only the Good. Hold all men and women in thoughts of love. This is the Path of Wisdom. It is God's way of Happiness. It is the road to True Success.

Meditate much on this lesson. By meditation you will find the Christ within. When you have found the Indwelling One, you will enter into that higher consciousness which our Lord called the Kingdom within. You will then realize that all things are yours and that all achievement is possible if you believe it to be possible. All fear of lack and limitation will pass away, to be replaced by a sense of absolute repose, a consciousness of immense and universal power.

*

Do not be satisfied with reading this Lesson and then putting it on one side: try instead to read it every day and meditate quietly and calmly upon it. Carry it with you so that you can study it at times which would otherwise be wasted. Reading, however, is not sufficient: it is necessary to 'do' the course: to become a 'doer' of the word and not a hearer only. Fill your life with prayer and affirmation: be sure to make living contact with your Divine Source, God, at least once every day, and in so doing you will become more efficient in your work and service, for the Power of the Spirit is INFINITE.

WEEK FOUR:
CHOOSING AN IDEAL

WHAT IS NEEDED now is not strain, or striving, but quiet persistence. The Kingdom of God cannot be taken by storm or entered by violent or even anxious effort; but we can put ourselves in the right attitude of willingness, so that when we are called to go up higher (experience a fuller realization of Truth), we shall be ready.

Our Lord tells us not to put ourselves in the topmost room, but to occupy the lowest room, so 'that when he that bade thee cometh, he may say unto thee, Friend, go up higher'. This parable has other meanings, but it has a lesson for us, which is that we cannot put ourselves into the Kingdom. No amount of effort can give us entrance. We may exalt ourselves by affirmations of: *'I am this wonderful thing'* or *'I am that still more wonderful creature, or being'*, but the end of it all is that we are abased. 'For whosoever exalteth himself shall be abased; and he that humbleth himself shall be exalted'.

The use of such affirmations as *'I am Life'*, *'I am Spirit'*, *'I am Conqueror'*, and so on, merely inflates the personality, deludes the mind and puffs up the pride. (In very early stages, however, some form of *'I am'* affirmations may be helpful, such as 'I am health', *'I am success'*, etc.)

Not by self-exaltation, nor by anxious effort can we find the Kingdom. We have to wait patiently upon God, to keep ourselves in the right attitude of humbleness and willingness: then just at the right time we are asked to enter more fully into the life of the Spirit. Then Truth is revealed to us, and we are freed for ever from fear, worry and care, simply because we know the Truth. Then are we conscious of our oneness with Christ—we realize that we are one of the Divine family. Only a small and humble member—but, blessed thought, still a member.

In Lesson IV, you are told of the value of an ideal. It is better to have any ideal than none at all. That is if the ideal is something higher than one's present life. To keep a gin palace might be quite a lofty ideal of comparative respectability to some.

An ideal, held in the mind, always draws us on. A man has an ambition to achieve material success. He holds his ideal in his mind and earnestly follows it. Mind, Spirit or Life, whichever you like to term the invisible Power which ever works on our behalf, brings to him opportunity and material out of which he builds a worldly success. As he succeeds, so does his ambition grow, until, instead of him creating a success, his success rules him with a rod of iron, and his life becomes one of complete slavery to his ambition. He, metaphorically speaking, gains the whole world and loses his own soul.

Yet the law that leads such a person, and finally drives him or her into such a miserable condition, is the same law by whose aid we find God and Heaven. By taking Christ, the Archetype, Who is God's only-begotten Son, as our ideal, we not only are led on and ever on, becoming changed more and more into His Divine Likeness, but a time arrives, sooner or later, when Christ takes complete control of our life and is revealed to us, and in us, as our real Higher Self and Redeemer. Born in us, from above, by the Spirit (mystically conceived by the Holy Ghost), He grows in us and finally absorbs our personality, or lower self, altogether. Then it is that we understand what St Paul meant when he said: 'Yet not I, but Christ liveth in me'. Then, also, it is that we understand what is meant by the words: 'But as many as received Him, to them gave He power to become the sons of God, even to them that believe on His names which were born, not of blood, nor of the will of the flesh, nor of the will of man, but of God'.

Some students seem to know by intuition just what the qualities of the Christ or Archetypal character are: love, wisdom, power, mercy, forgiveness, compassion, steadfastness, patience, and so on, and can meditate upon such abstract qualities. Others find in the life and teaching of Jesus a key to the Divine Christ-Ideal Character, which forever leads us on to find perfection, not in anything that we ourselves do, but in the Divine Archetype with whom we become one. Jesus Christ came to reveal God, the Supreme Being, to us in the form of a Father of Infinite Love. He also came to reveal to us the perfect Divine Man: the Lord from Heaven, clothed in human form. He did not come as an Immortal—those superhuman beings, of whom Melchizedek was one, who possess the power of appearing in a form visible to man, and then disappearing again, whenever they choose. (All fourth, or super-, dimensional beings can do this.) But He, the Lord from Heaven, took upon Himself mortality. The Representative of Heaven, fresh from the Presence of the Father, put on the body of mortal flesh, and overcame temptation, death and the grave in order that we might be saved by following in His footsteps. If the Lord had come as an Immortal, it would have helped us not at all. It would not have assisted us to know that two thousand years ago an Immortal appeared, masqueraded as a man and then disappeared. All that he (the Immortal) might do and say would be very wonderful to us, but it would not help us at all, for what might be possible to him, as an Immortal, would be impossible to us, who are merely weak, mortal men.

But Christ came as a mortal man. A fully-human man with all the weaknesses of humanity to overcome. If He had not overcome, He would have given in to temptation, and would have died, as all mortals do, and that would have been the end of the whole matter.

Christ overcame, and in doing so made it possible for us, in spite of human weaknesses, to overcome also. He Who trod the winepress alone has made it possible for our feet to follow. He who has abolished death and brought immortality to light through the gospel, gives to us eternal life through oneness with Him.

Therefore, is it any wonder, that in the life and character of Jesus Christ our Lord, we find those qualities of strength, love, wisdom, steadfastness, patience, etc., which we desire most of all to be incorporated with our own character? Can there be any higher, nobler or more perfect ideal to hold before our imagination? Many have tried to do without Christ, but they have all failed. It is only as we hold this Divine Ideal before us that it becomes possible to live the truly spiritual life, free from sin (but not free from temptation), which leads to Divine Union. It is necessary to emphasize the fact that we are tempted, and it must be admitted that we may fail many times. Directly we use the name of Christ and take Him as our ideal, the forces of hell seem to be let loose. This must ever be so, for we must be tested and proved at every point and at every step.

All failure, all surrender to temptation, is due to relying on the personality, or the strength of the ego, instead of standing steadfast in the strength of the Spirit. So long as we keep hold of the hand of our beloved Elder Brother, and 'be not afraid', we are safe. As soon, however, as we let go the hand, and trust to our human strength and will, fear takes hold of us, the Light is obscured, and the adversary beats us as easily as sunlight melts snow. Of ourselves we can do nothing. 'Yet not I, but Christ liveth in me' must be our constant watchword. The Christ can never fail, and if we stand fast in Him, we too can never fail.

We see then that we have to take Christ as our Ideal and that by so doing we enter definitely the Path of Attainment. Through making Christ the Centre of our life, we set in motion forces which culminate in our union with the Divine. Without Christ we can do nothing. He is the Lord from Heaven, born from above of the Holy Ghost, within us. Finally, He possesses us altogether and we become one.

This, however, cannot be accomplished without passing through many temptations or tests. Life to the awakened soul consists mainly of tests and experiences. Everything that happens—or rather, comes to pass each day—is a test. Every person we meet, every task we have to perform, every situation in which we may find ourselves, is a test. It all depends upon how we deal with each situation as it arises, as to what our life shall be. If we avoid, or try to avoid, unpleasant duties or responsibilities which we dread, we create trouble for ourselves, for the experience will repeat and repeat in ever-increasing unpleasantness until we do handle them in the right way.

But, apart from every detail of our life being a test, we are bound to meet with big temptations. At times all the powers of hell will appear to rise up against us. These big tests foreshadow a step forward in spiritual things. Before a step forward in spiritual experience is possible, it is necessary that we be tested and tried in various ways, and then if we are found worthy we are promoted to something higher.

The life of Spiritual Attainment, then, is one of constant test and temptation. No progress can be made otherwise. We are, so to speak, balanced on a razor blade with hands clutching at us on every side. No wonder we are enjoined to watch and pray that we enter not into temptation! This brings us to the remedy. One way to cut the ground from under temptation, and to weaken its attack, is meditation in the quiet place. By meditating every night and morning in the Silence, we become filled with Divine Power and are thus able safely to pass through temptation. By meditation we become more and more like Christ: our secret thoughts become cleansed, our character becomes built up: we become more thoroughly possessed with the desire to live a blame-less and spotless life: we become filled with the Power of the Spirit: even the substance of our physical frame becomes more refined. Because of all this, temptation, although severe, is over-come, not by our own strength, but by the Power of the Spirit.

I am more than ever convinced that thought-control by itself cannot save us from falling. It is only the influence of the secret place that can keep us. Thought-control is a vital necessity, but with-out meditation daily in the quiet place, it is well-nigh useless.

We said just now that Jesus Christ took upon Himself all the weaknesses of mortal man and overcame so that we also might overcome. How did He overcome the weakness of the flesh? By prayer in the Silence. The quiet inner sanctuary—the shut door, communion with the Father in secret—these were the means whereby our Lord overcame. Without them, He could never have become the Strong Conqueror. We, also, can certainly not overcome without making use of the same means. We cannot overcome by hoping or wishing, but only by doing as we are taught by our Lord.

Show me a man who has overcome in the great battle of the soul and I shall behold one who has spent much time in quiet meditation, and persistent waiting upon God. Show me a man who has fallen by the way and never lifted up his head again, and I shall behold one who has neglected the means of Grace our Lord employed, and by the use of which He overcame.

'Now unto Him Who is able to keep you from falling, and to present you faultless before the presence of His glory with exceeding joy, to the only wise God our Saviour, be glory and majesty, dominion and power, both now and ever'. Amen.

Yours in the One Service,

HENRY THOMAS HAMBLIN

INSTRUCTIONS IN PROGRESSIVE REFLECTIVE MEDITATION

The result of this method of progressive meditation is that the good effect of hours of patient meditation can be recalled and made use of by the uttering of a few words, or even one word, or by the thinking of one thought. Thus, in the space of, say, fifteen minutes, as much real, constructive work can be accomplished in the quiet place, as in hours of ordinary meditation.

First of all, let us review what meditation is and what it accomplishes.

Meditation is the holding in the mind of a thought of God,

or aspect or quality of the Divine Character, and the turning of it over and over so as to allow the Illumination of the Spirit to reveal to our consciousness all its various facets of Truth. By our so doing, a flood of understanding comes to the soul, and new thoughts, ideas and aspects of Truth come to us. We do not discover Truth, but by turning over the thought in our mind the Light of the Spirit reveals Truth to us.

By our meditating in this way, Truth is revealed to us by inward spiritual illumination. It rushes into the soul and we feel its power and inspiration. If, when this takes place, we quietly bask in the warmth that this inward understanding and revelation bring, just in the same way as one can bask in the rays of the sun, whatever quality of Divine Mind that we meditate upon is built into our own character. The more we bask in this manner, the more we become changed.

But there are so many things that we need: we come so far short of the Divine Character, that it would take us nearly all day to meditate in this way upon all the qualities that we find are necessary if we are to attain to the full stature of Christ. Therefore, we must find some means whereby the process can be shortened without being impaired.

Also, to meditate in the ordinary way, at great length, might produce mental fatigue, through having to remember all the various things upon which we have to meditate. By progressive meditation, this mental fatigue also is avoided.

When we hold a subject or idea in the upper mind, allowing the searchlight of the Spirit to play upon it, a cloud of other thoughts, ideas and meanings come flowing in, like bees attracted by a jar of syrup. Not all at once, but day by day something is added, until as a reward for patient persistence we not only know far more about the subject upon which we have been meditating, but we understand and realize and *feel* the wonderful inner truth which it contains. When we *feel* the Truth, then is the time to bask in Its rays; and the more we bask in this way, the more do we become changed into the Divine Likeness.

Many students experience this feeling in the form of a warm glow. They experience a feeling of actual physical warmth which spreads outwards from the region of the heart. For my own part, I experience it in the form of a delightful feeling of rest, calm, peace and joy, sometimes accompanied by a sense of mystical light, such as cannot be described. Others have only a feeling of calm, happy conviction—and in this there is rest and peace. It does not matter which form our experience may take: it is good, and all that we need do is to bask in the feeling or realization.

It may take a long time to reach this stage of knowing: not only the weeks, or even months, spent in building up and up, until realization comes to the soul; but also in going over the whole ground each day.

For instance, let us take as our subject of meditation 'All is Good'.

In order to realize this, we have to pass through a gradual unfoldment of Truth on the subject. The mind at first has to realize that there is no evil purpose in God's Scheme, and that there is only one God and one Scheme. Next, that there is no evil Principle, and that there is only one Principle and this is Good. Next, that what appears to be evil may be Divine Justice in operation. Next, that apparent evil may be good in disguise. Next, that because we can know only in part, what appears to be evil may be only one side of a perfect whole. Next, that evil may be something out of which good and order and progress are evolved, and therefore cannot be evil in actuality. And so on, almost *ad infinitum*. As we meditate upon the subject, fresh ideas come to us, each bringing more light and understanding. For instance, Good is omnipresent: therefore, Good is here. Good being everywhere, there can be no room for anything else; therefore, all is Good. Finally, we reach a stage of understanding, or realization, in which we know, in our very soul, that Good is the only reality, and that all evil is lack of Good, and that while it has a temporary power in this consciousness, must pass away. This understanding, or super-knowledge, brings a feeling of joy, peace or glow, as the case may be.

Having reached this stage, the work leading up to it should be repeated day by day until the *feeling* is always obtained, and we can bask, at will, in the warmth and sunshine of the truth that all is Good

Having been through the Course, you know that the principal thing to be accomplished is to realize the reality and truth of Truth. Every thing already *is*, all that is necessary being that we should realize inwardly this great truth. The effect of true meditation is to bring Divine Light and understanding to the soul. Arguments are good, so long as such arguments are based upon Truth—that is, if they are made from the standpoint of the Universal Mind—but reflective meditation is far better. If the subject of Good is held quietly in the mind and lifted up, so to speak, to the Light of Truth, and the various aspects of the subject, as here enumerated, touched upon, then other thoughts and ideas will come direct from the Universal Mind and flood the consciousness with light and understanding.

These instructions will be continued in our next letter.

LESSON IV

Dear Fellow Student of Truth,

In this lesson, you are taught how to bring the Inward Power into expression: it teaches you the value of practical Idealism. Progress is possible only through the following of the Highest Ideals: therefore make up your mind, here and now, to follow the gleam—to reach after the highest and best.

Do not be persuaded that 'it does not pay' to follow high ideals. Believe me, it is the only thing that does really pay, in the real and wider sense of the word.

No matter how alluring the temptation to sacrifice your ideals may appear, it is false, and will lead you to disappointment, unhappiness and failure. There is only one Path for you to tread and this is the following of your highest God-given ideals within your own soul. All other paths are false and lead to misery and despair.

Follow the gleam, and all joy, achievement and attainment will be yours.

Affirming for you the inward growth which follows the highest strivings, I am, Yours in Truth and Service,

HENRY THOMAS HAMBLIN

SPECIAL THOUGHTS ON DIVINE SUPPLY

Thought IV

Consider the inexhaustible nature of the Infinite Supply. Behind the prodigal profusion of Nature stands a Divine Idea. Ideas in Divine Mind are inexhaustible and infinite in extent and degree. Meditate upon the way Nature persists, year after year, showering her abundance upon man—yet the supply fails not. Behind Nature is an inexhaustible source of supply. This source is the *Divine Idea of Abundance.*

What we see on the surface of things—Nature's prodigal and, apparently, inexhaustible abundance—is only a microscopically tiny part of the reality. God's Idea is infinite in every direction and in every possible manner—far beyond our finite comprehensions—and the farther we endeavour to trace it back, the more we realize how impossible it is for us either to comprehend it to any degree, far less ever to exhaust it. Who can exhaust God's Idea?

Therefore, meditate upon this wondrous truth. Take it with you into the quiet, or Silence. Steep your mind in this wonderful idea—the inexhaustible and limitless nature of the Divine Supply. Become impregnated with the idea to such an extent, that even to think of it causes a glow of joy and a thrill of anticipation to pass through you. Say and think the following:

'God's Abundance is infinite: it is available for all of us now'.

Divine Abundance is like the ocean; no matter how much you may take out, it is impossible to make it grow less. Also, it makes no difference to the ocean if you take a cupful out, or a bucketful. It is the same with Divine Supply. You can think in a small way and receive only a cupful, or you can think in a larger way and receive a bucketful. You are the only loser if you take only a cupful, and if you take a thousand bucketfuls no-one will be any the poorer.

Do not, however, waste anything. There is a law of economy in Nature and the Spiritual World, which must be obeyed.

Therefore, all who would aspire to the abundance consciousness must avoid waste, and learn to manage his or her affairs in a thoroughly efficient manner. Before being entrusted with abundance we must learn to be wise stewards. Riches are not ours to hold and keep, and never can be. They are merely for us to use, for the benefit of our fellows, and the glory of God.

LESSON IV

THE IDEAL

The first step in Self-Expression is the formation of an ideal. No-one has ever achieved anything worthwhile except through the following of a high ideal. Whoever follows an ideal and reaches up towards higher things is bringing the Inward Power into expression. The Power is Infinite. It is yours to call upon: it can be limited only by your doubt, unbelief and fear. If you follow Christ as your Ideal, then: 'There is no noble height thou canst not climb; All triumphs may be thine in Time's futurity'.

When you create an ideal and follow after it, you come into line with the most Ancient Wisdom: you come into harmony with the Eternal Purpose of the Divine Scheme. In *The Message of a Flower* is expounded the great truth that the universe, including man, is the unfoldment of an idea. The perfect ideal exists in the mind of God, the Creative Mind, and therefore within everything and everybody lies inherent and Infinite Perfection. Within YOU is hidden God's Perfect Man: within everyone, even the most debased, is the Infinite Perfection patiently awaiting unfoldment. Within everything is the dynamic urge towards God's Perfect Ideal.

Perfection is reached only through much striving, persistence, perseverance and overcoming. In man, God's ideal can be attained to only by reaching up to the highest and best that we know. 'Be ye perfect' (or, ye shall be perfect), the Great Way-Shower said, 'even as your Heavenly Father is perfect'. This is the grand ideal towards which we must strive—absolute perfection: nothing short of this, nothing less. It is by believing in, and affirming, this indwelling perfection and goodness of Christ that we can bring it forth into expression. If we say that we are poor and weak, diseased and miserable, we become poor and weak, diseased and miserable: for we, by our negative thought, cut ourselves off from our Divine Source. If, however, we affirm that within us is the perfect Christ, and realize our oneness with Him and His life and Power; if we believe the promise that we shall be perfect even as our Heavenly Father is perfect, we bring the Inward Power into expression, and live a life of victory and overcoming.

Within each one of us is the Indwelling Christ, and the teaching of Paul the Apostle proclaims this truth. It is plain to all who can understand the spiritual significance of Paul's teaching, that he refers to the Universal or Indwelling Christ. This Indwelling One is in you and in me—He has been born in us from above. As we unfold the mummy wrappings of our soul, we behold His glory; we realize that there is no separation, that God's Perfect Man and the true Self are one.

Emerson tells us to 'Hitch our wagon to a star'. Is there any brighter star than this 'Sun' within the soul; this Divine Ideal of Perfection which is ours in deed and in truth? With our face turned towards perfection, we come into line with our glorious Destiny, into harmony with God's Will and Purpose: we fit into our niche in the Divine Scheme. When we reach upward after perfection, we begin to work in the way that God works: therefore we can never fail.

What is called the 'New Psychology' teaches us that if we form an ideal and hold it in the mind; that if we think from the standpoint of that ideal, and live our life from the standpoint of that ideal, then a time will come when our ideal will, in turn, create us. This is true. If, therefore, we make God's Perfect Ideal, the indwelling Christ within the soul, our ideal, and think from this ideal, and live our life in the light of this ideal, then a time will come when the Indwelling One will take charge of our life and recreate us in His image, and we shall find that we are one.

Now Christ is not only within us but He is also above us. He is both immanent and transcendent. By worshipping Christ, by adoration, by reaching up to His transcendent perfection, by the humbling of our little 'self', the Christ within us grows; and as He grows, so our weakness and failings become less and less.

The great Ideal, then, is that Christ should live in us and grow in us, finally taking complete charge of our life. We have to humble ourselves and exalt Christ in our thought and attitude of mind and soul. *'Of myself I am nothing, but Thou, O Christ, art All in All'.* This is the attitude of mind which leads to Divine Union. Extreme humbleness of mind and humiliation of the personal self make it possible for the Christ in us to grow, gradually taking more and more the charge of our life, until He reigns supreme and is All in All. We do not lose our identity, but Christ becomes All.

At first we are as a Kingdom divided against itself. On the one hand, Christ—on the other hand, the personal ego. By denying ourselves, or by humbling this personal ego, and by glorifying Christ, the former is gradually overcome, and the Lord from Heaven takes its place, to our eternal joy.

It will be seen, then, that all arrogant, self-assertive affirmations, as usually taught, such as, *'I am Life'*, or *'I am Spirit'* (meaning Christ, or God) inflate the false personality and smother the Christ babe within out of existence. This does not mean that we are to adopt a weak, negative attitude. Far from it. Like St Paul, we can say: 'I can do all things through Christ which strengtheneth me'. St Paul gives first place to Christ, and if we do the same then like this great apostle, we shall in our humble way attain also.

We, then, hold Christ as our ideal, and yield everything to Him.

Let us meditate upon these things.

'I live, yet not "I", but Christ liveth in me.'

'Christ is in us and is the hope of our glory.'

'I can do all things through Christ.'

'None of self, but all of Thee.'

Use the most helpful of these affirmations as often as possible, also the most helpful of others taught in Lesson III. By meditating upon these truths and by affirming them, you will hasten the time when you will find the hidden Kingdom. When you have found this, you will never lack any good thing. You will be led forth with peace: all the Divine Forces will hasten to minister to your eternal joy; you will find the work you have come here to do.

Continue to enter the Silence every night and morning. Endeavour to set aside regularly a certain time for yourself. If this does not appear possible, do the very best you can and make use of this combined denial and affirmation.

Man can never be hindered in his search for God, for all the gracious Spiritual forces are on his side.

Remember that those who have the greatest difficulties to overcome frequently make the most progress and become the strongest characters. Those who say, 'I cannot make good progress because I have not the time', never succeed. Such people, if they had the time and leisure, would find that they would not be able to make good use of it. On the other hand, those who make the best of things, no matter how difficult circumstances may be, find that when leisure and opportunity come to them, they are strong and capable of using them to the best advantage. Never put the blame on circumstances, for the cause is always within. Circumstances are only effects of causes within your own thought-life. Affirm leisure and opportunity continually and you will get them sooner or later, according to your faith.

WEEK FIVE:
VISUALIZATION

HTH speaks of the use and abuse of visualization as a technique. In this chapter, he twice refers to his own small book, The Message of a Flower.

MANY PEOPLE declare that they cannot visualize. Perhaps it is that they do not understand the meaning of the term. If we recall a day spent, say, at the seaside, we have to see in our mind the place that we visited, the people we saw and all the moving panorama of life which made up our day. We see the sea, the sunshine, the pier, the boats, various happenings—everything that was stamped on our memory, at the time, comes back to us in the form of a succession of pictures. This is memory. It is also visualizing.

Again, something is told us. 'Mr. B. has gone away to Switzerland.' We ask which Mr. B., and we are told that it is the short, stout Mr. B. with the florid complexion, whose wife always dresses so perfectly, who lives at Acacia Lodge, in Acacia Avenue. At once, you see the right Mr. B. in your mind—his shortness, stoutness, florid complexion, all complete; and this recalls many other peculiarities which your friend may have never noticed but which impressed themselves upon you. You also see Mrs. B. who dresses so exquisitely, and also Acacia Lodge. This is memory. It is also visualizing.

Again, you may wish to add bookshelves to your room. First, you think it would be nice to have them; next you imagine what the room would look like with the bookshelves in position, after which you begin to see the proposed fittings in detail. Whenever you look at the corner of the room, you imagine you see the bookshelves hanging there, filled with rows of your beloved volumes. This makes your fingers itch to construct the bookshelves, and often you say to yourself: 'I must make them'. The next thing may be that you see some wood that is 'just the thing', and soon you have the work under way, and great is your satisfaction when the bookshelves hang on the wall with your favourite authors carefully placed upon them. This is creative imagination. It is also visualizing.

Visualizing should be creative. When visualizing, one has to create or form an image in the mind. When recalling a scene from the past, this is easy to do because it relates to something one has already seen. True creative imagination, however, is the formation of an image in the mind of something that is to be. The sculptor can see, within the marble, the beautiful form of the statue that he is going to chisel. He merely chips away the superfluous stone, until the beauty of his own imagination is revealed in concrete form.

By carrying the image of Christ always in our mind, the superfluous wrappings which cover the soul are gradually broken away, until the indwelling Christ is revealed.

By picturing only the good, the beautiful and the true in our mind, eschewing all pictures of evil or untruth, only the good, the beautiful and the true are brought into visible manifestation.

It is, of course, perfectly legitimate to hold a worthy and righteous ambition in the mind. By so doing, we bring all our mental forces to a focus, and everything that we do is done in such a way as to have some bearing on the achievement of the object we have in view. Also, it unconsciously influences all our decisions. Every decision has some relationship to the accomplishment of the thing we have in view. Further, it also has the effect of putting into motion tremendously powerful forces which work invisibly on our behalf. This Spiritual Power, Force or Intelligence works for us while we sleep, while we play, and while we are engaged in other work. Opportunities open before us. The material that we need is attracted to us, and things come our way, by natural attraction, so that all we have to do is to make the best use of them.

How this law of mind acts even in the small affairs and duties of life is seen in the following. Imagine that you had to take over, say, a room, in which you, in future, would have to live or work. We will suppose that you find it in a state of dinginess, disorder and filth. Immediately you picture what the room would look like if it were thoroughly cleaned and tidied. You form visions of tidy shelves, orderly arrangement of articles and a clean and spotless condition generally. You may also picture a new floor-covering, new paint or wallpaper, a whitewashed ceiling and fresh curtains. You then set to work and all that you do is directed towards bringing the room as near as possible into the exact condition of order, brightness and cleanliness that you pictured in your mind. Further, you will not rest satisfied until your room expresses perfectly the picture held in your mind.

We have been speaking of creative imagination and not merely the ordinary pictures of our everyday thought. By creating a mental image of some desired achievement and consistently holding it before us, we put in motion tremendous forces. What is going to happen if we hold the wrong picture in our mind? Very great disharmony can be the only result. If the wrong course is persisted in, the result can only be disastrous in the extreme. Therefore, the more wise we become, the more we realize that Wisdom is the great thing that we need, so that we may be guided to do the right thing and to follow the right ambition.

We must not think, however, that we have to map out and plan our own lives. Really, we do not have to do this any more than we have to choose our parents or the country of our birth. Each day brings to us a series of experiences. Each experience can be dealt with in two ways. We can either deal with it constructively or destructively. Each experience gives us the opportunity to attain. The apparently unpleasant path of duty for duty's sake, of doing good although it can apparently bring us no reward, but only probable loss: this is always the path to follow. By giving up our narrow, selfish life, we gain the more abundant life of the Spirit, in which is fullness and complete satisfaction. But even if we always make a practice of following the difficult path, there will come to us perplexing problems when we do not know which road to choose; when we cannot see which course of action to take. Therefore, we again see that the great thing that we need is Wisdom. When we are guided by Infinite, Divine Wisdom, all our decisions are right decisions, and all that we do and undertake is in harmony with God's Will and Purpose, and with the perfect life which He has planned for us.

When we are led entirely by Divine Wisdom we hold only those pictures in the mind which correspond with our ideal life as it exists in Divine Mind. Each picture is a forerunner of that which is to be. The picture may alter from time to time, and develop, as greater possibilities open out before us, but it is substantially of that which is to be. If, however, we follow carnal or worldly desires (the desires of the personality), our mental pictures are not in harmony with that which is to be. Therefore, the result of such picturing can only be disharmony, disorder and disaster. The picture backed by desire creates for us more or less successfully, according to the intensity of our desire and our steadfastness in holding the picture in our mind; and all that is created in this way has to be broken down and, taken away from us, simply because it is not in harmony with our real and perfect life. We are apt to lament at such times and to bemoan our fate, but it is only Love bringing us back into the right path. If we were allowed to go on mis-creating it would be the worst thing possible for us; therefore Infinite Wisdom and Love (or, rather, the Law that is the outcome of them) break down what we build up, and take away that which we hold dear, in order to bring us into line once again with our glorious destiny.

Jesus came to transmute our desires and to wean us from earthly to heavenly things. To use our higher mental and spiritual forces in order to bring to us circumstances in which we can gratify our earthly and fleshly desires is the greatest possible un-wisdom. The more we misuse our powers in this way, the greater the resultant disorder and disharmony. In fact, the more we strive after earthly things, making use of our higher power in so doing, the more hell we produce for ourselves.

It is legitimate to hold a picture of good service and honest achievement in the mind, and to work up to it, so to speak, but earthly ambition should all be made subject to Christ and the inner spiritual life. We should follow no ambition for the sake of fame, vainglory, honour, power, wealth or position; but only as service to God and man. Our earthly desires have to be transmuted into spiritual aspirations. Not 'What can I get out of it?' or 'What is it going to bring to me?' or 'What fame, honour and adulation will it bring?', but 'How best can I serve my fellows, my day and generation, and my God?'.

Hold the picture of the Christ in the mind. Study the character of Jesus in the gospels and then visualize Him as your Ideal and Lord, and King. One who still desires carnal or earthly things, still loving the life which perishes, will find, upon self-analysis, that his ideal is not Christ, but a different being altogether, who offers the attractive baubles of life, ease, gratification, pomp, power, earthly love, sensation in some form, adulation, earthly praise, and so on. 'Choose you this day whom ye will serve.'

Finally, let a word be said about mental malpractice. The occult way of mis-creation is to form a mental image in the mind, say of money, or any other desired thing, every day, for say twenty minutes or so. While engaged in this practice, the will must be used very strongly, willing the desired thing to come to you. Given the right type of mind, this method is very effective. It brings results, but with it come sorrow and disaster. Finally, everything takes wings and flies away, the disillusioned one being left with his life in ruins.

In concluding this letter, let me again emphasize the fact that, having reached this stage, we must avoid egotism as we would the plague. Our prayer should always be *'Not I, but Christ liveth in me'*. The 'I am' affirmations elevate and exalt not the real Ego, but the false ego. 'Whosoever shall exalt himself shall be abased: and he that shall humble himself shall be exalted.' These are the words of Christ Himself. As already mentioned, such affirmations as *'I am success'*, or *'I am health'*, or *'I am self-confidence'* are helpful and legitimate. Autosuggestions such as these call into expression latent mental powers. They are legitimate because they simply call up powers latent in every individual.

Yet here again is another paradox. It is quite legitimate to develop one's personality, so long as we do not dominate others or use it in a selfish way, but this same developed personality must be surrendered to Christ or brought into captivity to Him. There is no greater joy than this.

Let us, rather than use affirmations that inflate the personality, say:

'O Christ, live in me and possess me utterly and completely. Take possession of all my thoughts and lead them in the channels of peace and quiet trust in Thee. Let Thy ways be my ways. Let Thy thoughts be my thoughts. Let Thy desires be my desires. Let Thy character be reflected in my character. Let Thy love fill me, flooding my soul and consciousness, then passing through me to others. Of myself I can do nothing, but Thou canst use me as a channel for Thy power to flow to others.'

'Take Thou possession of me, O Christ: I yield my flickering torch to Thee.'

All blessings be with you. Remember the secret: 'Not I, but Christ.'

Yours in His Service,

HENRY THOMAS HAMBLIN

INSTRUCTIONS IN PROGRESSIVE REFLECTIVE MEDITATION

Gradually, through meditating quietly in the way already described, there is built up in the mind and soul a wonderful structure of Truth. If the subject of Good, omnipresent, omnipotent and all-permeating, be held continually in the mind, and also made the subject of quiet meditation night and morning, innumerable ideas and flashes of Divine illumination and understanding, together with fresh knowledge derived directly from the Universal Mind, are added to the central idea. It is like building a heavenly palace of gems and precious stones. As heavenly ideas come to the mind, they are added to the structure that is being built around the idea of Good. We do not have to do the building. Everything fits into its right place, of its own accord.

It is customary to call pleasant experiences good and those which are unpleasant, evil. Yet they are both 'Good'. The human mind is so limited it can only think in pairs of opposites. On the surface, we see good and evil in conflict. We call disaster, adversity and bereavement or loss, evil; and prosperity, ease and enjoyment, good. Yet experiences teach us that the so-called good times are dangerous to our spiritual welfare, while what we miscall bad or evil times are beneficial to our soul's wellbeing. Therefore, the same experiences when looked at from a different standpoint are found to be the reverse of that which we supposed them to be; for what we called good we now call evil, while that which we called evil we now acknowledge as being good. In the lessons, also, we speak of good and evil as being relative and comparative. But this is not the Good upon which we wish to meditate.

When we become further advanced in understanding, we realize that all is Good, or the offspring of Good. Sin is thinking out of harmony with Good. Sin (in essence, wrong thinking), because it separates us from Good, brings in its train every possible negative ill. Suffering, lack, ugliness, disorder, misery, disease, sickness, death. But none of these things is evil. We call them evil, but they are the highest form of good that our sin, or wrong thinking, will allow to manifest. We fear death, looking upon it as evil, but we have to confess that it is often a friend in disguise, or 'a happy release'. Whatever comes to us is Good manifesting in the only possible form that we, by our sin, wrong attitude and imperfect thinking will allow to manifest.

What, then, do I mean by Good? Good is that which transcends what we call good and evil. Good, while it may include much of that which we call evil, which, of course, is only painful or unpleasant discipline, transcends all our ideas of good and evil, and our finite way of thinking in pairs of opposites.

From this One Source, Good, the pure and perfect stream of creation and life flows. This pure stream or fountain is Infinite Wisdom and Love, flowing from the heart of God, and this is the Source of all Creation (as it really is). All the laws of life and the universe are based upon Wisdom and Love. Therefore, there is no such thing as revenge or punishment from the Divine side. We punish ourselves, by our sin or wrong thinking, by which we separate ourselves from the Good, thus causing ourselves to suffer from every description of negative ill.

When we meditate on Good, we get beyond, or behind, what we call relative good and evil, the pairs of opposites of ordinary human thinking, the contending forces which, on the surface, produce disorder and unrest, making contact with our Divine Centre—the one pure and perfect Source from which all Life proceeds.

In this inner realm we find perfect peace and in place of unrest; perfect divine order instead of human disorder.

LESSON V

Dear Fellow Student of Truth,

By our mental pictures, we either bless or curse our life, build up or destroy. By our picturing the highest and best, our life becomes transformed. Let us therefore create pictures in our mind of beauty and perfection, for by so doing we are creating our future life. Instead of disease and sickness, let us picture God's perfect health and wholeness: instead of failure, let us see God's perfect Success: in place of ugliness, let us see the Infinite Beauty: instead of misery, let us compel our minds to behold the joy and happiness of God's perfectly expressed Idea. By persistently doing this we bring the Perfect Reality into expression, first in our own life and then in the lives of those around us. *We* must change before those around us can alter: *we* must become transformed within before our circumstances can be overcome.

Affirming for you the joy of mind-mastery and life-mastery,
I am, Yours in Unity and Peace,

HENRY THOMAS HAMBLIN

SPECIAL THOUGHTS ON DIVINE SUPPLY

Thought V

In Thought IV, we warned you against waste and extravagance. In this thought, we warn you against going to the other extreme. Do not, on any account, cultivate a mind of the pin-picking-up variety. While, under some conditions, picking up pins may be an admirable thing to do—as in the event that no more pins were to be made, or that they were very valuable and difficult to procure—yet in ordinary circumstances, such a habit shows a condition of mind unfavourable to success, and a mental attitude that keeps prosperity away.

There should be exercised, always, a sound economy—a making of the best use of material, time and opportunity, and an avoidance of waste; but economy should never be allowed to degenerate into a pin-picking-up habit.

This habit exhibits a wrong attitude of mind. It shows a tendency to think in a small, mean way; to cling to comparatively worthless things and to neglect great opportunities. It is possible for one to be so busy picking up pins that opportunities worth thousands a year are allowed to go by. It is possible to spend so much time over cheeseparing economies as to leave no time for great and useful achievements.

The time of even the poorest is generally of more value than the price of pins. Therefore, one who indulges in the pin-picking habit has no sense of values—he or she does not see things in their proper proportion.

One who picks up pins has his eyes glued to a tiny, restricted manifestation of wealth (a pin!), which he can see, and has no conception of the Infinite Wealth of the Divine Idea, which cannot at present be seen by him, but which is an ever-present reality. Confining one's attention in this way to the little which can be seen, stifles the imagination and compels it to produce a narrow and mean environment.

One who picks up pins generally has no conception of the glorious opportunities that life holds before him. He looks down amongst the dust at his feet and saves a pin, when he might be looking up to see all the abundance and riches which life is only too anxious to bestow upon him.

The pin-picking habit displays a lack of faith in the Infinite. It fears that there will be no more pins, therefore, valuable time must be wasted in picking them up. One who picks up pins and thinks in this narrow and petty way, utterly fails to realize the abundance and profusion of the Divine Supply.

Think in a larger way. Not about mean and petty things but in the consciousness of infinite abundance, always to hand, to those who realize that they live and move and have their being in the Universal Spirit (God), Who is the creator of all that is.

LESSON V

VISION, VISUALIZING AND MENTAL PICTURING OF THE DIVINE IDEAL

Visualizing is the true creative faculty of the mind. In Chapter II of *The Message of a Flower*, this creative process is amplified. 'In the beginning was the Idea, and the Idea was with God and the Idea was God.' (The word 'Idea' only partly expresses that which is meant by the word 'Logos'.) This means that at the beginning of this Cosmic Day, there was an idea imaged in the Divine Creative Mind. This Idea, being Infinite, included the whole universe, visible and invisible, down to the smallest detail, including you and me. This Divine Idea is being unfolded through countless

aeons in you and in me, and in everybody and everything. Within
each of us is hidden the Divine Idea. Outwardly we see the idea
but partly unfolded, but within lies the infinite perfection of the
Divine Vision. By retiring from the external world we enter the
Divine Mind and 'contact' the Infinite perfection of the Divine
Idea. We realize our oneness with it all. By finding God's infinitely
perfect Idea, God's Perfect Archetypal Man, the Christ within,
we hasten its outward expression. In the same way, if we refuse
to see evil in others and see only the good: if we see in them
God's Perfect Idea, we hasten its unfoldment and expression.
We therefore help to make the world a better place, not only for
ourselves, but also for others.

The small is a replica of the great. The atom is a miniature
solar system with a centre which corresponds to the sun, and
revolving electric particles which correspond to the planets. Man,
it has been said, is an epitome of the Universe. The Bible says
that man was made in God's image. The Hermetic saying is, 'As
above, so below; as below, so above'. From this it will be seen that
we can work effectively only as we work with God and in God's
way—the creative way. Mind is creative: all the universe is simply
an unfoldment of the Divine Mind; and man's mind, being part of
the Universal Mind, is creative also. Just as the Deity imaged or
visualized His perfect universe which is gradually being brought
into perfect expression through a process of evolution, so also can
we do great things, build up our life anew, and hasten our spiritual
evolution by using our mind in the same creative way.

The creative faculty is the power the mind possesses of building up a picture of its ideal. This picture is built up of mind stuff
and is a genuine creation. If the mind concentrates upon it persistently, all the invisible forces of life work together in such a
way as to reproduce the ideal in our outward life. Vision always
precedes achievement. Everything worthwhile that has ever been
achieved has first been imaged in its creator's mind. Every big
business is the outcome of vision. Speak to any man who has
built up a big business and you will find that he first saw the

possibilities, and visualized the expansion of his enterprise which afterwards materialized. Even a man who builds a wheelbarrow has first a picture in his mind of the exact kind of barrow that he desires to build. The difference between men is, as far as the achievement goes, one of vision. Two men may look at a swamp. The one sees a swamp and nothing more; the other sees waving corn, a wealth of orchards and rich meadow. He sets to work, gets other people interested, forms a company, drains the swamp and turns a desolate waste into a fruitful garden. His vision is translated into accomplishment. Without the vision, the swamp would have remained desolation and waste. It is the same with the higher life. 'Where there is no vision the people perish', said Solomon. It is necessary for us to carry with us the vision of all that we hope to be, of all that we hope to achieve. Whatever picture we hold in our mind will mould our life; let it be, therefore, a vision of the highest and truest aspirations of the soul.

There are two ways in which this creative faculty can be used. One can visualize God's Infinite Perfection and thus enter the real world of the Divine Ideal. By so doing, we come into harmony with the Divine Will and Purpose, into the Path of Destiny. We cease making trouble for ourselves; instead, we attract to us the Divine Forces and these 'hasten to minister to our eternal joy'. The other way is to force the mind to produce a picture, either of evil or of purely material success and power. Whatever is imaged in this way will become manifest in the life. This is the way of witchcraft, sorcery, mind-domination and hypnotism. It is evil, not because the powers and forces are evil, but because these Divine powers are used in the wrong way. By forcing our finite, human, personal will upon life and its forces, we are trying to coerce God, and all who do this are simply ground to powder. One can force success in this way, but unhappiness and loss of all that is worth having in life, follows in its train.

In the Divine Mind is imaged God's Perfect Ideal concerning each one of us. It is the Divine purpose that we shall ultimately be perfect even as our Heavenly Father is Perfect, and this perfection *already exists* in God's mind. By following our highest ideals, we get into harmony with the Divine plan; we walk the path that leads to the consummation of the Divine Idea. Therefore, by visualizing our highest ideals, we hasten our spiritual evolution: we bring harmony, peace and true success into our life. It is God's Will that we should be healthy. It is God's Will that we should have all our wants supplied. It is God's Will that we should be engaged in just that work in life which we have come here to do. It is God's Will that we should be happy, peaceful, joyful. It is God's Will that we should give ourselves to life and mankind in highest service and love. It is God's Will that we should show forth the fruits of the spirit. If we form mental pictures of these things, realizing that they all come from the Infinite Divine Supply: if we bathe ourselves, as it were, in the Eternal love, yielding up our finite self and false personality, surrendering our human will to the Divine Will and Purpose concerning us, we shall enter into perfect peace and freedom; our life will become successful in its highest and truest sense. This is the only way of true success and achievement.

Try to think in the form of mental pictures. When making an affirmation, try to picture what you are saying. Hold in your mind a picture of all that you hope to be and to achieve. Let everything that you visualize be in harmony with what you feel to be the Divine Will concerning your life.

In order to strengthen and develop the power of visualizing, the following exercise is given. It should be practised at odd times which otherwise would be wasted.

Take a flower, look at it carefully, observe its beauty of colour and form, thanking God for such a beautiful expression of His Thought and Love. Now close the eyes and 'see' the flower with your mental sight. Next trace the life of the flower and its plant back to its source. 'See' the lovely blossom close up slowly into a bud: 'see' the bud and the leaves disappear into the stem, the stem into a shoot, the shoot into the seed, and then within the seed 'see' the Divine Idea, which is the real and only 'cause'.

The same exercise can be repeated the other way round, beginning with the idea and working up to the completed flower.

Appendix

There are three kinds of visualizing. There is the visualizing of past events, the visualizing of ideals or achievement, and there is clairvoyance. (There is also the Black Magic form, but of this, more later.) The first is easy, the second is easy to some, but difficult to others. A boy may conceive, or receive, the idea of becoming a great man. He continually pictures himself, mentally, as great and successful. This mental imagery so influences all his decisions and actions as to make him become a relatively great man. What begins as a mental picture later completely masters the life. Thus one who visualizes worldly success and gives himself up to this ambition, becomes, in time, the slave of his success.

If, however, Christ is the Ideal held and pictured in the mind, then we become Christlike. If we hold the perfect character of Jesus continually before our mind's eye, we become more and more like Him.

It will be seen then how necessary it is that we hold the right ideal before us and picture only the highest, truest and best.

In contrast to all this you can picture the joys of Heaven, the harmony of the Spirit, or of this world freed from all sin and hate and imperfection. Such picturing is helpful in the extreme. Behind the changing imperfect world of the senses is the Perfect World of the Spirit wherein is love, Joy, Beauty, Order, and every pure delight. This is the reality, and by holding a picture of it, or if not a picture, a thought or idea of it, in the mind, we are drawn heavenwards. 'Set your affection on things above, not on things of the earth.' All honest achievement can be pictured in the mind. The more you achieve when inspired by a good motive, the more helpful you become to the world.

Above all do not neglect the Silence with its times of quiet meditation. Almost everything depends upon these.

WEEK SIX:
THOUGHT-CONTROL

PERSONALLY, I find it helpful to think of the subconscious mind as abdominal, or in the region of the solar plexus, the conscious mind as occupying the brain, and the superconscious as above the brain. No doubt, scientifically, this is absurd, but it is helpful to me. By raising the thoughts and consciousness to a region above the head, so to speak, we make contact with spiritual ideas—we enter, in time, into a wider place—a more expansive consciousness.

It is helpful, however, to remember that Christ indwells us, literally. We can look within and realize that 'Christ liveth in us'. Yet, at the same time, He is with the Father (God transcendent). It is Christ in us Who enables us to rise in consciousness to a higher plane. It is Christ in us Who is trying to find expression in purer lives, more perfect service and in thoughts and actions, the motive power of which is universal love.

We must not look upon the subconscious mind as necessarily evil, although it has animal propensities. These have been necessary for the preservation of the human race, as a higher animal. Now, when man is born again, becoming a spiritual creature, these old desires must not be suppressed, but must be translated into higher service.

The next discussion is about the control of the emotions. Hamblin tells us that it is extremely harmful to repress them; to do so is to sow the seeds either of nervous trouble or organic disease.

It is much better from a health point of view if we let our temper have a good fling, but it may be disastrous as far as our relationships with other people are concerned. Anger is a very powerful emotion and its nervous energy, when aroused, must be discharged. Rather then repress it and fight it down, it is far better to break a few things, in spite of the loss and damage this incurs, and the waste of valuable nervous energy. The great thing is that it allows the tremendous nervous energy, generated by the temper emotion, to escape. By so doing the health is not undermined. But what a waste.

Far better, the nervous energy of 'temper' must be consciously directed into other channels. This does not mean choking down our anger and then doing something in the way of work. What we must do is to say to ourselves, 'I will now use up this 'temper' energy by doing this digging' (or other useful work). Then the digging must be proceeded with *at once*. It spoils everything if we delay. While digging, we must consciously expend our 'temper' energy in the vigour with which we dig. The same energy, however, could be expended in mental work, just as profitably and effectively.

So long as we keep our faces turned towards the Light, and meet God in the Silence every day, we are safe; and although our progress may appear slow, or even nil, yet definite progress will be made.

HTH next speaks of how a balanced life can be found through meditating inwardly while remaining true to the demands of the external world.

On no account, then, must we give up our times of meditation in the quiet place. If some imperative duty calls us away at the time usually given to entering the Silence, we must find some other opportunity. If we are really in earnest, we shall find time. The difficulty is only temporary, and, if we are steadfast, it soon disappears. We then find ourselves with all the necessary time for meditation at our disposal. It is not always the one with the most time and opportunity who makes the best student. It is very often the one with the least time who makes the most progress. Our circumstances are always the best for us at the time, and we can never be hindered really, by lack of time in our spiritual unfoldment.

Further, we must not look upon the conscious mind as inferior or evil. It has its limitations, but without it we could never make contact with the world in which we live, and without such contact we could never gain the experience which we so much need. Life supplies us with wonderful experiences and opportunities. Life is a wonderful privilege as well as a glorious adventure. Therefore, let us make the greatest possible use of it by work and service, so that we gain the greatest possible amount of experience.

The ideal life is dual. It consists of an inner spiritual life which is eternal, and an outer life which, though temporal, is of the greatest value as an experience for the soul. He who lives both lives fully and well-balanced is truly successful. He may be very far from worldly success and be unknown to fame, but his life is truly successful, in the highest sense of the word.

Going back to the subject of the subconscious mind: in addition to acknowledging that this mind is not evil, although it has animal propensities and gives us many impulses that cause us trouble and sorrow, we must look upon it as a very faithful friend and servant. This wonderful and extraordinary mind of power and achievement will do anything for us, if we will only lead it aright. It will make a habit of anything that we repeatedly do. Indeed, that is the subconscious mind's duty. It is not evil, it is only trying to help us. If we do a certain thing every day, the subconscious will either do it for us without our conscious knowledge, or else give us a craving to do it consciously. If we do wrong, then a bad habit is formed, and it is as though we had an evil spirit within us, compelling us to repeat the wrong, in spite of our efforts to do better. If, however, we practise and repeatedly do something that is good, the subconscious mind soon takes a hand in the game and not only makes it easy for us to do the right or good thing, but gives us a craving to do the right or good thing.

We can therefore train the subconscious mind to produce good habits instead of bad. We cannot overcome evil habits by fighting them, because this directs the attention of the subconscious to them, thus increasing the trouble. Much, however, can be accomplished by building up good habits of such a character as will replace the bad ones, and also entice the attention of the subconscious away from the latter.

This however, is quite all right in theory, but unless we can make use of a power far greater than that of our personality, and draw upon wisdom far greater than our human wisdom, we get weary in well-doing, and drift back into the old life. We become backsliders. This is the fate of all who try to attain by their own efforts alone, and try to plan and guide their life according to human wisdom. By all means, let us build up character and good habits, by the use of a sound psychology, but we need something in addition. We need Divine Wisdom and the Holy Spirit. These can be found only in the quiet place.

By retiring into the quiet and repose of the 'Inner Life', and by raising our thoughts and consciousness to a higher plane, we get in touch with spiritual things. We touch the superconscious. That is, we commune with that which is above human consciousness. We enter the realm of Truth, which is inscrutable, in that it cannot be either described or understood intellectually.

By meditating in the quiet place, we come in touch with Divine Ideas. Divine Wisdom reveals to us the way we should go, and the Spirit gives us power to follow Truth, no matter where it may lead.

Meditating in the quiet place will set a poor habit-ridden soul free, at the same time helping him to build up good habits to take the place of those from which he is delivered. By meditating in this way, we become saturated by Divine Power so that all the difficulties of life can be overcome, and the most searching and trying temptations withstood.

By meditating in the quiet place upon those thoughts which we desire to occupy our mind during the day, we make thought-control and thought-selection possible. People often say that they cannot control their thoughts. They could, if they meditated upon Truth both night and morning, in the quiet place. It is only by such meditating in the Presence, that our secret thoughts can be cleansed, and the very source of our thinking purified.

There is some central point in the mind around which our thoughts revolve. It is exceedingly difficult to control the thoughts while that point, or central idea, remains unchanged. By meditating in the quiet place, this point becomes changed in some way, so that our thoughts revolve around a more Christlike idea. Because the centre or fixation point becomes changed, the trend of the thoughts changes also. It is true that we have to be constantly on the watch, controlling, restraining and guiding our thoughts into higher channels, but by far the most important thing of all is meditation in the quiet place.

Yours in the Fellowship of this Glorious Truth,

HENRY THOMAS HAMBLIN

INSTRUCTIONS IN PROGRESSIVE REFLECTIVE MEDITATION

We have still to clear the ground a little more, so to speak, before our palace of Truth can be erected.

You are probably desirous of agreeing with all that has been said about Good being the only Principle or Cause (and that, therefore, all is Good) yet you still feel that there is a malevolent evil, out of God's control, which is liable to attack us at any moment. That there are forces of evil we admit: but they, like our own sins, passions and wrongdoing, are due to an absence of Good. They are not an omnipotent power out of God's control, but are a negation or voidness. Mystically speaking, an archangel falls from heaven, becomes separated from his Divine Source, and can create nothing that has any real life in it. He creates, but such creations, having no life of themselves, must pass away. Christ (the archetypal Man, the only-begotten Son, the Spiritual Man created in the likeness of God, the Logos or Word) is The Truth and The Life. There is no other truth and no other life, really. All others are only a seeming or counterfeit.

Therefore, while there are powers of evil, they are a negation, or voidness. They can have no power over us if we refuse to recognize them, taking our stand firmly and wholly in Truth and Christ. One of the objects of our Lord's incarnation was to demonstrate this great truth by non-resistance. By refusing to resist evil and all the powers of evil, which rose up *en masse* against Him at the close of His life, Christ showed, once and for all, that they have no power over spiritual man, although they may torture the body. When they thought they had killed Him, Christ was in Hades, preaching the Gospel to those who died in their sins in the days of Noah. Here is a victory indeed. All the powers of evil can only succeed in sending our Lord to preach His glorious Gospel of Love to those in the dark regions of Hades, the place of departed Spirits.

When our Lord tells us not to resist evil, He does not mean that we are to give in to temptation, or to approve of, or condone, sin. What Christ does mean is that when we are wronged or persecuted we are not to resist. When an injustice is done us, or when we receive an injury, we are not to retaliate. This means that no matter how much others may attempt to hurt us, on no account may we attempt to hurt them. We may have to defend ourselves, or those under our protection, but we must defend only, not trying to hurt the aggressor at all. Some would even go farther than this, but most will find this standard quite high enough.

The great point is this. If we do not resist evil, it loses its power and defeats itself. If we do resist it, we invest it with power, perpetuating the disorder of our own life and the disorder of the world at large.

The secret of it all is that the Divine Order is always seeking to manifest itself, and does so if we cease violating the Law of Love. As soon as we cease trying to 'get our own back', cease resisting injustice and injury—forgiving and loving, instead of harbouring resentment—the Divine Order and Harmony begin to appear.

Whatever there may be on the surface in the way of apparent conflict between good and evil, due mainly to the limitation of our finite method of thinking (in pairs of opposites), and to our sin in thought and deed, behind, or underneath, it all is to be found the one Source, Good, from which flows the perfect, pure fountain of Wisdom and Love.

The object of our meditation is, then, to get behind, or above, all conflict, to the calm stillness of the inner Life of the Spirit. ('God is Spirit', says Jesus.) By our doing this repeatedly, all the disorder of our life is smoothed away, and the disorder of the world also is lessened.

LESSON VI

Dear Fellow Student of Truth,

Better than all attempts to influence the subconscious mind by suggestion is the raising of the thoughts to the Christ realm. Then Divine ideas flow to us, passing to the subconscious mind automatically. These Divine ideas or thoughts gradually change us until we become new creatures.

When harmful thoughts assail us, we should not run away from them, but should meet them boldly, affirming their Divine opposite, until they shrink away into nothingness. Nothing that is not of God can stand the light of Truth. There is a mental cowardice which, if given in to, makes us run away from all thoughts and suggestions of unpleasant things to which we are liable. These must not be avoided, but must be faced boldly by statements of Truth, until they are driven away or dismissed.

Then we can realize the reality of the Divine Perfection as something that is real and present now and always.

Yours in Unity and Truth,

HENRY THOMAS HAMBLIN

SPECIAL THOUGHTS ON DIVINE SUPPLY

Thought VI

Do not think that you depend upon man or material sources for supply. Your only source of supply is the Universal Spirit in whom you live and move and have your being. Just as, physically, you are surrounded by air, so also are you surrounded by Spirit. This same Omnipresent Spirit (the creative Life of God) is Infinite Wisdom, Intelligence, love and Creative Power. According to your faith in Omnipresent Spirit Substance to bring to you all that you need, you will receive abundance, pressed down and over-flowing—more than you can either ask or think.

Further, there is in you a spark of the Divine Fire. The real self, man, or ego, in you, is spirit—offspring of the One Eternal Spirit, Source, Creator and Ruler of all things. Because you, in reality—i.e., in your real self—are part of the Great Creative Spirit, you have only to realize your Divine Sonship, in order to enter into God's Abundance. All things are yours—you have only to realize this, inwardly, in order to bring the riches of the Divine Mind into visible manifestation.

So long as you think that your source of supply is limited to man, to business, to 'times', good or bad, to your own cunning, cleverness or smartness, you will be subject to these limitations. So long as you believe in limitation and think from the standpoint of human limitation, your life will be limited and filled with want or financial difficulty. It is only when you realize that you have only one source of supply and that this Source is God (Omnipresent Spirit), and that you are heir to all the Divine riches, by virtue of your sonship (your real self being a spark from the Divine Fire, or offspring of the One Eternal Creative Spirit); it is only then that you can become free from limitation, and enter into the free use of the Infinite Divine Abundance.

To think that your supply depends upon man, or upon manmade systems of trading, employment, or investment, is to limit yourself to these things. Whereas to realize that God, only, is your supply is to enter into freedom.

Your supply will come to you *through* material sources and human agencies, but *from* God (the Creative Logos). This is the vital essential truth for you to observe.

Therefore, declare and affirm continually, in the face of all sense-evidence to the contrary, that *'My only source of supply is God, and as His child I am abundantly supplied'*.

LESSON VI

THE SUBCONSCIOUS MIND AND THOUGHT-CONTROL

There is the subconscious mind: there is the conscious mind of the senses: there is the superconscious mind. At the bottom is the subconscious; this rises partly into our present limited consciousness, while above this is the higher or Christ-consciousness. The latter can be entered into only after much seeking. Some teachers speak of the subconscious mind as the devil, the conscious mind as the carnal or natural mind, and the superconscious as the spiritual or Divine Mind. The reason they do this is that the subconscious mind is more animal than spiritual and gives us a backward or downward pull. This, however, is not really evil, for it is essential to our highest development, because we cannot become strong without having something to overcome. Therefore, although this downward pull seems evil, it really ministers to our highest good. That is to say, it becomes 'good' to us only if we overcome the lower nature. If we give way to the downward pull then it becomes 'evil' to us, and very much so. The lower nature must be transmuted into, or raised up to, the higher. Then, and not until then, it becomes 'good' to *us*. Some teachers call the conscious mind 'carnal', or 'natural', because it accepts the evidence of the senses, which is almost invariably opposed to true spiritual wisdom. They also speak of the superconscious as the spiritual mind, because it is the Christ-mind.

But little need be said about the conscious mind. It gathers its knowledge from outside sources. It learns through the evidence of the senses; it accepts the great illusions of life as facts; it is deceived by appearances; it is also a clearing-house for thoughts and ideas. The Will can decide whether a thought coming into the conscious mind shall be rejected or allowed to pass down into the subconscious mind, there to be translated into action and become part of the life. The Will and the conscious mind stand at the gate of the subconscious mind. They either guard the life from evil, or they can allow negative thoughts to enter: thoughts which, in time, will hamper or even destroy the life.

The conscious mind is very small compared with the subconscious, soon reaching the limit of its resources. The subconscious mind has been looked upon as a reservoir of blind force and intelligence. This is an illusion, for the subconscious mind is capable of thought of a quality and capacity that staggers the finite understanding. The important thing is that the subconscious mind possesses immense power and a wonderful intelligence and can be influenced by the Will acting through the conscious mind. That is to say, by taking thought, or by controlling our thoughts, we can govern the subconscious mind. By governing our subconscious mind, we control our actions, for it is the wellspring of all action. By controlling our actions, we govern our life, for the life is for the most part the result of our actions.

Every thought that we allow to enter the subconscious mind influences it for good or ill: it is a command to bring forth action, either good or bad, according to its kind. Every thought that enters the subconscious mind must manifest some time in the form of action, or, if suppressed, will bring forth neurosis in the body. To allow poisonous thoughts to enter the subconscious and then to suppress, by force of will, the natural action resulting therefrom, is the quick road to nervous disease and great unhappiness. 'Cleanse thou me from secret faults', prayed the Psalmist, and he did so because he realized that the very springs of his life needed to be cleansed, rather than that he should attempt to cover up pollution. The secret of right thinking is to follow the highest ideal and accept those thoughts only which harmonize with it. By rising above the ordinary mind of the senses, we can behold the infinite perfection of God's Ideal Man, Christ, and if we will ever guard our thoughts and accept those only which correspond to this Ideal, we shall be creating our life anew.

'Instead of the thorn shall come up the fir tree: Instead of the brier shall come up the myrtle tree: It shall be to the Lord for a name, For an everlasting sign that shall not be cut off.'

Continue to enter the Silence both night and morning. Bless all creatures great and small and breathe upon them your love. See in them the Infinite good and perfection. Make diligent use of the affirmations, until they become part of your life.

Entering the Silence and times of quiet meditation are really the secret of the whole matter. If we neglect these, then all attempts at right thinking are in vain. Our thoughts always revolve around a centre. If this centre is not Divine, then our thoughts are not Divine, and no external efforts will ever make them so. By finding God in the Silence and by meditating on Divine Things, the Centre around which our thoughts revolve is shifted nearer to God, so that all thoughts and our subconscious thinking become more Godlike. In course of time, our Thought-Centre becomes entirely merged in the Divine.

The reason some Truth students make no progress is that they think that efforts towards thought-control and an intellectual study of Truth are all that is necessary. They are, however, dealing with powers beyond their control. What is needed is the quiet time when actual, living contact is made with the Divine Spirit. This entrance to the Divine Presence subjects us to spiritual influences which so transform us inwardly that the current of our thoughts is naturally changed, and with this change comes a reformation of our subconscious thinking.

GENERAL HINTS

Think cheerfully. Think hopefully. Refuse to admit that anything is hopeless or utterly evil. Affirm the Good: do not bark against the bad. Impute good motives to all. Think only of others in order to help them.

THIS IS THE WAY OF HAPPINESS

'Finally, brethren, whatsoever things are true, whatsoever things are honest, whatsoever things are pure, whatsoever things are lovely, whatsoever things are of good report; if there be any virtue, and if there be any praise, think on these things.'

THOUGHTS TO AVOID

Thoughts of envy, jealousy, self-pity, destructive criticism of every kind (for instance, never find fault with the weather, or your neighbour, or your circumstance), fear, worry, hate, revenge, impurity, pessimism, failure, sickness, disease, ill-health, weakness, poverty, lack, restriction of means and supply, unhappiness, hopeless grief, injustice.

THOUGHTS TO CULTIVATE

Keep your mind on thoughts of love, harmony, justice, unity, brotherly kindness, encouragement, thankfulness, true neighbourliness, courage, trust, peace, forbearance, purity, health, life, energy, strength, abundance, plenty, unlimited supply, happiness, joy, gladness, hope, cheerfulness, justice, accomplishment, achievement, overcoming and the final overcoming of good.

When a wrong thought comes into your mind, dismiss it at once before it can find a lodging place, and then turn your thoughts upwards to your Perfect Ideal. Affirm the very opposite of the thought you wish to conquer. Above all, do not neglect the Silence.

ADDITIONAL TEACHING
based on personal experience
and that of many students

You may proceed satisfactorily for a time, regulating your thoughts to such a nicety, that you may begin to congratulate yourself on your success. If you allow yourself to fall into this error, you will surely rue it, for self-congratulation is a mild form of boasting. Now boasting, no matter how mild, is fatal in spiritual things. It always causes a downfall. If a student writes to me in a boastful, self-satisfied vein I know that he will shortly come a severe 'cropper'. We can avoid such a disaster by continually turning to the Spirit and giving Him the praise. Like St Paul, we can say: *'Yet not I, but Christ'*.

Again, after going along for a time quite satisfactorily, and when you think that you have overcome your besetting wrong-thinking, once and for all, you may be assailed by a perfect flood of wrong thoughts, worse than any that you have known before.

This is merely a test. Therefore do not be alarmed. All will be well if you remain steadfast and will meet the difficulty in the following way. Turn to God and say: *'Thou alone canst save and keep'*. By so doing, you confess that your own efforts are of no avail, and that it is only the Power of the Spirit or Christ which can deliver and keep you. If you maintain this attitude of 'none of self, but all of Thee' you will be taken safely through the experience, without failing.

It took me years to find out this great secret, but since it was revealed to me during a very severe initiation by trial, wonderful progress has been made, and my days are filled with praise and thanksgiving for all God's dealings with me. During this experience things got so acute and despairing I had even to discard St Paul's affirmation 'I can do all things through Christ which strengthened me', and say instead: 'I am nothing, and I can do nothing, just undertake for me, O Lord.'

Then, once this lesson has been learnt, it never has to be learnt again. When the finite 'self' has been got out of the way, the Power of Christ's Spirit is liberated, giving us liberty and freedom from the bondage of sin and all that has held us down and kept us back.

It is wonderful, this life of the Spirit.

*

Depression must always be overcome, for it brings failure and negative ills into the life. We must resist the devil of depression, and then he flees from us. We can overcome depression by cultivating a spirit of joy, thanksgiving, and rejoicing. We can repeat the words: 'Health, success, happiness and joy', in the face of depression and discouragement, at the same time breathing deeply, and feeling lifted up above our troubles, to a higher plane of achievement, happiness and freedom. We have to feel the joy, the uplift and the spaciousness of deliverance.

With regard to avoiding criticism. What is referred to is negative, destructive criticism, fault-finding, imputing wrong and unworthy motives to others, picking holes in others, judging others, and so on. Our Lord said, 'Judge not, that ye be not judged; for with what judgment ye judge, ye shall be judges; and with what measure ye mete, it shall be measured to you again.' Some people sit for whole evenings criticizing other people, pulling their character to pieces, judging then harshly and unjustly; all the time inferring how superior they are themselves, and how much better they would act if they were in the shoes of the one criticized and judged. This sort of thing is most terribly destructive: not to the one criticized, but to the one who sits in judgment on his fellows. It alienates him from life, it darkens his closing years, and dooms him to a cheerless, unhappy old age.

Constructive criticism, on the other hand, is good and helpful if it is done wisely and without offence. If something can be altered for the better, then it is our duty to point out how it can be done. But we must be careful about putting other people right. We must not try to take the mote out of our brother's eye, the while a big chunk of wood is in our own. All this leads up to this: that most of the disorder in our life and the trouble we experience through other people is due to something wrong within ourselves. Through becoming changed ourselves, our outward life becomes changed. Instead of judging and condemning other people, we should try to see the Christ in them. It may be difficult at first, but, if we persevere, our life, in course of time, becomes transformed and glorified. Also our own character and disposition change for the better, much to the comfort and relief of those around us.

WEEK SEVEN:
NO EVIL IN THE PLAN

In this letter, HTH defines sin as 'acting out of harmony with Divine Law'.

BY THIS TIME, you are no doubt such a believer in the reality and omnipresence of Good, that you have no need to deny evil—that is, of course, an evil and malignant purpose running through God's Universe, or an eternal principle of malignant evil, co-existing with Divine Good Principle, or an evil and malignant, unfriendly purpose underlying all life's experiences. The only evil is sin—acting out of harmony with Divine Law, and falling short of the Divine Ideal. 'For all have sinned and come short of the glory of God.' Evil is not a thing in itself so much as a falling short of God's perfection. It is a privation or absence of Good. By sin we bring disorder into our consciousness and this manifests outwardly in the form of disharmony and suffering of various kinds. What we term evil is often the working of Divine Justice. It is only an appearance of evil. It is, in reality, Good in disguise, trying to do the very best for us, and is certainly not an evil purpose thwarting us and torturing us out of malice.

It does not matter whether we look upon the tempter as the subconscious mind, or believe that he is a great spiritual being, who is omniscient, omnipresent, and capable of reading our inmost and most secret thoughts. Whichever we believe does not alter the fact that test (temptation) and trial each form a necessary part of our spiritual training. We have to be tempted and we have to be tried, also we must reap as we sow, according to

Divine Justice, but none of these is evil. It is only Good, Infinite Wisdom and Love, working to encompass our highest good.

Life is good, and is always endeavouring to do us a good turn. But if we oppose it and fight it at every turn, how can it manifest the good that it is trying to bring into expression? Utterly impossible. So long as we fight life we keep the good, which would otherwise manifest, away. It is only when we realize that life is good and not evil; it is only when we co-operate with it, instead of opposing it, that harmony can be brought into manifestation. We are not to look upon life's experiences as evil, but as a necessary and valuable aid in our spiritual unfoldment. By fighting against life, we create needless suffering for ourselves. If we think that life is evil, we naturally are constantly up in arms against it. By fighting against its experiences we create great disharmony, and this confirms us in our belief that life is evil. Therefore, you see why it is that by believing in evil, that is, that life is unfriendly and has behind it a sinister design, and that therefore its experiences are evil and must be resisted, evil seems to meet us at every turn. As soon as one thing seems to have been fought and overcome, another so-called evil appears in its place.

Until we learn the great secret that life is good and friendly, and is always endeavouring to do us a good turn, it is natural for us to fight life. When we learn wisdom, however, we are very careful not to resist life's experiences, but to meet them with open arms, looking upon life as a friend who comes to bless us, instead of as an enemy who comes to destroy.

Most of the suffering of life is due to fear and panic. People are apprehensive of what life will bring them next. They fear unemployment, illness; disease, disaster, loss, failure, malignant fate. The foundation of their fear is a firmly rooted idea that life is evil. If they believed it to be good, and were to co-operate with it instead of opposing it, they would find, as many advanced souls have found, to their eternal joy, that life is good and friendly, seeking only our highest good. When this truth is apprehended fear passes away and the life is transformed.

This opposition to life and its consequent suffering and resultant fear are aptly illustrated in the popular attitude towards
disease, sickness and illness. These things, because they are looked
upon as evil, are fought, opposed and feared. Because they are
fought against as something evil, they increase and become more
painful and difficult to deal with. All illness is an attempt on the
part of Nature to cleanse and renew our body, thus bringing
about a state of balance, and a certain chemical condition of the
blood that is essential for health. If the illness is co-operated with,
instead of opposed, either mentally or by physical means, or both,
health is soon restored.

Nature is always trying to heal us, and an illness is her way of
ridding the system of rubbish, or of restoring that normal balance or condition of blood upon which health depends. If, however, her efforts are thwarted and the illness suppressed, Nature
will try again and again, if there is enough vitality left in the
patient, to find some other avenue, or form or illness, through
which the healing, restoring, balancing process can be accomplished. Consequently, if Nature is thwarted and suppressed at
every turn, there comes a time when she can do no more; and
because her vitality is exhausted, the body breaks down into organic disease. If, however, especially in the early stages, illness is
looked upon as a healing crisis; if, instead of looking upon illness
as an enemy to be fought, or the work of some malignant influence, it is co-operated with, then health is soon restored. Nature is
kind if we co-operate with her. We can only master her by obeying
her laws and by co-operating with her beneficent designs.

It must not be imagined from the foregoing that we advise
students to do without doctors. Until humanity is on an altogether higher plane, doctors and surgeons will be necessary; but
it is wise to choose one who relies more on the healing powers of
Nature than upon drugs or serums.

The harmful effects of repressive measures, by means of drugs
or even serums, are, I believe, mild and innocuous in comparison with the repressive influences of the mind and the destruc-

tive action of fear. This subject will have to be dealt with more fully in a later Letter. All treatment directed against illness, which is Nature's beneficent way of helping us and restoring our health, is harmful. All forms of repression are harmful, but mental repression is by far the worst, because it is the most powerful. Mental and metaphysical treatment directed against the illness or ailment as something evil, is extremely harmful. All 'treatment', or prayer, should co-operate with Nature instead of opposing her. Nature is the outer garment of God. While it is true that there are higher and more powerful laws than those of Nature, yet they must not be invoked in order to thwart or oppose Nature's beneficent processes and designs. There must be harmony on all planes, spiritual, mental and physical. Our circumstances are always the best for us at the time, and the only way they can be altered for the better is by ourselves becoming changed. This can be done only by meditation in the Silence and in quiet yet persistent waiting upon God.

The question arises, how is the student to enter into an inner knowledge of Truth and realize that all is good, for then it would become a simple matter to think and act from this higher standpoint, co-operating with life instead of fighting against it? The answer is that there are two ways by which this may be accomplished. One is by co-operating with life and meeting all experiences and discipline as friends, denying that life is evil, affirming continually that it is good, that good is always trying to manifest, and that everything is working together for good. This will prove to him, in the long run, that he is on the right road at last. The other way is by meditation in the quiet place, realizing the Omnipresence and Allness of Good. If this is done regularly, patiently and perseveringly, good is seen in everything, and gradually it is recognized more and more that there is no evil purpose, principle or design in life, and that Good is an omnipresent reality, because God is Love.

Desiring for you an ever-increasing understanding of Truth,
Yours in the One Service,
HENRY THOMAS HAMBLIN

INSTRUCTIONS IN PROGRESSIVE
REFLECTIVE MEDITATION

AS we have already seen, Good may include both good and evil, or what we call good and evil. Good transcends all our finite conceptions It is something far greater than our puny ideas on the subject of good and evil. We might argue about relative good and evil until the end of time, but we could never arrive at any understanding or clear decision. We can arrive at an interior understanding of Truth only through a spiritual awakening. Truth can be apprehended only by the soul, through direct knowing. No-one can explain Truth, for the reason that It transcends all finite conceptions and is entirely beyond the human intellect. Whereas the finest intellect is baffled in spite of a search for Truth, continued and persevered with, it may be for many years, unceasingly, the soul, through meditation, receives a flash of illumination whereby it *knows* the Truth which forever sets us free.

The great paradox is this, that while Good may include what we term good and evil, it transcends them, at the same time excluding even the faintest idea of imperfection. All the perplexities of life and a relative universe can be solved only by meditation upon THAT which transcends them all: which is *All* and yet transcends all. The dividing line between the false teaching and the true is this: whereas the former bids men to seek after things, the latter bids them to seek the Source of all things. In our Lord's words, to seek first the Kingdom of Heaven, or God, after which all things needful are added. The Kingdom of Heaven is a state of consciousness wherein we realize our complete oneness or at-one-ment with our Divine Source. When we reach this state, or even something remotely approaching it, we realize how utterly futile is seeking for results, making demonstrations, and so on. Finding the Kingdom is so transcendent that everything else is flattened out into nothingness.

We meditate, then, upon God as the Supreme Being, Source and Essence—Good. Transcendent, beyond and above time, space and sense, behind all pairs of opposites, always beyond our highest aspirations.

Brushing aside all thoughts of time, space, conflict, opposing forces, becoming, progress, evolution, unfoldment, we direct our attention calmly and quietly upon that which was and is and ever shall be; the one eternal *is-ness*, who is always complete, perfect, whole and sufficient in itself.

Therefore, we begin our meditation proper by thanking God that there is no change, conflicting forces, or violence, disorder or even becoming, in the secret, inner place of the Spirit, but only perfect calm, repose, divine order, and so on. While some students are capable of meditating upon abstract ideas, the majority are helped by picturing something that will act as a symbol of perfect repose, wholeness, and the stillness that is not inactivity, but is the effect of activity in perfect order, wherein is absolute poise, balance and effortless accomplishment. We shall speak more of this in our next letter.

LESSON VII

Dear Fellow Student of Truth,

There are two things of the utmost importance that you need to realize, and which when realized transform the life.

The first is that there is no malevolent, evil purpose in life at all, but that your life is cradled in love by God Who is Love itself. God is Love and God has planned your life, and is looking after you every step of the way. The purpose behind your life is Love, directed by infinite Wisdom. When you realize this, your life becomes wondrously transformed.

Secondly, although there is disorder, violence, evil, tragedy and horror around you, yet none of these things can touch you, if you 'dwell in the secret place of the most High'. They may come near you, but they cannot touch you. All the Divine Forces are on your side, protecting and upholding you, so long as you abide beneath the shadow of the Almighty.

All is well, for all is Love.

Yours in the Love of God,

HENRY THOMAS HAMBLIN

SPECIAL THOUGHTS ON DIVINE SUPPLY

Thought VII

Do not envy or covet other people's prosperity or riches. One who does this unconsciously relegates himself to the ranks of the poor and hard up. To covet or envy perpetuates a state of mind which effectually keeps one out of the abundance consciousness. One who envies another's prosperity is admitting to himself that he is an outsider—that he is poor, needy and does not possess the same amount of prosperity the other person possesses. This acts as an autosuggestion to the subconscious, which, accordingly, manufactures circumstances for us which are poor: ones which are mean and filled with financial care.

Therefore, one who envies, or covets, his neighbour's goods or prosperity manufactures for himself poverty, lack and financial trouble and difficulty. There is no escape for him, for life is governed by infallible, undeviating psychological law, and so long as he works against them he must suffer. *He reaps exactly as he sows.*

Further, do not resent the success, progress and prosperity of other people. In its destructive effects, this is far worse even than envy and covetousness. Not only does it effectually keep a man out of the abundance consciousness, but it robs him of his health and happiness, and makes him do very foolish things which bring him much loss and suffering. Harbouring resentment warps a man's judgment, making it impossible to arrive at impartial decisions, thus effectually preventing him from being successful in his undertakings.

None of us can enter the abundance consciousness so long

as we admit to our inner self that we do not possess abundance or prosperity. By envying others, we admit that they possess prosperity and that we do not. Therefore, we must cease envying, coveting or resenting other's prosperity and rejoice with them over it. Having done this we can realize and affirm that all abundance is ours—abundance and prosperity that is unlimited. By becoming steeped in this thought or idea of unlimited abundance, our circumstances become changed; for the Infinite Life, of which we are an individual manifestation, expresses itself either in the form of beauty and abundance, or ugliness and poverty, according to the nature of our thoughts and the attitude of our minds.

Therefore say and affirm:

'I rejoice in other people's prosperity. Divine abundance is mine and is free to all.'

LESSON VII

NO EVIL IN THE DIVINE PLAN OF YOUR LIFE

We live in a realm, or consciousness, wherein good and evil are forever in conflict. Behind it all is Christ, or the Kingdom of the Spirit, in Whom, or in which, there is no evil, but only infinite perfection, harmony, order, peace.

In the outer life we see every form of disharmony, disorder, disaster, tragedy, sin, suffering, ugliness, misery. These are all the result of sin, or separation from God and the Spiritual Kingdom of Divine Perfection.

Now the mercy, love and wisdom of God are so wonderful that even the tragedies and disorder of life are overruled for good. Indeed, they are not due to a heartless *karma*, but to the law of sowing and reaping transformed by Divine Grace. Because of this, every experience, no matter how painful or terrible, is something which is trying to help us back to God. Therefore, when we leave off sinning, and every thought is brought into captivity to Christ, we cease creating personal disorder and disaster in our own life, and thus are saved much suffering.

But we may still feel that we are the victims, or may at any moment become the victims, of the forces of violence. We may fear and dread accidents, malignant disease, infection, false accusations, calumny, and other evils. We may fear these things, not so much for ourselves, as for those whom we love. There appear to be forces of evil and disorder rampant on every hand. Evil, malignant powers seem to be plotting our downfall. Who can feel safe? Who will be the next victim? How can we escape? How can we find a refuge, a place of safety?

At this point, HTH commends to us the very comforting Psalm 91, which includes the verse, 'He shall call upon me, and I will answer him', and makes further quotation from it in the ensuing passage.

This Psalm was written by one who had entered into a higher consciousness, or it was given by the Lord or Divine Mind, speaking through the Psalmist, who transcribed the message. In any case it is absolute Truth. It speaks of the inner Kingdom of the Spirit in which there is no disorder, tragedy, or disaster, but only harmony, beauty, order and peace. It tells us also that we can enter into this Kingdom and dwell therein, and that because of this no evil can come near us.

'He that dwelleth in the secret place of the most High shall abide under the shadow of the Almighty.' First of all, we see that there is a secret place, an inner *Sanctum Sanctorum* of the most High, to which, marvellous though it be, we can have access. It is not merely a secret place in our own soul, but a place of hiding in God Himself—the most High. In this inner, secret place we can *dwell*—that is, live in it always. Not merely make contact with it at times, but dwell continually in it.

Those who live in this secret place shall abide under the *Shadow of the Almighty*. Not the shadow of an angel, but of the *Almighty*—the All-Perfect, All-Love, Infinite God. Because of this, no forces of evil or disorder can affect us. We are perfectly safe in this secret hiding place. So long as we abide in God, or in this inner King-dom of the Spirit, for us, *there is no evil.*

'It shall not come nigh thee' is the burden of this Psalm, be-cause of this abiding. 'No weapon that is formed against thee shall prosper.' No matter how helpless and unprotected we may appear to be to outsiders, we are protected absolutely by the Infinite, Almighty, One God.

There can be no evil in your life if you dwell in the secret place of the Most High. No matter what may happen around you in the way of accidents, disaster, pestilence, and so on, they cannot 'come nigh thee'. 'Angels shall bear thee up in their hands, lest thou dash thy foot against a stone.' Enemies may plot your downfall, but no weapon shall prosper against you, 'Because thou hast made the Lord, which is my refuge, even the most High, thy habitation: there shall no evil befall thee, neither shall any plague come nigh thy dwelling.'

If upsets come to you in life, you need never look upon them as evil, for they will be simply experiences which have come to help you to know God better and to advance you in your spir-itual life. Because you abide in the Secret Presence of God you will know that all is good in your life, and not evil, and that diffi-cult times need only a little patience to make it possible for the Divine Good and Order to appear.

Because you dwell in the secret place and abide in God, and because you love Him with your whole heart, desiring only that God's Will should be done in your life, and that you should be led entirely by the Spirit—because of this, everything in your life must work together for good, and everything that we call evil must be overruled for good also.

No matter what apparent evil may beset you, if instead of brooding over it, thinking about it, worrying over it, and fearing it, you turn to God Who is not only the absence of all evil, but is the positive Divine Good itself, the only Reality, the only Power, then Divine Order will surely appear in place of the disorder. In order that your faith may be increased and strengthened by testing, your deliverance may be delayed for a time, but deliverance will surely come, although often in an entirely different way from that which you expect.

If you believe only in Divine Good, affirming at all times that Good only can come to you, and that no evil can enter your life, because you abide in God and His Presence is always with you, then, in course of time, it will be revealed to you by direct spiritual understanding that for you there is only Good, that evil can have no power over you, and that you are perfectly safe, both now and for all eternity.

Although there is no evil purpose attending your life, and God's will concerning you is that you should have good and ever-increasing good, yet all of us have to be tempted. If we overcome the temptation we are very much better and stronger for having passed through it. If, however, we give in to the temptation to think wrong or sin-thoughts, we have to reap their bitter fruits.

The beginning of all sinful action is, of course, in the thoughts. To me the only way to keep the thoughts pure, noble and true is continually to turn to Christ, saying, *'Thou alone canst keep'*. Then the evil thought dies away. If we turn away from the evil thought to Christ, or God, in this way, it cannot live, for it has no real power of its own.

By 'sin-thoughts' I do not necessarily mean thoughts of murder, revenge or sensuality. Every thought that is not in harmony with the Divine Principle of Good, that is not in correspondence with the Law of Love, that is not from the standpoint of God's Perfect Idea, Christ, is a sin- or wrong thought. Wrong thinking is thinking upon a lower standard than the Divine, for such thinking must obviously be incorrect, for there is only the Divine Perfection and everything else falls short of it.

By turning to God and Christ in this way, and by seeking the Secret Place of the Most High and abiding in it, we are not only preserved from all the apparent evil of life, but we are kept from-the power of temptation and sin.

HOW TO FIND THE KINGDOM

How, then, can you find this inner Kingdom of the Spirit, this secret place of the most High? Simply by quiet persistence in turning away from the life of the senses and finding your Divine Centre. In order to find our Divine Source, Christ, we have to raise ourself to the Transcendent Divine. We cannot reach That which transcends all, for it is ever above all, but Christ reaches down from above, and in Him we find the secret place of the most High. We are helpless ourselves, but in Him all things are possible.

If this is not perfectly clear to you, you need not puzzle over it at all. All that you have to do is to become quiet, forget about external things, and then reach up to God and Heaven, or higher and better things. Christ does the rest. Sooner or later you will become conscious of the Divine Presence. You will then become conscious of immortality. Not of yourself but through Christ, Who has proved Himself to you to be the Way, the Truth and the Life.

A regular time must be spent every day in seeking after God. The more earnestly and systematically this is done the greater your progress will be. Everything depends on your quiet times of meditation in the secret place.

Also during the day you should recall the Truth to your remembrance, and the calm and peace of the secret place, by using a simple statement of Truth. When faced by apparent evil, danger and violence, or fear, you can say: *'God is my defence'*, or *'no evil can come nigh, nothing can hurt or destroy, saith the Lord'*, or *'Thou art my rock and my defence: in Thee will I trust'*.

Finally, every experience in your life, if met in the right way, and handled in a spirit of co-operation instead of antagonism, will admit you to a deeper understanding of God and a more intimate knowledge of Him and His love and care. No difficulty or trouble will come to hurt, but only to help.

ALL IS LOVE, AND ALL IS WELL.

WEEK EIGHT:
AFFIRMATIONS AND DENIALS

In this letter, HTH continues to speak of denials and affirmations, speaking of times when we feel assailed by the greatest difficulties and temptations: when things outside ourselves and unwanted, seem to have the greatest hold over us. He also develops a very radical view of illness. In the next paragraph, remember his earlier definition of sin as 'acting out of harmony with Divine Law'.

AT SUCH A TIME let the student deny the claim. Let him say: 'I deny that this sin has any claim, or hold upon, or power over, the Spirit'. At once the claims of error are severed, as though by a sword: the Sword of Truth. Where before was complete darkness and bondage, light and freedom and the promise of greater freedom are at once seen to be present.

Of course the denial must be followed by the same truth put in positive form—i.e., an affirmation. 'Thou art in me and I am in Thee. We are one, and sin can have no dominion over me'. Or the same truth might be expressed thus: 'Because Christ is in me and I am in Christ, I am one with Him, and no sin can have dominion over me'.

The question may arise: 'Why should I not say: "I deny that sin can have any power over me", or "I affirm that because I am Spirit, I am free from the law of sin and death"?' The reason is this. By declaring that sin can have no dominion over us, we merely inflate our false ego, or human personality. 'He that exalteth himself shall be abased', said our Lord, and if we deny and affirm in this way, we exalt our finite personality, trying to

make it equal with God; and therefore, we are bound to fail, and
that disastrously. Denials and affirmations have no value, except
they be based upon, and are statements of, Truth. If they proclaim error, then they cannot deliver us from error. Instead of
declaring that sin or the flesh can have no power over us, we
have to declare that they can have no dominion over Christ, or
Spirit. This is absolute Truth, for Christ has overcome sin and
temptation once and for all.

Therefore, because we are one with Christ, He in us and we
in Him, sin and the flesh can have no dominion over us, for we
'are hid with Christ in God'. It will be seen, then, that whereas if
the Truth is stated correctly in the form of denial and affirmation, it delivers us from the bondage of sin, denial and affirmation used wrongly only bind us the more completely to error and
the claims of sin and the flesh.

Truth expressed in the form of denial and affirmation can be
applied, successfully, to every experience of life. There is no situation, no matter how baffling, that cannot be overcome by stat-
ing Truth clearly, establishing oneself in It, and refusing to move
from It, or to be frightened out of It.

For instance, if we are ill or sick, we can deny that our illness
is either evil, hurtful or malevolent. A small percentage of pain
and suffering is physical, the rest is purely mental. As soon as we
cease either to fear or to be antagonistic toward our illness and,
instead, begin to rest quietly in the knowledge that it is a beneficent natural process, the sole object of which is to save us from
the effects of our sins, both against natural and spiritual law, wrong
thoughts, emotions wrongly dealt with, and so on, and all things
are working together for good, if we will only let them do so, the
principal cause of our suffering is removed, and a speedy recovery is made, or, at least, a good recovery. That is to say, instead of
the sickness, illness or healing crisis being suppressed, either by
physical or mental means, and Nature being forced to relinquish
her beneficial healing and cleansing processes, so as to cause
symptoms to disappear (but which really means that the trouble

is driven back into the system to cause far greater difficulty in the future); instead of this, Nature is co-operated with, the beneficial process of cleansing and restoring the body proceeds unimpeded (in fact it is encouraged in its lifesaving work), and a complete cure takes place. The patient is not injured by the illness, but by its suppression, and by the fear that a belief in illness as an evil and malevolent thing produces.

The denial cuts right down to the root of this amazing error. We see at once there can be no evil purpose or malevolent design in any experience that come to us; for there is no evil purpose or malevolent design in all God's Life, which also is our life, hidden with Christ in God. We should have to be apart and separated from our Divine Source for evil of any kind to come to us, and, as we know, this is impossible, for, 'I only know I cannot drift Beyond His love and care'.

The Divine Presence is with us always. We cannot even escape from It, and this Presence is Love. Omnipresent Love enfolds us, surrounds us, interpenetrates us—therefore nothing can come to us that is not good. We know all this, of course, but an illness may make us forget it. A high temperature may distract our attention so that our thoughts are thoughts of error instead of Truth. The denial cuts to the roots of our doubt, fear and erroneous thinking, and reveals once again to us the Truth; so that we can say: *'Since only Good can come to me, I know that all is well and everything is working together for good'*. Our illness then becomes transformed. We see that it is a friend helping and blessing us: that it is the highest form of good that we will allow to manifest. By denying that any experience can be evil, and by affirming that all is good, we come into harmony with the real truth of things, and by holding before our imagination a true vision of health and wholeness, we hasten our recovery to a higher state of health than ever we have yet known.

This problem arises here: 'What of malignant disease, such as cancer?' I do not believe in such a thing as a malignant purpose in Nature. I believe that Nature is always seeking to do the best thing for us, but repression and suppression of illnesses (which are really, if treated aright, healing crises) make it impossible for her to bring about the state of equilibrium which we call health. It is in order to save us from such things as cancer that Nature throws us into fevers and eruptive illness. If these are suppressed and wrong habits of eating and thinking continued, poor Nature is powerless to avert the catastrophe. So long as people indulge in hurtful emotions, or repress emotional energy; so long as they think that life is evil and look at life from the standpoint of evil; so long as people stuff themselves with food every day of their lives, instead of fasting at times and eating very little always; so long as people eat harmful food, or that which has been denuded of the elements most essential to life; so long as Nature's healing crises are suppressed instead of encouraged and co-operated with, cancer and other so-called 'malignant' diseases will continue to flourish. Co-operation with life and Nature's good processes, instead of antagonism, is the secret. When we alter our attitude towards Life and Nature, we alter our conduct.

While denial and affirmation should always be used so as to co-operate with Nature, instead of trying to suppress her, yet there is no reason why we should not follow Truth to its logical conclusion, or trace everything back to its Source (Spirit), and thus find that there is nothing to heal. While we admit that Nature's fevers and healing crises are a beneficial process, a kindly effort to cleanse the system of accumulations of morbid or waste matter, we can also realize that 'in Spirit' there is no waste or morbid matter at all, therefore there is nothing to be eliminated.

Further, accumulations of morbid matter must have a cause. Having ceased, by extreme moderation in diet and by hygienic observances, to violate Nature's Laws, we know that there can be no physical cause. Therefore the cause must be mental and spiritual. We therefore next realize that 'in Spirit' there can be no disharmony, friction, violence, or anything that could cause any accumulation of morbid matter, by saying: *'I thank Thee, because in Spirit there is no disorder or disharmony, but only perfect Divine*

Order in which, as a child of Thine, I share'.

By proceeding in this way, we do not work against Nature at all, but in perfect harmony. At the same time, we get behind, or beyond her, realizing the great Eternal Verities of the Spirit.

Again, we may be faced by poverty or financial ruin. Day and night we are oppressed by a sense of evil, calamity, and approaching doom. Imagination magnifies our trouble and pictures awful conditions, from which it seems to be impossible to escape. Money all gone, business ruined, too old to make a fresh start, nobody wants us—and so on. What shall we declare in the face of such a trying experience? This is similar to our position when we are tempted; in fact, it is a form of temptation or test. We are tempted to doubt God's ability or willingness to supply our needs. Therefore, just as before, we say, *'I deny that poverty or lack can have any power or dominion over Spirit'*. At once we see where we really stand. Christ the Archetype, the perfect Divine Creative Word, the only-begotten Son of God, can never be restricted in any way. Because we are in Christ and He in us no lack or want can touch us. We may not be able to see a way out of our difficulties; we may not possess any money; we may not know where the next meal is to come from—but the Eternal Son can never lack and we are safe in Him. The Spirit by which all things are created can never know loss or restriction. In Spirit we live and move and have our being, therefore what applies to Spirit applies also to us, and supply sufficient for our needs must surely manifest if we have faith and faint not.

Yet again, we may be faced by circumstances which seem to hem us in like the walls of a prison. There seems to be no way of escape. Our life may be so difficult and confined that it appears to be hopeless. Difficulties may have closed in upon us until we seem to be bound hand and foot, unable to move or do anything. It is obvious, that, humanly speaking, nothing can be done. This is true so long as we look at our trouble and difficulties. But if we turn from them, looking to God, our Divine Source, and deny that Spirit can be restricted or bound, affirming that Spirit has perfect liberty, we are set free. All these experiences are merely tests. If we deny their power over Spirit or Christ, and affirm our oneness with Him, all our troubles are revealed to be nothing but tests. When the tests have been faithfully withstood, we see that Infinite Good and Love have been behind them all the time, and that we have been led by them to a life that grows richer and fuller, day by day.

The Path of Attainment consists of a series of tests and experiences. Life to one who has entered the Path consists of nothing else, except, of course, opportunities for service. But even these are, in a way, tests also; for it depends upon how we deal with each opportunity, no matter how small or trivial, as to whether we succeed or fail in the Spiritual Life. I believe that it is often dealing wrongly with apparently small things (neglecting opportunities for service, or trying to avoid unpleasant duties) that lands us into much larger difficulties. Difficulties, if grappled with at once, are comparatively easy to overcome (the difficulty is in ourselves and not in the difficulty itself), but neglected or 'dodged' they increase until they challenge us in the form of a grave calamity (so-called).

The larger tests of life bring us right to the limits of our resources. Trouble brings us up against a blank wall in which there is no opening, or possibility of an opening, apparently. When we have exhausted everything, even prayer and meditation, and admit that of ourselves we can do nothing; and when we cease trying to put our life right, according to our own finite ideas of what it should be, saying: 'Thy will be done', instead of, as it almost always is, 'My will not Thine be done', we are delivered, very often, in a very simple manner, apparently. It is necessary that we should be brought to our very extremity in order for us to yield ourselves so completely to God as to make it possible for His Will, Love and Wisdom to act through us.

No experience that comes to us in life can be evil, for everything comes to us through the working of a law that is not only absolutely just, but is more than this, because it is based upon, and is, the outcome of Infinite Wisdom and Infinite Love. Therefore all our experiences are the outcome of Infinite Wisdom and Love, being Infinite Wisdom and Love in expression, therefore they are good. We should continually praise God for all experiences, the unpleasant as well as the pleasant. All experiences are good, the painful as well as the enjoyable—equally.

The wise soul does not ask for an easy life, but for more strength and wisdom with which to meet life as it is.

Yours in Fellowship of Truth,
HENRY THOMAS HAMBLIN

INSTRUCTIONS IN PROGRESSIVE REFLECTIVE MEDITATION

The symbols given in these letters are offered as suggestions only. For That which is beyond all pairs of opposites, and which I sometimes call the Repose of the Infinite (not meaning sleep, but the stillness of unimpeded activity), I sometimes use the symbol of a mental picture of a globe spinning on its axis at a speed which makes it appear motionless. Upon this globe are painted concentric circles, perhaps unevenly, yet the higher the speed the more perfect the circles appear to be. All crudeness and imperfection are 'swallowed up' by the speed at which the globe revolves. Imperfection disappears.

It is the same with our symbol. To our imagination, it presents a picture of perfect order: activity at so high a rate as to appear as stillness. No matter what disharmony we may encounter, no matter what idea of violence or disorder, one trained in meditation can lose it in the stillness. At first we find our symbol disturbed, to the extent that we are disturbed by what has happened or threatens to happen. When we are disturbed, the circles on our symbolic globe will not fall into their perfectly true and symmetrical form. But as we quietly meditate, denying that there can ever be any disorder of any kind in Spirit, the circles resume their perfect inherent symmetry. We then are at rest in Truth. When the circles again become true, the disorder has been overcome and we are again one with our Divine Source.

Again, I sometimes liken the perfect, reposeful, unimpeded 'Activity in Stillness', or 'Harmonious Cause', to the Cosmos. The latter is, after all, a poor representation of the former, but its wonderful order and precision convey to our minds just the right idea of harmonious, effortless, reposeful precision that we need. The Cosmos, when regarded as unaffected by man's disordered thinking, presents a wonderful picture of order, calm, wholeness, completeness, balance, poise, and so on, utterly transcending all our finite ideas on the subject. By picturing in the mind some sort of idea of the Cosmos, with all the perfect working of the heavenly bodies in their passage through space, never hurried, yet never late, always in their right place, at the right time, neither one second too soon, nor one moment too late, the orderly working of the Cosmos conveys to us a correct idea, although a limited one, of the One Perfect Causeless Cause whom we adore as our Divine Source and centre.

Yet again, we can sometimes contact the 'Stillness of the Infinite' through a sublime sunset, the dawn of a perfect day, the silence of mountain peaks, the inspiration and awe of vast spaces—these may bring to us a realization of what THAT is which is behind it and of which these things, lovely though they be, are only but a feeble expression. Afterwards, by recalling whatever it was that raised the feeling, or brought realization to the soul, we can at once enter the Stillness and find ourselves in the Presence of the Most High.

When realizing this stillness, or calm, or oneness which is behind all the change, opposition, struggle, disorder, and disunion of the surface life, we seem to enter into a larger place. Time, decay, change, death, all finite limitations, are left behind, and we know ourselves to be one with THAT which changes not.

LESSON VIII

Dear Fellow Student of Truth,

The great good we are seeking is Realization. We seek to know, in an intuitive and spiritual sense, the Infinite Perfection which, lying behind the apparent imperfection, exists here and now. Evolution tells us that creation is proceeding majestically without hurry towards perfection. On the other hand, intuition and interior knowledge tell us that the perfect expression of the Divine Idea is the Reality awaiting our discovery.

The way to Realization is choked by the false evidence of the senses and erroneous beliefs: these can be cleared by means of denials. Cleansing the mind by the use of denials prepares it to receive Truth.

Remember that Denials, Affirmations and Visualization are only means to an end: they are only aids to Realization. These things do not perform miracles, but realizing God's Infinite Perfection works wonders in the life.

Yours in Service and Truth,
HENRY THOMAS HAMBLIN

SPECIAL THOUGHTS ON DIVINE SUPPLY

Thought VIII

Do not wish or long for better circumstances or an easier life. By wishing and longing, you admit to your inner self that you have not the thing which you desire. Whatever the inner self accepts as truth becomes actualized in your external life. If, therefore, by wishing and longing, you impress upon your inner self that you do not possess the thing you desire, you never will be able to have it. You will forever be a daydreamer, a mere wisher, but never a doer.

Wishing, longing and daydreaming must be resolutely pushed on one side, to make room for constructive thinking. Instead of saying or thinking, 'I wish I had Jones's income', or, 'I only wish I had Brown's opportunities', say, 'Jones's income, large though it be, is nothing to what my Divine heritage is. My abundance has not yet manifested, but when it does it will leave Jones's idea of ample means far behind', or, 'My opportunities may not yet have appeared visibly, but inwardly, in actuality, or in creative spirit they are mine and when they manifest, as they will do, they will be glorious indeed'.

Never on any account say. 'Because I am poor (or my means are so slender) I cannot afford this or that thing that I need'. This is arguing and thinking from the standpoint of limitation—it is cultivating the pittance-a-week mind. This attitude of mind keeps more thousands of people down in the depths of poverty, than anything else. Many people write to us saying: 'I should like to take your Course but my means are so small I cannot afford to'. So long as they preserve this attitude of mind they will never be able to have the Course, nor to buy anything that is worth having. If, however, they were to reverse the thought and argue not from the standpoint of limitation, but from that of God's unlimited abundance, they would find that their circumstances would change, so that they could have and pay for everything that they need. Instead of saying: 'I wish I had this, but I cannot', or, 'I would like a certain thing, but am too poor to have it', say:

'Because all the Divine Abundance is mine and all men's, all the things and opportunities I need are coming to me.'

LESSON VIII

THE PHILOSOPHY OF DENIALS

The question naturally arises: 'If there is no real evil (that is, absolute or permanent evil, or a principle of malignant evil), why deny it? Why try to negative a negative?' The answer is that the cause of all negative conditions is found in a settled belief in these things in the subconscious mind. 'As a man thinketh in his heart (subconscious mind) so is he'. It is the constant thinking by this great inner mind that determines largely what our outward life shall be. Our conscious thinking affects our life greatly, according to the quality of the thoughts sent down into the subconscious mind, but this great inner mind does a vast deal of thinking of its own, and, according to its dominant note, so shall our life be. It is because our subconscious mind believes in evil, as a principle or omnipotent power, that apparent evil is produced in our life; for what is held in the mind becomes manifest in the life.

It is seen, then, that this inbred belief in evil must be eradicated from the subconscious mind before any real progress can be made in the new life. Therefore, in time, by denials we remove this wrong, dominant note from the inner life and replace it by a belief in a God of Love, Whose purposes are kindly and prompted entirely by love. My experience is that it is not possible to cast out a firmly-rooted wrong belief from the subconscious mind without the use of denials. To affirm good is not sufficient: it is like sowing seed in ground choked by weeds. First remove the weeds of beliefs which are enmity against God: then there will be room for the seeds of Good and Love. Therefore I advocate the use of denials, for they cleanse the subconscious mind and alter its dominant note. Until this cleansing is accomplished, all attempts at progress are as building upon sand.

Whatever dominant idea is held in the subconscious mind becomes the centre of life's activities. All the invisible forces of Nature work together to mould the outward life after the pattern set by the central, dominant note. I have repeatedly been struck by the fact that those whose life is one long struggle with poverty have a deeply-rooted belief in limitation and lack. It colours all their thoughts: it cramps and distorts their mental outlook: it unconsciously dominates all their actions. All the forces of their life are devoted to creating poverty and limitation. Life can do nothing else: it has no other pattern to work to, and what is held in the mind, especially the inner mind, must manifest in the life.

It is the same with ill-health. Converse with one who is never really well, and you will often find he or she has an intense belief in sickness as an unavoidable evil: the whole life, in consequence, revolves round this central belief or obsession, producing in the body an outward manifestation of that which is held in the mind. Again, take the case of one who cannot succeed in any task to which he puts his hand. No matter what work he may take up: no matter how bright his prospects may be, he never makes good: he 'falls down' before the first obstacle. He is probably sober and industrious: he laments his own failure, yet he cannot succeed. If we examine his mind, we find that its central idea is lack of all self-confidence: an ever-present dread and fear that evil in the form of bad luck is dogging his footsteps.

Obviously, then, the only thing to do is to eradicate from the subconscious mind those wrong beliefs in evil of various kinds which spoil the life and prevent or mar its perfect fruition. The quickest and most thorough method is by the use of denials. Whoever will persistently deny the evil in his life, and affirm in its place the Infinite Good, will sooner or later enter into a spiritual realization of the fact that what he has denied does not in reality exist, and that what he has affirmed, namely that there is only the Infinite Good, is true. When this realization comes to your soul, you will know that the subconscious mind has been cleansed of its wrong beliefs. You will also know that you have penetrated to the Infinite Wisdom.

In the same way that you deny that evil exists in God's Divine Idea, so, also, can you deny poverty and all lack, for these form no part of the Divine Ideal. You can also deny sickness and disease, for they do not exist in the Divine Idea. If you try to form a mental picture of God's ideal world, to which, with majestic deliberation, all Creation is progressing, you will find neither disease nor sickness, poverty nor lack. By dwelling upon the ideal and denying these negative states and conditions which form no part of the Divine Idea, we set in motion forces which eradicate them from our life.

By denials you can rob all negative forces of their power, for they have no power except that with which our thoughts and fear invest them. If a person desires to mind-dominate you, his intentions can be thwarted by a silent denial. If you go into an infectious room or hospital, you can protect yourself by using a denial such as this: *'I deny that this infection can affect me in any way'*. You can also form a mental picture of God's Infinite Perfection, and realize that in the True Reality there is no sickness or infection. You may be surrounded by apparent difficulty which you can meet with the denial: 'I deny that these difficulties can defeat me'. Or, in some cases, you can deny that they exist at all, for difficulties and troubles generally are found to be non-existent when we approach them boldly. Then we wonder how it was that we were ever afraid.

Some metaphysicians banish pain by denials, and anyone else can do likewise if he or she is sufficiently in earnest. If the denial of pain, as existing in God's Perfect Idea, is followed by a realization of His Perfection, then the pain will temporarily disappear. Denials, however, do not heal or build up: they kill the wrong thought, but they do not replace it by the necessary good. Denials, therefore, should always be followed by affirmations of God's Infinite Perfection, Reality and Substance, with a full realization of each affirmation. Each time that we realize God's Perfection, we bring It more into expression, in our body, our life, and in the world around us. Therefore, we not only benefit ourselves but also the world at large, thus making it a better place for the sons of God and the daughters of the Most High wherein to live.

Deny every thought which you want to kill, every evil you wish to eradicate, every habit you desire to break. Do this and follow your denial by affirming the very opposite of the thing denied. As you affirm it try to visualize it also. Remember that you are affirming that which is true of the Spirit, and denying that which is not true of the Spirit. It is only the Spirit that is true and real.

Try to form a mental concept of God's perfect ideal world,

or the world that you know, beautiful, and free from all sin and hate, filled with love, joy, harmony, goodwill and peace. The more frequently you do this, the more perfect will your outer world become. As you affirm a state or condition of perfection, try to 'see' it inwardly. This inner vision is spiritual: it is through the eye of the soul that you see the great Reality. This faculty can be developed and at the same time the power of concentration increased by means of visualizing exercises. These can be practised when on railway journeys, or at other odd times which otherwise would be wasted.

Visualizing Exercise

Close the eyes. Think of the paper upon which this printing appears. Trace it right back to its source, picturing every stage of its many changes: first at the place where you bought the book, then at the printer, then at the paper mill, then in the form of pulp, next at the wood-pulping mills, and lastly as the tree in the forest. Try to see it all clearly as though it were a cinematograph film put through the machine backwards.

WEEK NINE:
WHOLENESS

Letter IX begins with a discussion about how we succeed and fail on the spiritual path, reminding us that when we fail there is always opportunity given to rise again 'with faces still turned towards the light'. When we measure ourselves, it should be not against others on the Path, but 'by the higher standard of the Immaculate Christ'. The rest of the letter describes a way to move forward, by the use of affirmations.

AFFIRMATIONS can be used either in a right or a wrong way. They can be used in order to increase our understanding of Truth and to help forward our spiritual development, or they can be used in an attempt to alter our objective life and to avoid the experience that Infinite Wisdom and Love, or the Law, founded upon them, would, entirely because we need it, bring to us. In other words, they can be misused for the gratification of earthly desires instead of the furtherance of the Spiritual life.

It is not easy for some students to seek first the Kingdom of Heaven, and then to let God add the material blessings, yet this is the only way. If a student's attention is taken up with 'getting results', or in making 'demonstrations', he can never find the Kingdom. Those who went after the loaves and fishes never became true disciples, neither were they admitted to the inner mysteries. One who sought Truth, however, was told to sell all that he had and give to the poor, as a preparatory step to the Kingdom.

Those, however, who sought first the Kingdom, may have been, in a worldly sense, poor, yet they never lacked that which they needed. Also, and this is of far greater importance, they found the treasure: the pearl of great price. They became rich indeed.

Affirmations help us to find the Kingdom. They do not take the place of meditation in the quiet place—they reinforce it. In our meditations we find Truth and bask in its rays. During the day we might forget Truth and become enslaved by the appearance of evil, if it were not for statements of Truth.

Statements of Truth bring back Truth to our remembrance.

Truth can be stated either in a negative or positive form, either as a denial or an affirmation. Both may be necessary, although denials become less necessary as we learn, habitually, to abide and live in Truth. By denials we cut right to the roots of error, so that we realize where we stand; by affirmations we fill our consciousness with the very substance of Truth.

Too much importance should not, however, be attached to the use of statements of Truth. They are nothing in themselves. They bring back Truth to our remembrance—that is all. The idea that if we deny an unwanted thing enough times and with sufficient vigour, it will disappear, and that if we affirm a desired thing sufficiently, it will appear, must be discarded.

Divine Wisdom and Love have designed for each one of us a life that is perfect *to us*. Each life is different, but each is perfect, as it is imaged in Divine Mind. We can only be happy, our life can be successful only, if we live the life that Infinite Wisdom has planned for us. Therefore, we must not call our life evil, and then try to alter it by denials and affirmations. Instead we must realize that life is good, and then look at it with different eyes. It is hard at times, in some circumstances, to believe that life is not evil and sinister in motive and character. When faced by apparent evil, and by an apparently evil purpose, we are tempted to lose faith. But by denying that there is an evil purpose in life, and by affirming the All-ness and Omnipresence of Good, our faith is maintained, and Truth is brought again to our remembrance.

What we have to affirm, then, is not material needs, but the

All-ness of Good; not the gratification of some earthly desire, but the Omnipresence of Love; not something in the bank to keep us from want; but the Divine Presence, the One and Only substance, which is the One Source of all that we need, both Spiritual and temporal.

I am not now much in favour of trying to hasten or force one's spiritual development; but there seems to be a legitimate field for the use of affirmations in the unfoldment of the higher qualities of the soul. An affirmation is a prayer that assumes that which we declare is already an accomplished fact. Jesus told us to pray as though we have already received that for which we pray. This is because God does not have to do anything for us at all, in reality. Everything is accomplished, and everything that we require is ours already: all that is needed is that our consciousness should open to perceive the truth of the matter. By prayer, or affirmation, we do not create anything, we only bring the Truth to our remembrance; we merely open our eyes to behold that which has always been waiting for us.

When we have received a gift from a friend, we always thank him or her for it. Therefore, when we pray knowing that what we pray for is already ours, we should give God thanks for it. All our affirmations should take the form of thanksgiving. For instance, if we desire most of all the gift of the Holy Spirit, we thank God for the gift that is already ours, by saying: *'I thank Thee, Father, for the gift of the Holy Spirit'*. If, for a fuller understanding of Truth, we say: *'I thank Thee, Father, for a deeper and richer realization of Truth'*. If, for a sense of Divine Union, we say; *'I thank Thee, Father, because in Christ I am one with Thee'*. If we persevere in this way—not of course, neglecting our daily meditations in the quiet place—the things that we affirm will become real in consciousness. That which always was is brought into conscious manifestation. In other words, the Truth is brought to our remembrance.

In addition, during the day, when possible, the thoughts should be raised and the word Wholeness (and also Perfection, Completeness, which are included in the wonderful word, 'Whole-ness') should be repeated as a prayer or affirmation. By doing this the Light of the Spirit of Truth reveals things to us of which it is not lawful that men should speak.

Let us continually affirm and give praise for the Good, the Beautiful and the True. Let us give thanks for the perfect life God has given us—for virtue, character, love, goodwill, service, brotherhood, harmony and wisdom, and so on; for the list is a long one. Let us do the same for our friends and all mankind, even our enemies.

The life of affirmation should be the life of praise. Continual praise brings us nearer and nearer to God, until we live continu-ally in the Divine Presence; after which nothing else matters very much.

'I thank Thee, Father.'

But there must be real gratitude in the prayer.

Yours in Praise and Thanksgiving,

HENRY THOMAS HAMBLIN

INSTRUCTIONS IN PROGRESSIVE REFLECTIVE MEDITATION

Whatever symbol may be used, when we enter into a larger con-sciousness, we should remain in quiet meditation upon the sym-bol, breathing deeply and easily. The sense of expansion which is experienced is a form of cosmic, or universal, or super-, con-sciousness. As we enter into the calm stillness and peace of the Infinite, our consciousness expands until it seems to embrace the whole universe.

As we contemplate and meditate in this manner, we behold all things through the eyes of the Christ, or Archetypal Divine Man, and we become conscious of the reality of the Divine Order. Probably the first thing that we realize is a sense of wholeness.

In the Divine Presence all is Good. There is nothing else but Good. There is no limitation, no incompleteness, no imperfection, no disorder—only perfect Wholeness.

Good therefore implies Wholeness. By meditating upon the former we are led to the latter as the next step in our progressive meditation. We therefore hold the idea of Wholeness at the top of our mind, allowing the Light of Truth to shine upon it and illuminate it. As we do this from day to day and from week to week, we begin to sense, or inwardly realize, what Wholeness is. It cannot be described, simply because it is a state that transcends both the finite mind and finite language. We can, however, realize what Wholeness is, in the soul. Wholeness includes completeness, perfection, order, yet seems to transcend them all.

In course of time, Wholeness becomes associated in our mind with Good. Ever afterwards, to think and meditate upon Good calls up a sense or realization of Wholeness.

LESSON IX

Dear Fellow Student of Truth,

Good is omnipresent, but it can be discerned only by those whose eyes have been touched by the Quickening Spirit and opened to behold the Heavenly Vision. The Infinite Perfection is inherent in everyone, in everything, in every circumstance. Eyes blinded by sense-illusion cannot see It, but those who diligently seek find the Omnipresent Good in everything they see.

It is the greatest Occult Truth that, by getting away from the imperfect life of the senses, beholding the finite Perfection of the Divine Idea, affirming Its reality, and, so to speak, calling upon It to manifest Itself, we hasten Its miracle working. The methods vary greatly, but the underlying principle is the same. It is the antithesis of Black Magic, which forms an image in the mind, and, by willpower, compels it to appear. One who works by means of Black Magic imposes his human will and desires upon Life's forces and thus encompasses his own ruin and downfall. On the other hand, one who calls the Infinite Good into expression is working in harmony with the Divine, thus blessing himself and causing others to be blessed.

Yours in Unity and Service,

HENRY THOMAS HAMBLIN

SPECIAL THOUGHTS ON DIVINE SUPPLY

Thought IX

We should never endeavour to get something for nothing, or attempt to get something from another by being smart or sharp. We should never try to get things for less than their proper value, or to be a bargain-hunter. Above all, we should never buy anything and not pay for it, or buy something that we cannot afford in the hope (very slender hope) that we may be able to pay for it.

We must not think that because we 'best' another person in a deal, or get something below its true value, or buy something and never pay for it, that we can be any richer for so doing, for such is far from being the case. In reality, one who does these things is immeasurably poorer, for he shackles himself with the chains of a perpetual poverty, which nothing can break.

One who does these things shuts himself out of the Divine Consciousness of abundance, for by doing these things he impresses the idea of poverty and limitation upon the subconscious mind, which, in consequence, manifests poverty in the life. We must always remember that whatever is impressed upon the inner mind is externalized in the life. If we act meanly, then a thought of lack and limitation is impressed on the inner mind, then, in consequence, lack and limitation are manifested in the outer life, by the inner mind, which is infinite in power, but which expresses itself in the form we give it by our thought and attitude of mind.

One who enjoys abundance would never do any of the things we have mentioned. One who has more than he can possibly need would never, unless he were demented, stoop to mean or dishonest practices, in order to 'make' a few pounds. It is only those who have 'poverty' minds who act in this way. They argue from the point of view of lack, restriction and limitation, thinking that because their means are so small, they must use all sorts of tricks and subterfuges in order to get more for their money.

Those who would be free from the 'poverty mind' should endeavour to deal not only justly with others, but also as though they were the possessors (outwardly as well as inwardly) of great abundance. While they must live within their present income, they should continually affirm their oneness with the Infinite, and that all the Divine Abundance is theirs now (spiritually and in actuality), and will surely manifest outwardly also. It is helpful to repeat, over and over again when faced by appearances of penury and adversity,s

'*God's Abundance, Divine Plenty.*'

LESSON IX

HOW TO BRING THE INFINITE GOOD INTO EXPRESSION

We have seen that through the pursuit and visualization of a high ideal we help to bring the Inward Power into expression. We have also seen that by denials we check the vicious thought–circle within the subconscious mind which is the cause of most of our troubles. We now have to deal with the constructive power of affirmations. Just as, by the use of denials, what we call evil is checked and begins to disappear, so also by the use of affirmations the rout of the enemy is completed and the Infinite Good appears. Some metaphysicians teach that there is only the Infinite Good and that this is obscured by a mist of so-called evil. By denials, so it is asserted, the mist is diminished, until at last it is possible by the spoken word of affirmation to make the Good appear. We are as magicians: we possess the power to dismiss the bad genies and evoke the good. Another manner by which this teaching may be illustrated is to liken the Good to the light of the sun, and evil to the darkness. This, although far from perfect, is a useful analogy. The sunlight is positive: it has a very real existence: it has power. Darkness, on the contrary, is negative, simply the absence of light: it has no power of its own. Darkness has no terrors to one who does not fear it; but to one who fears, it contains dreadful phantoms. Infinite Good is the eternal reality: it truly exists: it is positive: it alone has power. Through doubt and fear, wrong beliefs and material outlook, the true light is obscured from the uninitiated, and they live instead either in the darkness or dim twilight, seeing not the heavenly vision. By the use of denials, the wrong beliefs and material conceptions are dissolved, letting in the light of the Infinite Good. How can I tell you of the joy which comes to the soul when it realizes that evil is not the reality, but that Infinite Good reigns: that the darkness has been dispelled: that henceforth there can be only light and joy, overcoming and victory? It cannot be described, for there is not language which can do it justice. It is a state which transcends happiness, even as a mountain towers above the plain.

Again, it has been said that just as beauty is something which exists in the soul, and that, by the unfolding of the soul, the eternal loveliness is revealed (see preface to *The Message of a Flower*), so also is it with the Infinite Good. As our eyes are opened through the influence of the Divine Spirit, so is the Infinite Perfection revealed to our gaze. We are thus able to understand why it is that of two people placed in entirely similar circumstances, one will see evil and the other good. One can see faults only in his neighbour and the other only virtues. The life and world and universe of the former are filled with evil, but the latter is surrounded by the Omnipresent Good.

None of these analogies is perfect, but they are useful if they help you to realize that there is, in reality, only the Infinite Good: that what we call evil is a negative shadow which passes away as we apprehend the Truth. There is also another aspect of good and evil. It is obvious that as there is only one Creator and He is perfect, therefore none of His creations can be evil. If there is only one Creator, then there is only one creation, and if there is evil, it must be in that creation and must be the work of the one Creator. Therefore, to believe in evil is to believe that God, the Creator, is evil and a creator of evil, which is absurd. Thus we are placed on the horns of a dilemma: either there are two Deities and two creations, or there is no evil. Either we must believe in two Infinite Beings and two Creators, or we must deny evil. If, then, we take the Universal as we find it and refuse to see evil in it, believing that it is one harmonious whole composed entirely of Good, we see that good and so-called evil must be relative. We see that all is good, but that there are various grades of goodness. We see, also, that the mire below, out of which we have climbed appears as evil; and we see all that is above us as perfect good. In course of time, when we have attained to a higher state, we shall look back on what we think now is perfect good, and see it as relative evil. We shall also see that evil is only that out of which good evolves and therefore is not really evil, but only a form of good.

It does not matter which point of view you take, so long as you realize that there is only the one Creator and one Power: that all life is good and that there can come into your life only that which is good. The purposes of God are all kindly: all the influences which come around your life are for your highest good. All things are yours: conscious immortality, joy and happiness, achievement and overcoming, health and abundance. Joy! Joy! Your life shall henceforth be a continual unfoldment of joy unspeakable! By denying evil and an evil purpose, you break the spell which has held you captive, and, by affirmations, reveal all the wonders of the Omnipresent Good, bringing them into expression in your life.

The great point about affirmations is this: they assert that Infinite Perfection exists here and now. God is, not will be, perfect. Behind the apparently imperfect stands eternally the Infinitely Perfect. Things are not what they seem: the Truth, which stands behind this changing life of time and space, is that Perfection is a fact here and now. It is here, and by the eyes of understanding we can see it. It is at our doors: we are face to face: all that we need is the seeing, understanding sight. Get hold of this wonderful, transforming, illuminating fact: that Infinite Perfection exists now, and can, by means of affirmations, be brought into expression or manifestation! This is the secret of all wonder-working, all miracles, all healing. Every time that you realize the Infinite Perfection and affirm it, you work a miracle in your life.

Once you get away from the spell of belief in evil and imperfection, realizing that there is only the Infinite Perfection and Omnipresent Good, your affirmations will bring into manifestation all that is good. The belief in an omnipotent malicious and evil power or being is a drag upon your life: until you get rid of it you can never make progress. When, however, you free yourself from this belief in a dual Power, there is nothing to hinder the working of your affirmation. Whatever you affirm, provided it is not ignoble, will come to pass. Be mindful to affirm only the Good. Do not affirm wealth, or power over your fellows, for these bring not happiness, but only added care. If, however, these things come to you unsought, look upon them as tests of your faithfulness: as a responsibility which must be faithfully discharged. Instead of wealth, affirm that all your wants are supplied, day by day, by God's Abundance. Neither is it wise to affirm an easy life, for it is only by overcoming that we can become sufficiently strong to climb the steep ascent to God. Do not affirm material things so much as spiritual, though you are entitled to affirm the supplying of all your physical needs, for there is no reason why you, any more than an angel in heaven, should suffer want. Let your mind be concerned sufficiently about material things, but no more. I believe in a man or woman expecting success in everyday affairs, for God is not a failure, but Infinite Success which we should share. I also believe that all should expect perfect health, without which individual service to life and humanity is imperfect: that each should become efficient, and spare no effort in the quest of self-improvement: and that wise prosperity and abundance are in accordance with the Divine Will. Man also should enjoy the love of others in exchange for the love that he bestows upon them, although we must learn to love universally, without demanding any return. Therefore these things should be affirmed daily, both night and morning, and the more time that is spent, in reason, upon them, the greater will be the results.

The greatest matters, however, are those concerning the soul. Let your chief aim be towards the development of soul-knowledge and spiritual understanding. Let your greatest desire be to enter into the realization that Infinite Perfection exists here and now. By so doing you will bring it into manifestation.

AFFIRMATIONS

'Now and always, according to grace, I am established in the consciousness of Omnipresent Good.'
'No sense of evil can control consciousness, for I am controlled only by Divine Love.'
'I rejoice and am thankful for my freedom in Omnipresent Good.'

DAILY ROUTINE

Enter the Silence or meditate upon the above statements of Truth, night and morning. Seek only the Good, the Beautiful and true. Follow the gleam. Let your life be a continual manifestation of the highest and best.

When you meet difficulty, retire into your inner self: deny that it can baffle you, and affirm that the Infinite Power within you will carry you through. *Then immediately go forward and conquer.*

WEEK TEN:
TRANSMUTATION

NOTHING IS TRUER than this, that 'As a man thinketh in his heart, so is he'. Our life is just a reflection of what we are inwardly (not as others see us, and not as we think ourselves to be, but as we actually are); and, as Buddha says: 'We are made up of our thoughts'. Therefore, our life is the result of our thoughts. It is either good or evil according to the nature of our thoughts. If we think from the standpoint of evil, of limitation, of imperfection, then evil, limitation and imperfection are manifested and expressed in life.

We always think from a centre, and our thoughts revolve around a centre. Not only must we endeavour to reverse our wrong thoughts, but the centre from which wrong thoughts spring, and around which they revolve, must be changed entirely. It is necessary that we should watch our thoughts, carefully, guarding the threshold of our mind, for by this and by meditation our centre becomes changed.

There are many who desire to use their mental powers for good, yet their lives still manifest disorder, and express imperfection and limitation. This is due to the fact that the centre from which they think and around which their thoughts revolve has not been changed.

We can think only from one of two standpoints, or centres. We can think from the standpoint of one who is inside the Kingdom, or from the standpoint of one who is outside the Kingdom. We cannot, however, think entirely or perfectly from the former standpoint until we are actually inside the Kingdom. We may try to think rightly and should and must always try to do so, but we cannot do so perfectly until we are inside the Kingdom. Endeavouring to think rightly, however, and to conform all our thinking to the Christ standard, helps us to find the Kingdom. Meditation, however, is the inner Path to the Kingdom, but it must be backed up by disciplined right thinking.

What is the Kingdom of God, or Heaven? It is a state of consciousness wherein we realize our oneness with God. All error is due to the error of separateness. All sin, suffering, ugliness, misery, disease, are due to separateness, or the idea which possesses us that we are separated from our Divine Source. We cannot, of course, in actuality, be separated from God, but in consciousness we are. In the Adam consciousness we all die (become separated in consciousness from our Divine Source), but in the Christ consciousness we are made alive. Which means that, in the lower consciousness, we lose our sense of oneness with the Supreme ONE, but when we are raised into the Christ consciousness, we realize our oneness with the One Source of all Life, Love, Wisdom, and Power.

In mystical language, this is described as the Divine Marriage, the union between the Redeemer and the redeemed, who then become one.

This entering into the Higher Consciousness is really the crux of the whole matter. We are either in the Kingdom, or we are outside of it. If the former is the case, all is well: and is known to be well, if the latter, things may appear to go wrong, although, in reality, all is well also, in a real, interior sense.

When we are in the Kingdom all things work together for good. It could not be otherwise, because of our at-one-ment with Good. When we are at-one with the Holy One (the Whole One), all that we think, say and do is in harmony with Truth and the Divine Order. Therefore, Divine Order is manifested in our life. We look at life from an entirely new standpoint, we think from a new centre, and our thoughts revolve around this new centre. It is not difficult to think Divine thoughts when we live at our Divine Centre. True it is that we may fall and backslide and display all the weaknesses of wayward children, suffering in consequence, but, in the main, we live at our Centre and all our thoughts and our general outlook are those of Truth.

Therefore, the great secret of right thinking is to find and enter the Kingdom of God, and then to think in the perpetual consciousness of Truth, instead of that of human error and limitation. But, and here is another paradox, while we cannot think rightly, unless we enter the Kingdom, at the same time it is equally true that we cannot find the Kingdom without right thinking. It is by continually trying to think from the standpoint of Truth that we seek the Kingdom, and he that seeketh findeth. Although we realize that we cannot think from the standpoint of Truth until we find Truth and know what it is, yet by trying to think in harmony with Truth, we ultimately find Truth. Always endeavouring to think from a higher, finer, nobler and richer standpoint, combined with meditation, gradually brings us to the Truth, because our conception of Truth continually opens, widens and expands until we know what Truth really is.

Until we really know Truth and enter into the Kingdom, all attempts at right thinking are difficult and more or less against the grain. When, however, we know the Truth and have entered the Kingdom, right thinking becomes easy and natural. Whereas, formerly, right thinking was the exception, and wrong thinking quite natural, now, having entered into Truth, right thinking is natural and comparatively easy, while wrong thinking is unnatural and against the grain, producing a feeling of repugnance if, or whenever, indulged in.

By entering the Kingdom we become spiritual beings in place of the material creatures we have hitherto been. We become one with 'the Lord from Heaven', ceasing to be of the earth, earthy. As spiritual beings, we think as spiritual beings, have a spiritual outlook, and live a life that is spiritual while yet in a body of flesh. We practise, naturally, the Presence of God, are at all times conscious of this abiding reality, and live and act accordingly. We realize that we are spiritual beings, living in a spiritual universe, governed by spiritual laws, possessing transcendent powers which will become ours to use to the glory of God, as soon as Infinite Wisdom sees that we are experienced enough, and sufficiently reliable and steadfast, to be entrusted with them.

Through being spiritually-minded, we think spiritually, i.e., rightly, in accord with Truth and Divine Order, instead of in line with error and human disorder. By so doing, we become changed, in character, in personality and in our physical body also. First the brain cells become changed. The cells which formerly were charged with energy to explode at any moment, at the slightest suggestion, into wrong thoughts, go out of action, responding less and less to the stimuli of harmful or erroneous suggestion, until at last they fail to respond at all. Instead of these, there is brought into activity a new set of cells whose function is right thinking—i.e., the thinking of spiritual thoughts, thoughts in perfect harmony with Truth; thoughts which are Truth itself, being those of Wholeness, Perfection, Love, Peace, Joy and Life Eternal. This spiritual thinking, in time, spiritualizes the body. First the brain is changed, and then the body. The face and its expression become changed and spiritualized. One can always recognize a spiritually-minded person without speaking to him or her. Just as the face of Moses shone when he descended the mountain, so also do the faces of the regenerated spiritual men and women in this wonderful age, shine to those who are able to recognize that which is spiritual.

The face becomes more spiritual in expression, losing, as many do in death, the coarseness, hard expression or careworn look common to mankind. The Spirit indwelling the man or woman begins to shine through his or her face, after which It spiritualizes the body, so that it becomes a true temple of the Holy Spirit.

It must not be thought that the way is easy. Before each step forward, there is a severe testing time. The old nature wars against the new, the lower against the higher. If we are steadfast, however, the higher nature must always win, finally. Great temptation spells greater victory. The harder the test, the greater the step forward. Christ has overcome sin, the flesh, and every temptation, and in Christ and through Christ, Who lives in us, we are more than conquerors.

Now the way to the Kingdom is twofold, or dual, but it is always through Christ. 'I am the way, the truth and the life, no man cometh unto the Father but by Me', said Jesus Christ. 'I am the door: by Me if any man enter in, he shall be saved, and shall go in and out, and find pasture', our Lord said also. The way is twofold. First, we endeavour to bring all our thoughts into captivity to Christ. This is the way of work, or effort—very necessary and very good. Second, through the good offices of the Spirit or Christ, we meditate upon Eternal Truth, and find the Kingdom through quiet waiting upon God. This is the way of quietness and contemplation—also very necessary and very good.

Regarding meditation, this is dealt with under the title of Instructions in Progressive Meditation, but with regard to thought control the following may prove helpful.

Although we may not yet have realized the Truth, we can bring our thoughts more and more into line with Truth. All that we have to do is to form an idea of Good in the mind, and to raise our thoughts continually to it. This idea can be related to all the common things of life, such as health, supply, happiness, etc. By holding in the mind an idea of perfect health and wholeness, a perfect idea of abundant and unlimited supply, a perfect idea of brotherly love and harmony, we come very near to the Truth. If we hold these ideas firmly in the mind, refusing to entertain any thoughts lower than these, we form a mould, or matrix, which shapes our life. But the good effect that it has on our life does not satisfy. We become possessed with an ever-growing desire to know the Truth in a special sense, so that we become one with God, *and know it*. Having attained to one thing we hunger after something much higher.

Now with regard to right thinking. Although the student may

not have yet entered into the Higher Consciousness, he should endeavour to think as though he had. He should try to think from the standpoint of oneness with God. 'Because I am a child of God', or 'Because I am one with Thee' should always be the standpoint from which thinking is done. The best way to become possessed of a certain blessing, that is to bring the blessing already ours into consciousness, is to assert and believe that it is ours now, and to thank God for it, because it is already ours. Therefore, although we may not yet realize our at-one-ment with our Divine Centre, we should believe and declare that we are in Christ and thus one with God. In this way our consciousness gradually becomes merged into the Christ Consciousness, which is the Heavenly Marriage—the union of the Redeemer and the redeemed. The lower consciousness is redeemed and absorbed by the Higher, or Christ-, Consciousness. After which nothing else matters very much.

If you are ill or sickly yourself, assert that you are a child of God, one with the One Source of Life, Health, Wholeness, Love, Harmony, Joy, Beauty, and so on. Therefore, you *are* perfectly whole. Think from this standpoint, always.

Whatever disease, sickness and ill-health you may meet with in others, or experience yourself, refuse to acknowledge them, but see only the perfection of God's Wholeness as it really is, and would appear, if it were not obscured by the disorder of man's wrong thinking (sin, falling short, etc.). Endeavour to see only God's Perfect, Divine, Spiritual, Archetypal Man, the Christ, and nothing short of this, holding firmly at all times to your idea, or mental picture, of wholeness and perfect wellbeing, which you have in your mind. Refuse also to talk sickness, to think sickness, to discuss sickness; but turn instead to your idea of Divine Wholeness and Perfection, declaring this to be true.

In the same way, deal with the matter of supply. Do not picture wealth, do not desire wealth, but hold in your mind your highest conception of unlimited abundance as a reality now in Spirit. Assert continually that you are a child of God, and that no child of God can suffer want, but always has access to the Divine Supply. Believe utterly and affirm with praise and thanksgiving that God is able to supply all your need now from the Invisible, either in money, or in kind, independently of people, trade, investment or any other human or material agency. Know, believe, affirm, and praise God, because there is no limitation in Spirit, and know that God can fill your life with every good and necessary thing. There is no need to hoard. If a poor man had permission to go to a shop and get as much food, daily, as he required, how foolish he would be if he were to carry a hundredweight of food on his back, for fear he should go short. The only commonsense thing for him to do would be to go daily to the shop and obtain enough to meet exactly the day's needs. It is the same with Divine Supply: one who realizes the Truth only looks for sufficient for his daily needs, but he knows that infinite abundance is always at hand. That is why he has no desire to be rich in a material sense, i.e., to hoard up wealth or to hold or possess things. The way of happiness and real opulence is to pass good things on and not selfishly to keep them.

My space is now exhausted, but room must be found to remind you that when confronted by the appearance of evil, a denial may help recall the Truth to your remembrance. When faced by disease, you can deny that disease can have any dominion over Spirit. When faced by lack, or financial difficulty, you can deny that these things can have any dominion over Spirit. Therefore, because you are a child of God, living in the Spirit, health and abundance are yours now. Commence, therefore, praising God for them, although at present one or the other may not be apparent to mortal sense.

Greatly desiring for you an ever increasing understanding of Truth,

Yours in the Great Service,

HENRY THOMAS HAMBLIN

INSTRUCTIONS IN PROGRESSIVE
REFLECTIVE MEDITATION

Meditation upon Wholeness brings us, in course of time, to the truth of ONENESS. The former is a transcendent truth, but the latter is, I believe, even greater.

It is impossible to describe, in finite language, the meaning of Oneness. It can, however, be held in the mind, in the quiet place. Then the light of illumination of the Spirit of Truth, playing upon it, reveals its truth and meaning to our soul, but not to our intellect, because it transcends the human mind entirely. It can, however, be felt, or experienced, in the soul.

First is revealed to us Oneness in itself. The Oneness of the ONE, which is the Oneness of the Whole.

Next is revealed to us that we are each, individually, included in the One. This stupendous truth cannot be comprehended by the intellect but can be realized by the soul.

Knowledge of the stupendous truth of Oneness, of which we form a part, can only be felt or realized by intuition, or direct revelation. It is a spiritual experience, having nothing whatever to do with the intellect. Indeed, the more intellectual a person is, the more difficult it is for him to grasp the Truth. It is necessary, as our Lord said, for us to lay aside our intellectual pride and become as a little child, if we are to enter the Kingdom of God.

Realizing our oneness with the One is of course the supreme realization. When the Redeemer and the redeemed become one, the Heavenly Marriage, or Divine Union has taken, place. We then know ourselves to be one with the Changeless One, enthroned with Christ, our older brother in heavenly places. We then know ourselves to be one with the supreme Good; and therefore only Good can come to us, and we, ourselves, can only express Good.

First, then, we meditate upon God as the Supreme Good. This suggests Wholeness, which, when realized in the soul, leads us on to Oneness.

As we hold this idea in the higher part of the mind with the Light of Truth playing upon it, we realize that there is only The One. Stupendous and blinding fact, but there it is. By meditating upon it we enter into Truth.

SPECIAL THOUGHTS ON DIVINE SUPPLY

Thought X

Those who would develop the abundance consciousness must learn to give: in other words, to tithe. The practice of putting on one side at least one-tenth of the whole income, and giving it to the cause of Truth, is one of the essential means of developing that perfect trust and confidence in the Infinite Supply without which the higher consciousness is impossible. So long as we cling to our money we cultivate the limitation and lack form of consciousness ('I have only so much, therefore, I cannot give this'), but if we let go, we loosen our hold upon material things, and learn to rely more fully upon our spiritual supply—God.

The more we learn to let go our hold upon material symbols and learn to rely upon our Spiritual Source (the Spiritual supply that lies behind all material things), the more we enter into the Abundance Consciousness.

To many, it is like drawing teeth to give part of their hard-earned money to the cause of Truth, or for the alleviation, or palliation, of the sufferings of others. They feel that they are throwing away the planks that alone can keep them from absolute poverty and privation. Yet it has to be done, for those who would develop the abundance consciousness must learn not to rely one whit upon material things, and this is best accomplished by giving away a goodly slice of that which they already have.

When this habit is once established in the life, complete reliance upon Spirit is possible—but not before. I admit that this is not easy, but it can be done, and, if it is done, it is wonderful how Spirit looks after us. One man I knew who early learnt to 'tithe', became so prosperous, that he was able later in life to give nine-tenths to God's work and live amply and comfortably on the one-tenth. I know another man who always tithed and has been looked after by the Spirit in a wonderful manner, in spite of the fact that he apparently did everything possible to make himself poor.

Tithing and giving must not be done as an investment. It should be done in order to bless others, and to express a willing-ness to run the risk of poverty which such an act, from a human standpoint, seems likely to entail.

Thought for reflection and affirmation:

'I give freely and willingly, leaving the rest to God.'

LESSON X

Dear Fellow Student of Truth,

The altering of all our thoughts from negative to positive is one of the greatest things in life. It is the secret of all achieve-ment and progress in the higher inward life, and also of all true success in the outward life. This polarization of thought, i.e., changing thoughts from negative to positive, is at once the most difficult task in life, the most important, and fraught with the most far-reaching consequences. By changing your habit of thought you change your life, at the same time creating brighter, happier and more successful conditions for the future. There is no need for us to be anxious about the future, for we have the satisfaction of knowing that every thought that is changed from negative to positive is a stone built into the edifice of our future life. Thus by polarizing our thoughts we bless ourselves today: we make the rest of our life here richer and fuller: we build up character which is the only thing we can take with us when we come to the end of this brief journey.

Yours in Unity and Service,

HENRY THOMAS HAMBLIN

LESSON X

THE TRANSMUTATION OR REVERSAL OF THOUGHT

The outward life is the result of our thoughts, both conscious and subconscious. By making use of denials and affirmations throughout the day, we can reverse every evil or undesirable thought from negative to positive. By this means, we can completely change direction of our thought-stream and guide it towards God and Life, instead of allowing it to flow in the direction of darkness and death.

Thought-control, as you already know, is the greatest accomplishment possible in this life. He who overcomes his thoughts becomes master of himself, his actions, his life, his circumstances. It has been said that every thought is a prayer, and in a sense this is true. How careful, then, should we be to guard every thought!

It will be helpful if we imagine our subconscious mind to be a separate person who is waiting and listening, as it were, to our every thought. Let us endeavour to allow only thoughts that are positive, constructive, and harmonious to reach the ears of this waiting, listening, untiring friend; for if we let negative, destructive, or disharmonious thoughts pass through the door of the Will, he will act upon them, knowing no better, and thus produce disaster in the life. 'Hush! he is listening' must be our watchword. If we carry this thought strongly in our mind, it will render us far more alert and watchful regarding our thoughts than would otherwise be the case.

I have already said that the great secret of thought-control is to find God's perfect Ideal within the soul, and then cast out all thoughts from the mind which do not harmonize with the Inward Vision. To deny the power of an evil thought is to destroy it. Denials are destructive, they disintegrate and break down beliefs and thoughts. We have seen that by denials, it is possible to eradicate agelong beliefs and thus remove their evil results from the life. It is also possible to destroy harmful thoughts by means of denials, and by affirming their opposites, to flood the subconscious mind with the healing, harmonizing, constructive influence of thoughts which are in harmony with the Divine Purpose of the Universe. The Divine Purpose of Life is the increasing expression of Good. Our every thought which is not in harmony with this purpose is destructive to ourselves. It not only hinders our spiritual unfoldment but also robs us of health, happiness and success. On the other hand, every time we destroy an undesirable thought and in its place affirm its opposite, we come into harmony with the Divine Plan: we replace destructive by constructive action, and thus produce harmony, peace, happiness, health, and success in our life.

Again: 'Every thought is registered in the brain by a change in the structure of its cells. By changing one's thoughts from bad to good, cells for good thinking will develop; others productive of evil will shrink'. These words are from an authority on psycho-therapeutics and are valuable because they reveal the physical effect of thought on the brain. Such evidence is encouraging because it shows us that the effect of right thinking is to alter the brain cells so as to make future right thinking easier and wrong less so. It gives us a physiological basis for our contention that the effects of right thinking are cumulative. It also explains why it is that the first effort is more difficult, and why progress eventually becomes easier and more rapid.

If, therefore, the effect of destroying wrong thoughts and replacing them by good is to shrink the cells hitherto devoted to bad thoughts and develop those devoted to good, we have the means in our grasp by which we can, in a sense, re-create ourselves. Literally, a new brain of a higher type is created to replace the old imperfect brain. Thus we have it in our power to compel ourselves to become men and women of a higher type. We see by this how perfect and kindly is the Divine Purpose, for when we seek after higher things, all the Divine Forces come to our aid.

The secret, then, of consciously building up a higher type, is the turning of undesirable thoughts into good, or rather the killing of evil thoughts and affirming their opposites. This calls for great vigilance and watchfulness, but the Divine Wisdom has provided for our help and reward in the law of habit. Like all laws, it can be used constructively or destructively. We can use it to produce either good habits or bad. If we will perseveringly deny all undesirable thoughts as soon as they appear and affirm their opposites, there will come a time when this will become a habit and will be done automatically.

*

Now lay aside this lesson and just think for a few minutes upon this great truth, trying to realize its significance.

*

This is what the Apostle Paul meant when he spoke of converts being transformed by the renewing of their minds. By finding the Christ within the soul and conforming all our thoughts to that grand ideal, we become transformed, by the renewing of our minds into the likeness of the Divine Image.

By the persevering use of denials and affirmations, the mind can be renewed, the life transformed, the cells of the brain altered, the subconscious mind cleansed and trained to direct life's forces towards a manifestation of God's Perfect Idea. There is no height to which we cannot, in process of time, attain. Dazzling indeed is the possibility that lies before us, but the fair vision is not all-sufficing: we must work out in detail, thought by thought, our own salvation. It is not easy at first to watch every thought but it is quite possible. By patience and perseverance, control of thought can, in time, be obtained. At the outset you will be astonished to find how wrong and harmful your thought-habits are and how your thoughts revolve round a certain centre. If your health is not good, you will find that a thought of ill-health, as a fact, is the centre of your life. This is not the result of your ill-health: your ill-health is the result of your fixed habit of thought. Your way of escape from sickness and ill-health is through denial of every thought of sickness, disease, ill-health and imperfection, followed by the affirmation of God's Infinite Perfection. You do not deny that those things exist in the world of the senses, but you do deny that they exist in God's Perfect Idea. When you affirm God's Infinite Health and Perfection, try to raise the consciousness to a realization of what these things really mean, believing in your heart that you will, before long, manifest them in your life. When you hear others talking about poverty, sickness, failure and ill-health, reverse the thought and think of God's Perfection, which can be manifested, if we will only think aright. Proceed in this manner, and in time the necessary change of thought will become a habit with you, transforming your life by the renewing of your mind.

SIMPLE EXAMPLES

First the attacking Negative Thought, then the Denial, and, finally, the Affirmation.

Example no. 1

ATTACKING NEGATIVE THOUGHT:

You are miserable, life is drab, things are all at sixes and sevens, you are depressed. What is the good of life anyway, and of trying any more?

DENIAL:

'I deny that I, a child of the Spirit of Joy, can ever be miserable, or that life is drab, or that life is not worth living, etc.'

AFFIRMATION:

'I am happy because I am a child of God, kept by His love; by grace I am heir of heaven and joint heir with Jesus Christ. Joy, joy, I am full of joy, for all

is well, all is love, and all things are working together for good.' And so on.

Example no. 2

ATTACKING NEGATIVE THOUGHT:

You are not well. That is a queer pain you have. What if it be the beginning of such and such a disease? Everyone succumbs to disease. How do you know what you can escape? And so on.

DENIAL:

'I deny all negative ills any power over me, because I am a child of God. Neither sickness nor disease can affect a child of God who takes refuge in the Almighty.'

AFFIRMATION:

'I am a child of the Spirit, and therefore express in my body the perfection of God's Life and Power. Health is all of God, therefore I open myself to the inflow of God's Life, Health, Wholeness and Power. I give thanks for Omnipresent Wholeness and Health.'

Example no. 3

ATTACKING NEGATIVE THOUGHT:

Your position is most perilous. At any time your source of income may fail, and you become penniless. Conditions get worse and worse, you are getting older. What of the future?

DENIAL:

'I deny that circumstances can have any power over me. No lack or limitation can affect a child of God who looks to the Spirit for supply.

AFFIRMATION:

'I am a child of God, the One Source of all substance and plenty. I am eternally established in the Inexhaustible Riches of the Spirit.'

Example no. IV

ATTACKING NEGATIVE THOUGHT:

You are just as sinful as ever you were, just as impotent, just as far from the Kingdom. You are making no progress. Troubles get worse instead of less. Why not give it all up, take your ease again, and cease this fruitless search?

DENIAL:

'In Spirit there can be, and there is no failure. Because I am in the Spirit, there is no lack of progress in spiritual things, for nothing can hinder man in his upward spiritual climb.'

AFFIRMATION:

"'I live, yet not I, but Christ liveth in me". Because I am in Christ and Christ liveth in Me, I pass steadily along the Path to glories unspeakable.'

The above are crude and clumsy, but they will help you to make better use of denials and affirmations. They can also be condensed and combined together. For instance, Example No. III might be combined something like this:

'No child of God can ever lack, for the Spirit is the Source of all Supply. I am (or man is) eternally established in the inexhaustible riches of the Spirit.'

Continue the nightly and morning regime as usual. Enter the Silence and contemplate the Infinite Perfection of God. The more you do this, the greater will be Its manifestation both in your life and in those around you. Send out your love to all. Serve your fellows in ministries of devoted service.

WEEK ELEVEN:
CHARACTER AND HABIT

In Lesson XI, HTH concentrates on what he calls 'character-building'. Although this does carry its conventional meaning, it is clear from the outset that what he refers to us something rather greater, something we might prefer to refer to as 'soul-building', the building of qualities of soul, or the building of the Christ character into our own being.

LIFE CONSISTS only of experiences. It is simply a training school in which we build up character and learn through experience. Life and its experiences are the great Initiator. Every day brings experiences which, if dealt with in the right way, build up character. If we deal with them rightly, character is built up, and life, because we become strong, is found to be comparatively easy. If we deal with them in the wrong way, life becomes increasingly difficult and painful. People often say: 'I cannot think why all this evil and trouble come upon me'. If they were to examine themselves, they might find that in some test they had failed, that some experience had not been met in the right way.

Trouble never comes without reason. The normal is harmony and peace. All trouble and difficulty are for the purpose of building up character. They show that in some way we have fallen short of the required standard. They come to us simply because we lack certain qualities of character. If we meet them in the right way, we pass on from victory to victory. If we fail to do so, they multiply and increase until life is a literal hell.

It is most important that we should realize that life consists of a series of tests, presenting us with an opportunity for us to meet certain experiences by which we attain to higher things. Therefore, we should always thank God for every experience of every day, no matter how unpleasant it may be. When the person meets with a disappointment, he feels 'very hard done-by', and thinks that life is treating him badly. Instead of which, he should give thanks for the opportunity it gives him of growing into a higher state of consciousness through character growth. All life's experiences are good, both pleasant and unpleasant. Every experience gives us the opportunity of rising to higher things. Without these experiences we could not rise, therefore we should at all times praise God for all life's experiences, both bitter and sweet. The experiences are small, the tests minute as a rule. Great tests may and do come, but almost invariably the experiences that we have to meet are small and comparatively insignificant. So much so, they may be overlooked. Such a small duty, or detail, or service, may appear to be not worthy of notice, yet upon these small things all our future depends. It may be that we meet with one needing help. We may be in a hurry, and therefore we are tempted to say: 'Let someone else see to him or her'. We dare not do this, we cannot afford to do so. If we do, we shall meet with a duty which will demand a great sacrifice. We may be sure of this, that if a person who needs help comes to us, or is put in our way, it is a test, or experience, specially provided for our benefit. It presents us with an opportunity by which we can advance in the real life—that of the Spirit.

Or it may be that some apparently small detail of our work is the test. We have the opportunity either to scamp it or attend to some comparatively significant detail at some personal inconvenience, or to let it go. No-one will be any the better, so it may seem, if we do it well; and no-one the poorer if we let it slide. But it is a test. By it we either rise or fall. If we let it go, character deteriorates and this brings bigger tests and more unpleasant experiences.

When I was a poor, vacillating, weak unstable creature, after much vicissitude I began to notice that people were successful, while I remained unsuccessful, because they were strong characters. I liked them no more on this account, as the weak always resent the strength of those who beat them in the race of life. I also noticed that these successful people expressed their character in their work. They never shirked anything. They always faced the music. There was no detail too small for them, no problem which they were not prepared to investigate down to its most minute detail. No matter how small and apparently unimportant a thing might appear to be, they attended to it with the greatest care. In fact, they did willingly all the things which I had been shying away from and avoiding. This is, of course, the secret of true success—to express character in our work: to face the music, to choose the difficult path of duty and service, rather than the way that is easy at the time.

In spiritual life it is the same. Work and spiritual experience are all mixed up. The business of life is the training for the soul.

Daily, if we look out for them, certain experiences will be offered to us, certain tests: very insignificant they may appear to be, but really of vast importance. We meet a certain person; we are led to go to a certain place; we go down a different street from usual; we receive a certain letter, and so on. Why this thing has happened is the question we should always ask ourselves.

We build up character, then, by being more faithful and efficient in our work and service: by meeting all life's experiences, no matter how apparently trivial they may be, in the best possible way: by choosing the apparently hard, unpleasant and difficult path, instead of the way of pleasant ease.

*

From what has been said, it will be seen how hopeless and foolish it is for us to desire to be taken 'out of the world', away from its difficulties and troubles, in order to live a dreamy, mystical and spiritual existence of no use to anyone, including ourselves. We have to get away from the idea that the spiritual life is one thing, and the hard facts of life, and the difficulties and duties of everyday existence, another. We can build up the character that endures, and the qualities of spirit which belong to eternity, only through meeting life's difficulties in the daily round and the common task. The one who is steadfast in his work, putting character into all that he does, and who attends faithfully to detail, is building for eternity: whether he knows it or not, matters little.

We can, however, build up character not only by meeting life's experiences in the correct manner, but also by meditation. This particular aspect of meditation will be dealt with in later letters.

Now with regard to habit. The subconscious mind needs something to do. Let us therefore build up good habits, for by so doing we not only 'kill' bad ones, but we also add to our character. If we have been in the habit of being unpunctual, let us cultivate the good habit of strict punctuality. We cannot expect others to be punctual with us, if we ourselves are not punctual to the minute. Still less can we expect those over whom we have authority to be punctual if we are frequently late ourselves.

It is these little things that build up character. If we are faithful in the small things, it is easy to be faithful in the large affairs of life, for we then possess the character which enables us to deal with them. All this involves sacrifice. Every day we must be willing to sacrifice some part of our own ease, comfort and enjoyment for the sake of duty, efficiency, or in order to help the weak. We cannot be selfish and at the same time build up character.

As an unstable, vacillating creature who has by the grace of God been able to overcome, at any rate to a certain extent, his weaknesses, let me add this testimony. In the past, whenever I have shirked a duty, or avoided an unpleasant experience, or dodged something which I ought to have done and would have done if I had not been so cowardly, I have had to suffer most severely for it; suffering which lasted for years and which probably still operates in my life today. That God can overrule everything for good is something for which to be thankful, but does not alter the fact that by neglecting or avoiding the small duties, we fail at tests which have been specially prepared for us and this may affect us during our whole life.

Desiring for you an over-increasing understanding of Truth.

Yours in the One Service,

HENRY THOMAS HAMBLIN

INSTRUCTIONS IN PROGRESSIVE REFLECTIVE MEDITATION

Because there is only the One, and the One is the Whole, we are included in the One.

Hold this idea in the higher part of the mind until the Light of Truth reveals its wonderful truth to you. Because there is only the One, we can never be separated from our Divine Source. The belief in separateness, i.e., believing that we can ever be separated from the One, is the greatest of errors, and the sin for which we have to suffer most. When our Centre is shifted and is made to coincide with the Divine Centre, we become one with God.

Because there is only the One and we are one with the One, we are one with all.

Hold the above in the mind, allowing the Light of the Spirit to play upon it until its truth is revealed to you.

Then pray:

One with the Universe. One with That which produced the Universe. One with all our fellow human beings—all one. One with every creature, both great and small.

One with the winds of heaven, and the mighty deep: the sun by day and the quiet orb by night. O Wonder of Wonders, how can I express my joy?

Because I am one with Thee, Thy Oneness is also my oneness: all sense of separateness is swallowed up in Truth.

Because I am one with Thee, Thy Completeness is also my completeness; all my incompleteness is swallowed up in Truth.

Because I am one with Thee, Thy Wholeness is also my Wholeness: all imperfection, or lack of Wholeness, is swallowed up in Truth.

SPECIAL THOUGHTS ON DIVINE SUPPLY

Thought XI

Our outward circumstances are the result of our thoughts, both conscious and subconscious. As our subconscious thinking is controlled largely by our conscious thinking, we shall deal with the latter first.

If we think in a small, mean way, our circumstances are bound to be small and mean. Thoughts have a habit of revolving around a central idea. If that central idea be small and mean, then every thought will be related to that which is small and mean, and smallness and meanness will be reflected in the outward circumstances.

Thinking from the central standpoint of small means must, inevitably, perpetuate a life of small means and restricted circumstances. If a rich man were to think in this way and allow his thoughts to revolve round a central thought of poverty, lack and fear of destitution, it would not be many years before his circumstances would be as poor and poverty-stricken as his thoughts. Conversely, if a poor man learns to think large thoughts of abundance and unlimited supply, then there is no power on earth that can stop him from rising, until his circumstances are as rich as his thoughts.

The writer has had plenty of experience, in years gone by, of poverty—that genteel poverty that cannot afford to go to the dentist until the teeth are ruined; that is appalled at the thought of a doctor's bill, or of the expense of a new suit of clothes. This kind of life is awful. Rent day is a nightmare and monthly accounts a source of continual dread. The writer knows by experience that thinking of all these worrying things, and thinking from the standpoint of inadequate means, develops a poverty consciousness. He also knows that by learning to think in a large way—in a more prosperous and opulent way, realizing that there is infinite plenty upon which we can all draw to an unlimited extent—breaks down the barriers set up by poverty-thinking habits, and allows the Infinite Abundance of Divine Mind to manifest in the life, to an ever-increasing degree.

Therefore do not think from the standpoint of possible restricted means, but from the standpoint of God's inexhaustible abundance. Believe that behind all that you see with your physical sight is the spiritual substance from which all things proceed, and declare that this will manifest abundance in your life, according to your abundance thoughts.

Remember that the One, Infinite, Universal Life expresses itself through *you*, according to the way you shape it. You can manifest it in the form of perpetual abundance if you will think only those thoughts which you would like to see objectified in your life.

LESSON XI

Dear Fellow Student of Truth,

Character building, not the having of a good or easy time or being successful, or popular, is the supreme object of life. Success, popularity, pleasure, pall on one in time. They are good things enough in their way but they do not satisfy. Character, when built up, is a source of eternal joy and satisfaction.

This lesson tells you how to overcome. There are two laws which, rightly understood and made use of, are of the greatest assistance to one who desires to overcome habit and weakness of character. They are: The Law of Subconscious Habit, and the Law of Polarity. Polarize your thoughts, raising them from negative to positive, from the sense-plane to the Spiritual, until this becomes a mental habit, and you will find that the whole life and character will become transformed. When you are armed with this knowledge, there are no heights to which you cannot climb.

Yours in the Unity of Service,

HENRY THOMAS HAMBLIN

LESSON XI

CHARACTER BUILDING AND THE OVERCOMING OF HABIT

Character is the only thing which we can take with us when this brief life is over. The main object of life is the building of character: if this is not achieved, our life here is more or less a failure.

Character is also the basis of all true satisfaction, of success, of health. No-one can derive any satisfaction from life who is not winning its battle, and the greatest victory of all is the overcoming of weaknesses and the building up of character. No-one can be successful in life, and remain successful, whose character is weak or faulty. One whose character is strong will pull through, time after time, where another less strong would go under. It is the small victories in everyday life which strengthen and make for victory when the severe testing time comes. It is the small failures and giving in to difficulties, the drifting with the stream, the avoidance of mental and moral exertion, that render one unfit for the battle of life and make us weak and helpless when the inevitable fierce conflict comes to the soul. Success in life is possible only to those who are strong in character: one hidden weakness is sufficient to wreck a career.

It was Philips Brooks who said: 'Do not pray for easy lives: pray to be stronger men. Do not pray for tasks equal to your powers: pray for powers equal to your tasks.' It is by overcoming obstacles and choosing the difficult path of achievement, instead of trying to avoid difficulty and seeking ease and security, that character is built up. To choose the easy task: to avoid the disagreeable duty: to 'flop' helplessly through life: to drift with the stream, seeking only ease, leisure, comfort and security, is the way of disintegration and death.

Character building, then, is our great objective, and our first aim is the overcoming of habits which we know to be undesirable. When these are overcome, great joy is experienced, but it is

soon revealed to us that there are other weaknesses to be conquered, and when these, in turn, have been mastered, we find
yet other parts of our character that need building up and
strengthening. Wrong habits are due to the wrong use of the
subconscious mind. This wonderful mind is perfectly willing to
produce either good action, or bad, according to direction. By
indulging in bad thoughts or by giving way to mental inertia and
lethargy, we produce a habit of thought, or a disinclination for
effort, which may paralyze our life: by repeated bad action we
cause the subconscious mind to reproduce that bad action automatically. This action of the subconscious mind is not evil: it is a
good quality wrongly applied. This willingness, on the part of
the subconscious mind, to produce habit, is the greatest help we
have in our upward climb, for if we will give it the necessary
direction, it will produce good habit instead of bad, thus making
character-building possible.

How then can bad habit be overcome and replaced by good
habit?

First, the greatest secret of all is meditation. In God we find
every trait of character that we desire to cultivate, in perfection.
By entering the Silence and keeping our attention fixed upon
Divine Strength, we become strong. By meditating upon God's
Patience, we become patient. By contemplating God's Love and
Compassion, we become loving and compassionate. By holding
the thought, at the top of our mind, of Divine Order, Precision,
Accuracy, Punctuality, and so on, we become orderly, accurate
and punctual. We grow into the likeness of that upon which we
meditate.

Supposing that your weakness is lack of perseverance, staying power, persistence, etc., you would enter the Silence with the
thought of Divine perseverance and endurance in your mind.
The great thing is to become perfectly quiet and relaxed, but at
the same time aspiring upwards to God, and then to hold the
desired thought at the top of the mind. Then remain quiet and
at rest. Presently the thought will expand and flood the whole

mind. Keep like this for as long as possible. Then pass on to other things. As a result of this practice, not only will it be much easier for you to hold the right thought at all times, but you will find that you possess staying powers and an ability to persist that will agreeably surprise you.

Secondly, there is the daily and hourly quiet striving after a better life: the ever-watchful vigilance which nips wrong thought in the bud and substitutes its opposite good thought. This transmutation of thought is, after meditation in the Silence, the greatest thing in life. By this means, you polarize your thoughts, rising from the negative pole to the positive. This in time, transforms the life, for all action is the result of thought, and all physical habit and weakness of character are the result of wrong and negative habits of thinking. Remember that the thoughts must be switched from the negative pole to the positive: that is, its exact opposite. For instance, if a thought of hate or dislike rises in your mind, deny that it can affect you (for by so doing you rob it of its power), immediately raising yourself to your highest conception of Universal Love. If an impure thought seeks entrance to the mind, immediately deny it and rise to your highest conception of purity. It does not matter whether it be a mental picture of a dawn at sea, or the snowclad peaks of a mountain range, or the Infinite Purity of the Absolute, so long as it is your highest conception of purity. If a thought of weakness assails you, deny it, and rise to your highest conception of the Power of the Infinite. Whatever negative thought may come to you, always deny it and immediately rise to your highest conception of its opposite. Everything has its opposite and each are the opposite ends or poles of the same thing. For instance, light is the positive opposite of darkness, heat is the positive opposite of cold, courage is the positive opposite of negative fear. Courage is not the opposite pole of cold, neither is light the opposite pole of fear. In order to get results, we must work scientifically and reach the positive pole or exact opposite of the negative evil we wish to defeat.

This process of thought-transmutation is of great importance.

By it you can transform your life, for the Universe, everything, is thought. By polarizing your thoughts, thus bringing them into harmony with the Divine, you transform your life, regenerate your body and actually alter your world.

This may seem rather formidable, but it is not so. It is troublesome at first to reverse all negative thoughts in this way, but you are helped by two very important things: (1) The effect of meditation in the Silence, which makes it very much easier for the thoughts to run in the right direction. Meditation in the Silence prepares a channel for the thoughts along which they can flow. (2) Right thinking becomes a habit. Some psychologists say that there is a physiological reason for this, which is that new cells are cultivated in the brain whose use is to promote and facilitate the thinking of right thoughts, while at the same time the cells used formerly for wrong thinking become atrophied and thus are no longer used. Be this as it may, the fact remains that by a little perseverance and quiet effort right thinking becomes a habit, and therefore just as easy as breathing.

Thirdly, it is impossible to overcome habit and weaknesses of character by fighting them. By fighting evil we increase its power; by fighting habit we impress it more firmly upon the subconscious mind. A bad habit can be overcome by cultivating a good one to take its place, a habit which must be the exact opposite of the one you wish to destroy. Just in the same way that you reverse your thoughts, so also must you concentrate upon building up habits which are the exact opposite of the ones you wish to overcome and destroy. If those who are captives will constantly deny and ignore their bad habits, refusing to recognize them, and instead concentrate upon and make ideals of their opposites, they will find that, in course of time, their chains and fetters will be broken: they will enter into liberty and experience the joy of overcoming.

Do not be dismayed if, after a period of apparently easy victory and triumph, the old habit rises up with all its old-time power, and stretches you flat upon the ground in ignominious defeat.

Instead of lamenting the disaster (which recognizes and there-fore increases the power of the old habit), simply pick yourself up, going on your way not thinking of your defeat, except to make a mental note not to allow yourself to be tripped up again in the same manner. Continue to go straight on, holding before you the ideal (the exact opposite of your habits) and following after it.

Finally, remember that by idealism we grow gradually into the image of our ideal. Hold constantly, therefore, in your mind a picture of the ideal after which you are striving. No matter how dim or blurred the image may be, it will draw you onward and upward. If you meet with defeat, hold fast to your ideal and rise from the ashes of your failure to conquer and overcome. Follow your ideal no matter how much you may be tempted to relinquish it. Cling to it: sacrifice, if necessary, everything for it; for this is the way which will bring you all that is worth having and living for.

The way is not easy, but the ascent is possible; and each time that you try, even though you fail, gives you strength for your next battle. The faithful subconscious mind will lend its aid, ever striving to build up good habits in the place of bad.

When you have overcome one habit or weakness, you can then pass on to eradicating the next, for the good habit will become au-tomatic and will leave you free to improve in other directions.

Before you lies the Path of Victory. Within you is the Infinite Power. Rise up, O conscious Sons of God and Daughters of the Most High!

WEEK TWELVE :
SUPERCONSCIOUSNESS

Hamblin's concept of superconsciousness, like his notion of the subconscious, should not be seen in a conventional psychological context, but rather as a concept of his own devising, one which is explained in this lesson.

SUPERCONSCIOUSNESS is of course the consciousness that is above our ordinary consciousness. It must not be confused with subconsciousness, dream consciousness, or astral consciousness. No psychic powers or experiences have anything to do with it. Superconsciousness is a higher state of consciousness altogether, which transcends at one leap all psychic states, astral planes, and experiences, bringing us into heavenly places, which is the Presence of God.

Superconsciousness is actually a state of consciousness, and is not entering into a place. Leaving the body, entering trances, visiting other planes, these are all psychic experiences with which we have nothing to do. Such experiences do not help the soul to realize its oneness with God. They actually hinder instead of helping. They are bypaths which, only too often, lead out of the true way of Eternal Life.

Superconsciousness is beyond, or behind, or above, the pairs of opposites. The conscious mind can only think in pairs—good and evil, right and wrong, light and darkness, and so on. In the superconscious we get beyond these limitations and *know* rather than think, the Truth, i.e., Wholeness, Oneness, instead of separateness, opposition, contending forces, and so on. This is the realm of absolute peace, calm, order, oneness, perfection, silence. In other words, we are in the Universal, or four-dimensional Consciousness: what some have termed the Consciousness of many dimensions.

At this stage of our unfoldment, we are not allowed to enter either fully or permanently into this larger state of consciousness. We can sit, whenever we like to enter, in the outer courts of the heavenly places, but we are still chained to our ordinary finite consciousness and the limitations, although less than formerly, of the physical plane. Later on, when we have learnt all our lessons, have attained to higher things, and have passed certain tests and initiations, our bodies will be spiritualized, or translated, and we shall dwell in the higher, or super-, or Christ-Consciousness continually.

One who has attained fully to the Higher or Universal Consciousness can disappear from human sight, and reappear, at will. He can heal the sick at a touch, or even without actual contact, instantaneously. He can perform Miracles and do mighty works. Our Lord attained fully to this sublime state and is now helping us by His Spirit to attain to the same stage also. Jesus did nothing that He does not bid us do also, even including loving all, and resisting not evil, even unto the uttermost—unto death if necessary. When He walked on the lake, Peter was allowed to do the same, failing only when he lost faith. The wonderful healing of Jesus was also duplicated by His disciples, and the early Church carried on the same, until it became steeped in materialism and lost the power. In the same manner the Spirit of Truth (the Spirit that raised up Jesus) is also leading us into the full realization of our oneness with the Infinite, so that we too shall dwell permanently in the same higher consciousness as our Lord. 'I go to prepare a place for you, that where I am there ye may be also'. This means not a place, or plane, as we mortals understand it, but a state of consciousness which we may share with our Lord. Nothing could be plainer than this promise. The state of consciousness into which our Lord has entered, and to which He attained through all the weaknesses of the flesh, may be ours also. It is just a question of attainment.

Christ, the representative of, or Lord from Heaven, naturally was Lord of all planes of consciousness, but that would not have helped us, if He had not given up all and taken upon the weaknesses and limitations of our present fallen consciousness, called by the Apostle 'sinful flesh'. Through taking all our limitations upon Himself and overcoming finally to attain again to the Heavenly Consciousness, Christ has conquered for us, and made it possible for us to attain also.

Now, the outer court of heaven is as far as we have got at present. Let us thank God for this, for it is a tremendous stride in the right direction. We possess the power at any moment to enter the fringe of the superconscious, in which we know by intuition, or direct knowing, things which it would be a sacrilege to discuss, that is, if we could discuss in finite language those things which pertain to the Infinite.

At any moment, we can rise above, or withdraw from the things of time and sense, to reach that plane of consciousness wherein we realize the infinite calm peace, perfection, wholeness, oneness and joy of That which changes not. In a moment, in the twinkling of an eye, we become changed: we pass out of our finite limitations into the wider place where 'the Lord God wipes away tears from off all faces'. In a flash, we know the peace which passeth all understanding: we realize the truth and reality of oneness and unity. Time and space are no more—we are one with the Eternal; at one with Christ in heavenly places. In a flash we are one with all creatures, all stars and suns, all angels, all gods—we are all one.

All the universe pulsates with joy indescribable. Every atom is filled with praise. All is well.

We reach this state of enlarged consciousness mainly through meditation. It may be somewhat difficult at first to enter this state of spiritual illumination, and it may be only at special times that we realize our oneness, not only with the Source of all things, but all things themselves. In course of time, however, it becomes increasingly easy to enter this state. At any moment we can enter 'this larger place of consciousness', and make contact with our Divine Source. The ultimate result of continually doing this, if we do not fail when the tests of initiation are applied, is that we live permanently in the higher consciousness, after having passed the final test of the greatness and sincerity of our love to others.

We must not only meditate; we must not only keep making contact with our Divine Source during the day, we must also live the Christ life every minute, meeting all difficulties as tests of our apprenticeship. We must not, of course, look upon 'having a good time' as the principal aim and object of life, but to become initiated into the mysteries of the Kingdom of God, and to enter into the higher consciousness. We must live the life of the Spirit while yet in the flesh, at all times being willing to be led by the Spirit, no matter where He may lead us.

We must at all times raise our thoughts to a higher plane. We must cease utterly to think the old thoughts of selfishness and narrow limitation, thinking instead in a larger, finer and more universal way. Instead of being self-centred, we must become universal in our outlook, thinking of others before ourselves.

Our Lord tells us that not all who say Lord, Lord, shall enter the Kingdom, but he that doeth the will of the Father. Again, our Lord tells us that it is only those who do His sayings, as well as hear them, who build on the Rock of Eternal Life. Again, our Lord demands of us that we forgive even as we hope to be forgiven of God, that we love God with our whole heart, mind and strength, and our neighbour even as we do ourself. Here is the infinite wisdom of Christ's teaching laid bare. The thing that prevents us from entering fully into the Kingdom of Heaven is self and self-centredness. By loving God with all our strength and our neighbour as ourself, we break down this barrier. The more universal we become in outlook, in thought and in love, the more fit we become for the Kingdom of God. By blessing and helping others, we bless and help ourselves more. By losing 'self' we find the *Self*. By losing our life, we find *Life*. By forgiving others, we ourselves find forgiveness.

We see then that it is not only by meditation and by thought control, but also by living the life that we find God.

The superconscious realm or state is the Kingdom of God or Heaven. It is the mystical Divine Union, when Spirit and soul become one in the Heavenly Marriage. The redeemed soul becomes one with the Redeemer: in other words, it lives in perpetual consciousness of its Lord's presence, and of oneness with God. This cannot be attained to unless we make constant contact with God by means of praise and prayer. If we continually lift our hearts in praise and thanksgiving and continually pray to God about every situation or experience that arises during the day, we find in time that we are living the Spiritual Life actually, and practising the Presence of God. The Divine Presence is then realized, in a very special sense, as being always with us. Like a pillar of cloud by day, and a pillar of fire by night, never leaving us, it indicates the Presence of Divine Power and Blessing. It shows that we are daily advancing more deeply into the Kingdom.

It is also necessary for us to

Rejoice at all times.

Seek the good in all people.

Seek the good in all things.

Seek the good in all circumstances.

Seek the good in all experiences.

Seek the celestial behind the material.

Seek the celestial universe here and now.

We also help our own spiritual unfoldment by praying for others. Also our spiritual progress is helped by meeting trouble and difficulty. After considerable experience I can say that it seems impossible to attain without overcoming difficulty and passing through trying situations. It seems that it is only by these that we can really learn to *know* God *intimately.*

Desiring ever for you the highest wisdom and understanding,

Yours in the Great Quest,

HENRY THOMAS HAMBLIN

INSTRUCTIONS IN PROGRESSIVE
REFLECTIVE MEDITATION

'For through Him we both have access
by one Spirit unto the Father.'

It is necessary for us to remember that it is through Christ that we become one with God. For some reason, we are naturally fallen in consciousness from the Divine Presence, which is perfect wholeness and oneness, and it is only Christ who can raise us up to our lost estate. Christ, the Divine One, knocks at the door of our hearts. Christianity is a 'heart' religion. We have to become as little children', 'feeling' our way, by intuition into the Kingdom, rather than 'seeing' our way by great knowledge. Christ stands at the door of our hearts and knocks for admission.

The King and Lord of Heaven and earth and all planes, pleads for admittance. O wondrous, stupendous truth! Shall we not hasten to let Him in?

Christ is God—the understandable, manifested aspect of God. We can reach the 'Father' only through Christ, just in the same way that we can make a person hear only through his ear. Therefore, let it be understood that all approach to Truth, and all our meditation, is done in and through Christ.

Through Christ we are one with the Changeless One. Christ is the Way, the Truth and the Life. By realizing this, we get away from the self and the personality which would otherwise keep us out of the Kingdom of Heaven.

We will continue our usual meditation upon:

GOOD, behind all relative states and opposing forces.

WHOLENESS, which includes Perfection and completeness.

ONENESS, which includes the Oneness of the ONE, and our at-one-ment, or oneness, with the ONE, and with the WHOLE.

LESSON XII

Dear Fellow Student of Truth,

This lesson is one of the most important of the whole series. The time has now arrived for us to rise from the changing, impermanent sense-life of apparent imperfection, into the superconscious realm of Reality. Here God's Infinite Perfection eternally abides. It never evolves, never changes: it *is*. This Perfection *is* here and now. It is the only Reality, and all else is a changing, fleeting shadow, a distorted reflection, a grotesque caricature of the one imperishable, unchanging Perfection. When we rise up into this higher consciousness—or, to put the Truth in another way, when we raise our consciousness from the lower self to the real Spiritual Self—we look down upon the sense life with all its follies, illusions, baubles, shams, suffering and evil and see It for what it is. It is as nothing, for our eyes have seen the Great Reality.

When you enter into this knowledge and realization, you become filled with Divine Power. You are able to bring the Invisible into the visible: to work miracles and wonders in your own life and in the lives of others. May it be so.

Yours in the Great Truth,

HENRY THOMAS HAMBLIN

SPECIAL THOUGHTS ON DIVINE SUPPLY

Thought XII

The 'thoughts' which have been sent to you previously have had for their object the changing of your conscious thought-habit. This tends in time to alter the *subconscious* thought-habit. In addition to this, however, it is necessary to make use of more direct means of bringing the truth about supply to the inner mind. This is by 'being still and knowing' and repeating a statement of Truth. This is explained more fully in Lesson XIX. The secret of success in this method is to become perfectly quiet and free from all thoughts of care and worry and external things. When one has got into the necessary quiet condition, a statement of Truth should be made and repeated over and over again in a restful, trustful manner. The statement of Truth may be quite simple, such as: *'All that the Father hath is mine'*, or some such words as these. Even the words prosperity, abundance, plenty, repeated over and over again will do.

But not only is it necessary to think rightly and to *'be still and know'*, but it is also necessary to meet all thoughts or suggestions of adversity, and lack, and poverty, and anxieties for the morrow, with short, sharp affirmations, or ejaculations of Truth, so that before these false suggestions can pass the threshold of our minds, they are destroyed or driven away. As soon as the suggestion of lack, or poverty, or anxiety enters our minds, it should be met with an affirmation of Truth, quickly. By saying *'God is my sufficient supply'*, or some similar statement, the false suggestion is nipped in the bud and destroyed.

In conclusion, remember these three things:

(1) To think right thoughts, as previously described.

(2) To be still and know the Truth.

(3) To meet all false suggestions with affirmations, or ejaculations, of Truth, quickly, before the former can enter the mind.

Doing these three things wholeheartedly and sincerely changes the mind and transforms the life.

LESSON XII

THE SUPERCONSCIOUS MIND

The Superconscious Mind is unknown to all but the initiated. It is the Christ or Universal Mind. The whole teaching of Jesus, when its inner meaning is understood, relates to this higher consciousness. This Universal Mind and Consciousness cannot be entered except after much searching after God, and then only when we are fit to enter. As a result of much time spent in the Silence and meditation upon God, we gradually learn to rise above our false outer self, and enter the wider and deeper Universal Mind and Consciousness.

When this state is attained, we think universally, we understand universally, and all life's trivialities fall away. We understand the meaning of all suffering, of life and of death: all the mysteries of life are explained. We cannot, however, explain these things to others, because there are no words with which to explain them. What we do understand, however, is that all is well; that all is love: that behind this life of mystery and illusion is God's Infinite Perfection existing here and now. We know, although we cannot explain it, that the real life is wonderful and grand beyond description and that infinite joy and felicity are ours. We realize that all is well with the Cosmic Scheme: that God makes no mistakes in His beautiful Universe. Not an atom out of its place, not a single plan miscarried—all is well.

In my earlier writings, I spoke of the Subliminal Mind as being the source of all inspiration and knowledge. I did so because I classed, superficially, for the sake of simplicity, the whole of the interior mind under the term of subliminal. Actually, however, the superconscious is above the conscious mind and apparently has its physical location in the apex of the brain. Therefore, although we start our studies by realizing the Immanent God within, we now proceed to find God Transcendent, in a higher realm of mind and spirit.

Many are the ways by which this superconscious is reached, and the method that may suit one may not be possible for another. There is the path of meditation and devotion. There is the path of affirmation. There are also other ways. Edward Carpenter, for instance, attained what he calls Cosmic Consciousness through thinking along lines of evolution. The best way is undoubtedly to follow all the roads, or, in any case, those which intuitively appeal to you. By meditating upon all the wonders and perfections of God's character, and surrendering yourself to His Will and Purpose, you enter the path of devotion. By serving the whole instead of yourself; by loving all your fellows and all the Universe and its Creator; by seeking to give rather than to receive; by seeing the Omnipresent Good in everyone, you enter the path of service. The latter is the path all must tread. By meditating upon the beauty of God's character as revealed in His flowers you enter the path of beauty.* This also leads to the realization that God's Infinite Perfection is a present reality, and is the only Reality. By affirming your oneness, or union, with Christ, you enter the fourth path. It matters not by which path you finally arrive, so long as you reach your goal. All who seek God and the Inner Kingdom, find it, for 'he that seeketh findeth'.

The whole burden of the teaching of Jesus was this Inner Kingdom, or superconscious realm of mind. This superconscious realm of mind and consciousness is the great aim of the new life. It is the goal at which all souls arrive. When the Kingdom of God, which is the superconscious realm within, is found, we have come to the end of our journey: we enter the secret place of the Most High; we become instinct with Divine Power; we find our true life in God. This was the teaching of Jesus, and by following it we enter into peace. He attained more perfectly than any other to this consciousness, for He was the perfect manifestation of the Divine Idea. It is when we touch this higher consciousness that we become able to help others: to heal the sick, to bind up the brokenhearted; to overcome, to become master of our fate, captain of our soul. We shall ever seek after God and surrender ourselves to His Will and Purpose if we serve our fellows and the Whole instead of our selfish self, yielding up our false self to the Universal Self. If we seek God in the flowers and other unpolluted beauties of Nature which He has given us for our Spiritual uplift and refreshment; if we affirm our union with Christ; if we ever seek the Infinite Perfect, Reality which exists eternally be-

*See also *The Message of a Flower.*

hind the changing imperfections, then we shall gradually unfold, and in God's good time, enter the Kingdom.

The great secret that is gradually being unfolded to us is this:
that in spite of all that has been said about evolution; in spite of
all the evidence which we have of the gradual growth from lower
types to higher; in spite of all the imperfection that we see around
us; in spite of the seeming reality of this material life; in spite of
the apparent marring of God's Perfect Creation by the disharmonious thought of man, yet God's Infinite Perfection stands
behind it all, eternally spotless and whole.

Dear fellow student, may the Spirit open your eyes at this
stage, even as He has opened mine, to this great fact, that the,
infinitely perfect Idea of God exists *now* in all its completeness
and beauty. It is not marred by the thought of man, although at
one time this theory seemed to be the only explanation of the
riddle of life. What has held our attention and deceived our minds
has been a caricature of God's Idea, a counterfeit of the Eternal
Reality. When we enter the superconscious realm of the mind
we realize that the only thing that exists is God's Infinite Perfection, which has never been ruffled or disturbed, and that all else
exists only in our finite lower consciousness, therefore having no
reality apart from human thought. Entering the Superconscious
means leaving the lower or ordinary consciousness, and rising
out of the distorted, counterfeit existence into the realm of Infinite Spirit. It means rising from the unreal into the only Reality,
from the impermanent and changing into the Unchanging and
Eternal. Words cannot describe the experience. There is a consciousness of great power and infinite spaciousness. The consciousness expands and embraces ALL. This is the realm of
power. It is when we realize that the sense life with all its material
framework which seems so solid has, although it is apparently so
real to this consciousness, no reality at all, that we are able, to
realize the Infinite Perfection, which is the one true Reality. Our
affirmation for this lesson will be taken from Edward Carpenter's *Towards Democracy*.

'Deep as the Universe is my life, and I know it.'

You will notice that the teaching is changing. What is truth at one stage is not truth at another, and as we advance so does our viewpoint alter and our apprehension of Truth become enlarged.

WEEK THIRTEEN:
WHAT IS REALITY?

SOMEONE HAS wisely said that there is no place but *here*, and no time but *now*. Someone also has said that there is no place but the Presence of God, and no time but the unfoldment of Good.

Time and space are not only merely modes in finite consciousness, they are also limitations of our present finite consciousness. They are nothing in themselves: they only mark the limits of the finite human mind.

P.D. Ouspensky, in his work on the fourth dimension, tells us that the higher animal, such as a dog, or a horse, is of two-dimensional consciousness. We, of course, enjoy a consciousness recognizing three dimensions. A dog, or a horse, can see only length and breadth, while we can see length, breadth and thickness, or solidity. Therefore, although a dog, or a horse, lives in the same world as we do, he sees something very different from the world that we cognize. Where we see solids, he sees only planes. Where we see the angles of a third dimensional object he sees motion.

In the same way, Ouspensky argues, the immobile angles and curves of the (to us unknown) fourth dimension may appear to be as motion. Motion then is not true motion but is a limitation of consciousness, in the same way that the motion caused by the angles of the third dimension sensed by a dog, is not true motion, but is due merely to the limitations of his two-dimensional consciousness.

Mathematicians show that there is a fourth dimension, although because it is beyond our present range of consciousness, they cannot agree as to what exactly this fourth dimension is. It does not matter very much, but the knowledge that we are living in a world of four dimensions, of which we can apprehend three only, is valuable to us, in that it brings home to us the fact that we are living in a universe which we can sense only in part. Just as the dog's world or the world sensed by a dog, is entirely different from the world that is sensed by us, although it is the same world in which we are both living, so also the world that we sense is not the world of reality. We know only in part.

We are spiritual beings living in a spiritual universe now. We are therefore subject to spiritual law, which is greater than natural law.

If it were possible to extend the consciousness of a dog, or a horse, to three dimensions, so that it could apprehend the same world that we apprehend, it would then see that the world which it formerly apprehended (the world of two dimensions only, of planes and motion instead of three dimensions and solids) does not really exist. It was an illusory world, having no reality, being merely a sort of caricature of the real, due to the limitation of his former consciousness. In the same way, if our consciousness were to be expanded to four dimensions, we should at once realize that the world of three dimensions only, does not exist really, but is only a misconception, or misunderstanding, of what the world or universe really is.

We are not then surrounded by *maya*, or illusion, but by Reality. That we can sense only three dimensions of it does not matter. We are in a greater—far greater—Universe than we can apprehend. We are living in the real Spiritual Universe now, and the only change that is necessary is in man. When man changes and comes into harmony with the Divine Order, all the disorder of his life will pass away, and the whole earth be filled with beauty and joy.

But imperfection is not merely due to our lack of understanding. Our world exists not only exteriorly, but also inwardly. We receive impressions from without, which we translate into a mental picture based upon our limited consciousness, and upon our state of mind and soul. Our world is not only composed of a mixture of what we sense from without, interpreted according to our state of consciousness, but it also reflects our 'sin', or wrong thoughts, or inward disharmony. In a sense, we create our own world. We each live in a world of our own, made up in the way just described, and also composed of our narrow ideas, petty ambitions, selfish aims, and self-centred interests. The objects of this teaching is to break these petty, narrow limits asunder, and to help the soul to realize that it lives in the real, perfect Spiritual World of Reality now: that what is needed is not a changed universe, but a new spirit within, a new spiritual consciousness: a change within, so radical that the Centre, around which the individual life revolves, is changed, or shifted in position, so as to become in perfect alignment with the Divine Centre.

It is possible to possess a most perfect optical apparatus either for photographic or projection purposes, and yet for it to be useless, simply because it is out of focus. The system of complicated combinations of lenses may be the superb result of the combined efforts of mathematician, optician and instrument-maker; yet, if it is out of focus, it is utterly useless, for the image or picture in either case is blurred and indistinguishable. But, directly the lens system is brought into focus, simply by shifting its position in relation to the screen, all the perfection of design and workmanship that have been lavished upon it becomes immediately apparent, and a crisp, sharply-defined image is cast upon the screen.

In the example, perfection at once appears as soon as an adjustment is made which brings the instrument completely into alignment with its designer's idea or intention, and when certain laws of optics, mathematics or geometry are obeyed or harmonized with. In no respect have the laws of the universe, either optical, mathematical or geometrical, to be altered, nor the design of the originator; but what is required is simply that the instrument should be adjusted completely in correspondence with the designer's idea and purpose.

It is precisely the same with us. All that is needed is that our individual centre, around which our life revolves, should correspond, and be brought into alignment with the Divine Centre.

We cannot do this of ourselves, but we can be willing. While we cannot do it ourselves, it cannot be done for us unless we are willing. The desire to come into harmony and union with God is aroused by the Holy Spirit, but the decision rests with ourselves. We must be willing—willing to surrender all to Infinite Love.

We are spiritual beings, living in the real spiritual universe now, and therefore we must live lives in harmony with the Spirit, become at one with our spiritual source, and obey the law of the Spirit, which is Love. The great thing that we have to do is to surrender ourselves entirely up to God, so that the Spirit remoulds us, so to speak, causing us to fit properly into the Divine Scheme. There can be no at-one-ment without abandonment. We must cast ourselves entirely upon God, making ourselves flexible and plastic in His hands; then we can profitably meditate upon our oneness with our Divine Source, with the Spiritual Universe, and with the Law of Divine Being.

Although we have to give up, or lose, our life in order to save it; although we have to surrender all (even our will, the most difficult thing to do) in order to find God, yet we lose nothing. We reap a hundredfold. We gain eternal life and peace and joy indescribable, which fade not away.

Who can describe the joy of the knowledge that all is well and that we are safely home? I cannot. But all can experience it if they will make the great surrender.

Greatly desiring for you this joy,

Yours in the One Service,

HENRY THOMAS HAMBLIN

INSTRUCTIONS IN PROGRESSIVE
REFLECTIVE MEDITATION

Before we can come into alignment with Truth, before we can become one with our Divine Centre and be united with the changeless Harmony and Perfection, we have to surrender ourselves entirely to Christ. Our highest conception of God and Truth is Christ—God made understandable to man. He is Lord of all aspiring souls. He it is who guides us and helps us by His Spirit. But we cannot make progress, and even the Spirit cannot help us, unless we surrender ourselves, our lives, our ambitions, our wills, all to Christ. This complete surrender is the strait gate, the narrow entrance which so few find, of which our Lord speaks. 'And few there be that find it.' So few are willing to make the great surrender. They are willing to enter the Kingdom by any other road than this. But they cannot, or will not, give up their selfwill and personality. But there is no other entrance than this, which is by surrendering all—everything—completely to the Infinite Love. If we do not make this surrender we build on the sand, we erect our edifice on a false foundation, so that when days of adversity, temptation and test come, it falls to the ground in awful ruin. All teaching which leaves out the great surrender to the Will of our Father in Heaven, as exhibited by Jesus in His Cross and crucifixion, is false. There must be the cross, when we give up all and surrender everything, before there can be the resurrection and the new life.

Therefore, in our meditation, we adopt an attitude of complete surrender and abandonment, saying: *'Not my will, Lord, but Thine be done. Just take me and my life and do with me and it just as Thou wilt. Bring me completely into my proper place in Thy Kingdom, the place Thou hast prepared for me. I herewith give up everything that would hinder or prevent my at-one-ment with Thee.'* This should be persevered with daily, for months, if necessary, until you are perfectly sure that a complete surrender has been made.

In addition we continue to meditate as before, especially upon our oneness with the One. The surrender not only makes this at-one-ment possible, but brings it very near.

It is necessary to persevere with these (or similar) words of surrender. We may think that we have surrendered ourselves entirely to Infinite Love (Christ), but we find that we still cling to self and to the things that chain us to the lower life. We have to be uprooted, out of the old soil of sin, vainglory, selfishness and pride, before we can be replanted in the Garden of the Lord. First one root branch is severed from the earth and then another, and as each comes away we think that we are entirely free; but we find that what has come away is only one of many root branches, that there are many others.

So we need patience and perseverance in surrender. It is useless and foolish to rush on before we have become liberated entirely from the old life, the old desires and the old selfwill. But when we have become entirely separated from the old life, and liberated altogether from selfwill and separateness, the Master plants us in His own Garden of Love.

LESSON XIII

Dear Fellow Student of Truth,

Behind the world which we cognize through the senses, and at the back of all the imperfection, falsities, tragedies and disorder of life, is the eternal Kingdom of the Spirit. It can not be discerned by the natural man. It can only be apprehended spiritually.

As the Spirit in us becomes quickened, so does the Kingdom of the Spirit become revealed to us. It is felt and recognized in our circumstances, experiences, and in our fellow men. Our life becomes transformed to the extent that we apprehend the eternal spiritual reality behind that which changes and passes away.

As our appreciation of the Spiritual increases, so also does the realization of immortality develop within us. We realize more and more that through Grace we are children of God and joint heirs with Jesus Christ. All this comes about by seeking God in the secret place, daily, and through continually directing our thoughts towards 'our Father', and raising them to high and better things.

Desiring for you an increasing apprehension of the Spiritual Kingdom.

Yours in the Great Adventure,

HENRY THOMAS HAMBLIN

LESSON XIII

APPREHENDING REALITY

Life is not what it seems. The sense-life appears to be the only real one, while the spiritual appears to be vague and unreal. The reverse is the truth, the inner Spiritual Kingdom being the only real one, while the outward life is not concrete, inexorable and 'fixed', so to speak, but is obedient to the Spirit.

Until we learn to live in the Inner Spiritual Kingdom and to be led by the Spirit, life may appear to be an evil, relentless tyrant afflicting us and thwarting us at every turn. When, however, we become possessors of the true spiritual vision, we find that nothing can come into our life that is not good, and that every difficulty is something come to help us on our spiritual pathway.

The disorder of our life is generally due to our own opposition, strife, antagonism and impatience. By resisting what we think to be evil, we create disorder and yet greater 'evil'. We have to learn the great truth of nonresistance, as taught by our Lord. While we have to refuse to give in to temptation, and must disassociate ourselves from all that is wrong, sinful, unjust, and so on, and must help the downtrodden and oppressed, yet as far as we individually are concerned we must learn not to resist. This is probably the most difficult lesson that we have to learn, but it has to be learnt by all who would find harmony and peace. If life is good—and it is—then obviously we must not resist its disciplines, but rather co-operate with then. This does not mean that we must resign ourselves to invalidism or poverty, but it means that we eliminate the cause of these things. If things are not right in our life, it shows that we have mismanaged things, or that we have not yet learnt certain lessons. We may have dealt wrongly with life, so as to produce disorder and suffering: or at any rate we have not yet mastered our problem.

We have not only then to acknowledge that life is not what it seems, that it is good and not evil, that it is kind instead of malignant, but we must live in the consciousness that life is good, and also think, speak and act in harmony with this truth.

The world that we see around us is real enough to our consciousness, but it is not the real world. By this I mean that we are surrounded by Reality ('In Him, God, we live and move and have our being'), and Reality is forever impinging upon us; yet, owing to our limited consciousness we cognize only a limited world of imperfection, instead of an infinite world of perfection. 'Now we see through a glass darkly.' We possess five senses which bring to us only a limited understanding. Because of this, we do not see things as they really are, but only as they falsely appear. Therefore, we are not in a position to criticize life or to say that it is evil, or that certain things are imperfect. Some people criticize and condemn God on insufficient evidence. We see only in part. If we knew the whole we would know and see that all is perfect.

But we cannot alter or extend our senses. It is true that some people's hearing and seeing extend to the astral plane, but this is not a thing to be sought, but rather to be avoided at all costs. Although we cannot extend our senses to encompass Reality, yet through intuition we can apprehend it. We can enter into a state of realization in which we know that all is well, and that a perfect Divine Order is the reality. Through meditation, prayer, and the Silence we make contact with Reality, not through the senses, but through intuition or inward knowing. We should not try to see visions, or practise anything unhealthily mystical, but only to know the Truth. A conviction grows up within us that all is well, and that all good is coming to us, and will always do so.

The material, sense life may be likened to a room lit artificially and with windows heavily curtained to keep out the light of day. The room is full of men and women gambling, quarrelling, sometimes fighting, at times sad and sorrowful, at others boisterous with a forced gaiety. They play with gaudy, gilded playthings, but can find no satisfaction therein. They seek pleasure in various forms of sensation, some innocent and some demoralizing, but the result is always the same—unrest and unhappiness.

But there is one among them who is dissatisfied with his life in the room. The things which captivate the others gradually lose their attraction for him, until at last he yearns for that which is real, instead of the artificiality of the life lived by his fellow occupants. His companions think he is a fool. Some treat him with contempt and derision, others hate him, but none understand him. At last he goes to the curtained window, and, after much searching, finds a small slit or opening through which he can thrust his head. He looks out on a smiling landscape. The sun has just risen, the dew is sparkling, the birds are singing, and all is rest, beauty and peace. When he has got over his astonishment, he turns back into the room in order to tell the others of his wonderful discovery. Surely, he thinks, they will rejoice to know of this, and will be as happy as I to know that there is such a wonderful and beautiful world on the other side of the curtain. But they laugh him to scorn. The wicked curse him, the good shake their heads, saying: 'There is a better land, but it can only be found beyond the portals of death'. So no-one listens to him or will believe him. But he will not leave them, so he spends the rest of his life endeavouring to persuade them to look through the curtain and see for themselves the wonderful beauty of the world outside. Twice a day, however, he puts his head through the curtain, taking a long hungry look at the smiling beauty that meets his enchanted gaze, and as he looks he becomes filled with strength and power, which enables him to continue his difficult and discouraging self-appointed task of trying to convince the people within the room of the reality of the greater world outside.

The Kingdom of the Spirit is the real, true and eternal. It is to be found just outside our present consciousness. If we are patient in our search for Truth, a time comes when we can draw aside the veil, or it is drawn aside for us, and we find ourselves in contact with the inner Spiritual Reality. We then touch the real and eternal, leaving behind the temporal. All the illusions of life and its unrealities are transcended and we are in the Kingdom of the Spirit.

By making contact with our Divine Spiritual Source and the Realm of Spirit, in this way, and by surrendering ourselves entirely to the Will of God, Divine Order begins to appear in our outward life. In the Kingdom of the Spirit is perfect Divine Order. Everything is in its right place, doing its right work, at the right time, and doing it perfectly. In it are perfect harmony and smooth working, like the flowing of a deep river. Whenever we make contact with the Kingdom of the Spirit, desiring only that God's Will (which alone creates Perfect Order) should be done, forgetting all about our troubles and disharmonies, then, if we keep quiet and allow the Spirit to work in Its own way, Divine Order takes the place of human disorder in our life and affairs. A beautiful healing process takes place, which restores the whole life, from its centre to its circumference. Whatever is wrong in our life becomes adjusted, not in the way we should expect or arrange for ourselves, but in the marvellous, simple, perfect way of the Spirit.

*

How can you find this inner Kingdom of the Spirit? By always seeking God in the Silence: by surrendering yourself entirely to the Will of God and the guidance of the Spirit: by bringing all your desires and thoughts into harmony with the Divine Good: by being patient and steadfast during the times of testing through which you will have to pass: by living the Christ life and walking in fellowship with your Lord: by being faithful at all times to your Ideal: by not straining after the Kingdom, but by being quietly persistent, fulfilling the conditions, and then to *wait patiently for him*.

*

The most important of all the above conditions is waiting upon God in the Silence. Find God every day and surrender all to Him, opening yourself to the inflow of His Infinite Life and Power. Do this without fail and all will be well, for *'He shall give Thee thy heart's desire'*.

WEEK FOURTEEN:
ONENESS

A THING MAY be all right in theory, or even in actuality, but if it is not ours in consciousness, it is useless to us. While we may, in one sense, be one with our Divine Source, if we are not conscious of it, if we do not realize it, this great truth is useless to us. Before the eternal verities can be of any practical use to us, they must be realized in consciousness—in the soul.

For instance, we may know, or believe, the truth that actually, in Spirit, we are perfectly whole and healthy, yet if we do not *realize* it in consciousness, we yet remain just as sick, ill or diseased as ever.

Separateness is the cause of all our disharmony, disorder, suffering and woe. So long as we are separate in consciousness from God, there cannot fail to be disharmony—for we are, as it were, out of gear, instead of 'in mesh' with the Divine Machine. Man has slipped 'out of gear', and the great task is to get back into our real place in the Cosmic Machine, into that place designed for us by God.

When once we get back to our God-chosen position, when once we become one with the One, disorder ceases, and the Divine Order appears. All that we have to do is to get back to God. We have not to do anything in reality (in one sense), but only to get back to God. It was because of this that our Lord said. 'Seek ye first the Kingdom of God and His righteousness, and all these things shall be added unto you'.

God and His manifestation are one complete, perfect Whole.

He is the One, and all Reality is in Him.

In order to realize Truth in consciousness we must continually identify ourselves with It. This we must do in three ways.

(1)   By meditation upon oneness, at-one-ment and surrender.

(2)   By affirming at-one-ment and surrender.

(3)   By living the Truth and acting according to Its dictates. In other words, living the fully surrendered and consecrated life.

It is useless merely to talk about Truth and wish and hope for the best. Many people do this and lament the fact that they make no progress. We must be forever identifying ourselves with Truth, if we are to become conscious of It as a power in our life.

By affirming the Truth at all times, we keep ourselves in an atmosphere of Truth. We remind ourselves by affirmation that we are in the Spirit, therefore we live the life of the Spirit. By affirmation we retain, or constantly bring back to our remembrance, Heavenly ideas, thus becoming Heavenly-minded. A Heavenly-minded person is often looked upon as a rare kind of being, yet he or she is simply one who has made a practice of holding Divine ideas in the mind in place of those of a material or worldly kind. In meditation, he or she touches the Spiritual Centre of Life and Truth, receiving Divine Ideas, and these during the day are recalled again and again to the mind, so that the soul feeds upon Heavenly food.

The secret of all affirmation is to declare our oneness with God in Christ. It is because we can claim oneness with God in, or through, Christ, that we can declare that all things are ours, or rather that we share all things with God. In Christ we are divine sons, joint heirs with Jesus. How wonderful, wonderful, is this surpassing love of God which draws us from the depths of separateness, misery and waywardness, to make us joint heirs with Jesus Christ.

Therefore our affirmation can be something like this:

'I thank Thee, Father, because in Christ I am one with Thee.'

Or, for quick use in the face of calamity, difficulty or danger:

'Safe in Christ—one with Thee....

The sacred name of Jesus Christ is an 'open sesame' in spiritual things. By using His name, which is above every name in Heaven and on earth, we enlist His power, His wisdom, His experience, on our behalf. He, who trod the winepress alone, is with us, ready to do great things for us.

Gradually, if we proceed aright, surrendering ourselves to God, meditating upon Truth, affirming It, and living It, we enter into a growing consciousness of our oneness with the One. We must, however, live the Truth, in the form of a fully-surrendered life, otherwise all our efforts are in vain.

We must live as though we are already conscious of our oneness with the Whole.

The Will of the Father is the plan of our Life. We have to live a life that is surrendered entirely to Love. We have not only to surrender to the Will of the Father and do everything that life demands of us, but we must yield up ourselves and our lives and our all to Love. We have to follow in the footsteps of the Lord of Love. Very humbly do we have to do this, for we are very weak and ignorant beginners in this great and wonderful life which all the saints and masters have lived before us.

We cannot become at one with God, unless we are fully surrendered to the Will of the Father and to the Lord of Love, living a life of obedience to the Will of God and the Law of Love. Until we do this, we are not in the right mental attitude that makes such a union possible. Until we become perfectly flexible and plastic we cannot become moulded into the Divine pattern. We cannot be half and half—half after God's pattern and half after our own—but we must be entirely made anew in the Divine likeness. This is possible only when we become fully surrendered to the Divine Will and Purpose, and softened by entire surrender to the Lord of Love, or the Love Principle.

Having surrendered our will, we must live the surrendered life, always seeking to do the Will of the Father and follow the Law of Love.

Gradually the roots of our being are loosened in the soil of self and earthly things: one by one they are disentangled from their clinging environment, until at last the Master frees us entirely (to the extent that we are willing) and re-plants us in His Garden of Love.

May we all be transplanted by the hand of the Great Gardener.

Yours in the One Service,

HENRY THOMAS HAMBLIN

INSTRUCTIONS IN PROGRESSIVE REFLECTIVE MEDITATION

And so, having made the great surrender, we come to the quiet place, where God abides, and find ourselves home at last.

The strife and the battle over, the tempestuous voyage at an end: Safe Home at Last.

We thank Thee, Father, because we, who were once afar off, have been brought near by the blood of Christ. It is only such love as this that could have broken our hearts, won our wills, reconciled us to Thee, and brought us into Thy Kingdom.

We thank Thee that In Christ we are forever One with Thee.

We, the willing 'victims' of Infinite Love, now meditate upon this truth.

Brought home.
At one, forever one.
No parting,
No more separateness,
Forever one
in Christ
with Thee.

And God wipes tears from off all faces.

LESSON XIV

Dear Fellow Student of Truth,

Politicians are finding that there is a law of Unity affecting nations which cannot be evaded or ignored. Scientists are discovering every day the unity which runs through Nature. These merely confirm from the outside that which has been known to the inner circle of Truth seekers for thousands of years. God and His Universe are one Complete Whole. God is ALL and is in all; the all is in the ALL, and the whole is one complete body.

Because we form an integral part of the Whole, it is impossible to hurt others without hurting ourselves: it is impossible to criticize or think wrong thoughts about others without setting in notion forces which will react, with disastrous effect, upon ourselves. We cannot, for the same reason, be selfish without impoverishing our lives, either in mind, body, or estate. On the other hand, the more we love, the more love we receive: the more unselfish we are, the more we are blessed. Divine law is epitomized in the words 'It is more blessed to give than to receive'.

Yours in Patient Service,

HENRY THOMAS HAMBLIN

LESSON XIV

THE ONENESS OF LIFE AND THE UNIVERSE
SERVICE : LOVE

As we have already seen, only God and His real or true manifestations possess reality and permanence, and these are one: together they form the Whole. There is the one Eternal Spirit which is 'cause': there is the real Universe, or realm of the Spirit, of which we form a part, which is 'effect'. Cause and effect are one. The idea of God as a being far removed and separate from His Children is the conception of the finite mind. Separateness is an illusion, for God is all that eternally is, and all His true creation is part of Himself. God is infinite Spirit and fills all space: there is no place where God is not. God is within us, the Divine Spark, or Indwelling Christ within the soul, Who is leading us back to the bosom of the Father. God is also all around us: we live and move and have our being in the Eternal Spirit. All is Spirit and Mind, and manifestations or expressions of Spirit and Mind, and these form one complete Whole, which is God. There can therefore be no separateness. The wave is not separate from the ocean: although a wave, it is still part of the whole ocean: the ocean and its waves are one. We see God's face in flowers and sunsets: we find Him in all the sights and sounds of Nature: we breathe in His energy, not only in oxygen, but, in a special and spiritual sense, the essence of the life of God. He is in us and we are in Him. In Him we live and move and have our being. God manifests Himself in and through us. He is in all that is. He is all that is eternal. All is one complete Whole. All is well.

If therefore, there is only the One; if we all form part of Christ's mystical body, there can be no separation, in reality, between us and our fellow men and women. Just as islands are joined together under the sea, and through being joined to and forming part of the earth are therefore one with all other islands, so also are men and women one through the common fatherhood of God. The water between islands produces an idea of separateness which is unreal, for it is only on the surface: so, in like manner, the illusions of the sense-life produce an appearance of separateness which has no reality. It is only illusion that separates us from our fellows: in reality we are one.

We are all one body animated by one life, and this is God. There is only one life, which is eternal, of which we are partakers and sharers. Seeing, then, that we are all one body, we cannot injure others without hurting ourselves. We can never elude the effects of our wrong thinking and doing, for they react upon us, and also help to make the world a worse place for us to live in. Similarly, it is equally impossible to think rightly and act harmoniously without ourselves reaping benefit, and making the

world a better place to live in. It is because of the oneness that
selfishness impoverishes the life. Selfishness intensifies the false
sense of separateness, and fills the life with disharmony, allowing
no outlet, and preventing the full inflow of God's abundance
and richness of life. It is impossible to receive abundance from
God if we refuse to give out freely: it is only as we give that we
can receive: therefore, it is more blessed to give than to receive.
To be self-centred and selfish is to build a wall round oneself
whereby life is rendered cramped and narrow, devoid of blessing and filled with disharmony. One becomes a plague spot, a
centre of discord, causing trouble and suffering to oneself, and a
source of disturbance to the world at large.

When we reach the Higher Wisdom, we realize and know, by
spiritual revelation, that we form part of the Complete Whole.
Our finite self, the false personality, falls from us, and we enter
the consciousness of the Universal Self. Then we know that all
men are one, and can each say: 'My enemy is as much myself as
I myself am; when I love him I love myself: when I seek to hurt
him I injure myself. By refusing to give, I impoverish myself: by
grabbing and keeping, I rob my life of all that is worth having'.

This 'oneness' includes all creation. Man is intimately related
to all life below him. He is the apex of God's work in nature. He
is Lord of Creation, but this lordship involves responsibilities
which demand of him that he should love all his humbler brothers and sisters. By inflicting cruelty on lower forms of life, man
brings, through the law of cause and effect, suffering upon himself. 'As a man soweth that shall he also reap' applies with equal
force to his treatment of the lower creation. All creation is one:
and we form part of it, and it forms part of God. If we are to
love God, we must love all His humbler works, for they all form
part of the One Whole. Therefore, let our thoughts towards all
lower forms of the One Life be those of love, and let this love
find expression in kindly action and conduct, and in a human
mode of life which entails as little suffering on the part of the
lower animals as possible.

The Path of Wisdom, then, is that of love and service. Love to the Whole and service to the Whole. This restores Spiritual Harmony.

First, let me speak of love. If we are to love God, we must love the Whole, for God is the Whole—therefore we cannot love God without loving all men, friends and enemies alike. Neither can we love all men without, at the time, loving God, for all are one. If you have been trying to love God, and, at the same time, have cherished a dislike of, or resentment against a certain person, then your efforts have been in vain. 'First be reconciled to thy brother, and then come and offer thy gift'. It is only when we learn to love universally that we come into harmony with God and His Universe, the law which holds it together, and the Divine purpose of our life. When we love universally, we love as God loves. By so doing, we hasten our spiritual unfoldment and bring happiness into our life: become centres of harmony in the world, and benefactors and helpers of the human race.

Secondly, love seeks to express itself in service. Instead of work being done to further one's own selfish ends, or because it simply *has* to be done, it is made an offering of love to life and the world and all mankind. Therefore, in future, no work can be scamped or imperfect, nor accomplished in a grudging spirit: rather will it be the willing service of love. Thus does love of the Whole lead to greater happiness, increased efficiency, stronger character, and enduring success. To love and serve universally brings supreme joy and happiness such as nothing else can give: doing one's daily task in a spirit of love increases its quality, thus adding to its efficiency: by doing one's daily task more thoroughly, character is built up: by putting character into our work, we lay the foundation of enduring success. Thus is God's law of compensation seen in operation: by giving our best to the world, the best comes back to us. It is only by giving that we can receive: it is by giving freely that we reap abundantly.

*

Take the thought which runs through this lesson with you into the Silence. Say to yourself:

'I am one with all my fellows and with the humbler creations as well. Just as islands are all one, being joined together underneath the sea, so also am I one with all my brothers in the common fatherhood of God.'

Get mentally in touch with all God's manifestations, and putting, as it were, your arms around them, rise upwards to the Infinite Love, and lose yourself in the ecstasy of union with the Divine.

MEDITATION

I close my eyes to other people's imperfections, I see in them the Omnipresent Good. Within them dwells the Infinite Love and Perfection; and when I cast the beam out of my eye, I shall see more clearly, not my brother's faults, but his perfections. In all my fellows is the Infinite Love, henceforth I shall see It, and help to draw it forth. In everyone I shall see something to admire and reverence—something to love.

And I shall not stop with people, I will look also for the good in every circumstance, in every difficulty, in every temporary, so-called failure. I will look for the good in every blade of grass and every opening flower; in the wind which blows and the sun that burns my cheek. Rain or sunshine, fair weather or foul, I will see good in everything, see perfection underlying all. Out of these will grow a new sympathy, a more extensive and embracing love, a larger and wider Consciousness, for everyone and everything are my brothers; each forms a part of the Infinite Whole. We are one with one another and the Universal Life and Mind of which we form a Part.

WEEK FIFTEEN:
JUSTICE

DIVINE JUSTICE! People shudder at the word. Yet what can be more beautiful than justice? Those who are always demanding justice in life, both for themselves and their fellow men, do not want justice from God. They are afraid of it, yet why should any of us be afraid of justice? It is the most beautiful thing possible. As we sow, we reap; and with what measure we mete it is measured to us again. Could anything be better? The scales are delicately and accurately adjusted. The pendulum swings exactly as far in one direction as the other. Absolute justice, could anything of which we can conceive, be better or more beautiful!

Man fears Divine Justice because it is associated in his mind with a revengeful God. Divine Justice to him is rank injustice. It demands the impossible for man, then punishes him with fiendish cruelty, for ever and ever, because he cannot meet its demands.

It is true there are many things which the finite mind cannot understand, such as the visiting of the sins of the fathers upon the children, and so on; but this is because we do not know all the facts of the case, our consciousness being so limited we can see only a part of a thing or event at a time, and not the whole thing or event. But we can rest assured that there is nothing but a principle of absolute justice, for without it the universe would fall into ruins. It is integrity and justice that holds the universe together, or rather support it, for it is love that holds it together. If there were the slightest flaw or failure in this principle of integrity and justice, the foundations of the universe would fail, and the whole structure crash to ruin.

The application of the Golden Rule brings success, harmony and happiness because of the underlying principle of justice which supports it. Doing to others as we would like them to do to us may at first seem to be a profitless undertaking. We may find that people accept much from us, yet give nothing in return; but, in the invisible, a spiritual debit and credit account is kept which balances all our actions and motives, rewarding us exactly, with impartial justice, according to our thoughts, words and deeds. It is glorious, this principle of Divine Justice!

Through this principle of justice we are able to make progress; but without it, such a thing would be impossible. If we did not reap as we sow, we could never learn wisdom. If we do an injury to another, and are not *truly* repentant, we must receive a similar injury ourselves in order that we may suffer in the same way. Through such suffering, we learn not to injure others again in the same manner. Such an experience, when it appears, may seem to us to be an injustice. If we are foolish, we resent it and try to 'get our own back'. This, of course, keeps the pendulum swinging, so that the whole process is repeated, again and again, until we learn wisdom.

Could anything be more splendid than absolute justice? If we sow to the flesh we reap corruption, but if we sow to the spirit we reap life everlasting. We have only to sow aright in order to reap, without fail, the most blessed harvest of which the Mind of God can conceive. All through life and the universe runs this perfect principle. It ensures for us always a square deal between God and ourselves. God always acts squarely with us, because He is Absolute Integrity and Justice (and much more); therefore, He could not deal with us otherwise.

God is not only 'person', He is also 'principle'. In the past, the personal aspect of Deity has been emphasized too much, perhaps. God, as 'Person', is limited to finite conceptions. God, as 'principle', is infinite and not subject in any way to finite limitations.

God is 'principle', and the universe is based upon 'principle'. God is the principle of absolute justice and integrity. Let us thank and praise Him continually for this! When we limit God to a person we are apt to fall into the error of attributing to Him our own frailties and limitations, making Him a God of revenge, punishment, retaliation, and so on. It is most helpful, for some reasons, to think of Deity as limited to a personal God, but in order to realize absolute Truth, we must get on to wider ground, thinking of Deity as undeviating Divine Principle.

All the injustice that we see in life is not due to a lack of a principle of justice, but to human violation of this principle. The principle is always present and is always acting. It is inherent; it is the very nervous system of the universe. Nothing can happen, or come to pass, that does not contain in itself the working of this immutable principle. The principle is always present, is always acting and we can never get away from it. For instance, we can never give a person a cup of cold water without some good coming back to us in return, 'somewhen, somewhere'.

Now, while the principle is always present, there is nothing to prevent man from violating it. He violates it daily and receives back something which he calls evil, but which is simply the working of the Divine Principle of Justice. Much of what we call evil, or bad luck, is simply the result of past violation of the principle of justice. If all men were to act justly towards their fellows, most of the disharmony and unrest of the world would cease.

In an inner sense, there is no injustice in life or the universe. Outwardly, however, we may see injustice being done on every hand—much, perhaps, to our perplexity. In order to find peace we must realize the inner truth of things.

We must remember that there is always the inner and the outer, the Spiritual and the material, the real or permanent, and the unreal or temporal. In the Spiritual, there is absolute justice always. In the material, there may be all sorts of injustices perpetrated daily, but they are not due to a principle of evil, but to violation of this principle. The great point is this:

That by identifying ourselves in consciousness with Spirit (Christ) and by being perfectly just ourselves, in thought, word and deed, we become raised above the injustices of men.

When injustices face us, individually, by identifying ourselves with Christ, by refusing to retaliate, and by meeting illwill by good-will, we find that everything works together for good, and that which looked like evil turns out to be the best thing possible after all.

When we come to examine ourselves, we may find that our attitude towards life violates the principle of justice. We are un-just to God, to man and to our real selves. Only to be just! What an impossible task! It is impossible, of ourselves; but if we seek the aid of the Spirit in meditating upon the subject, it is shown to us in what way we fall short, strength being given to us so that we can reform our lives.

We have, then, to live our life in strict harmony with the Di-vine Principle of Absolute Justice. Every thought must be abso-lutely just. What a task! Yet the Spirit guides and helps us if we seek His aid. We can help ourselves during the day by saying, 'The Spirit shows me wherein I err, and at all times helps me to be just in all that I think, say and do'.

Further, we must not retaliate when apparent injustice is meted out to us. When such a thing happens, we have to turn away from the appearance of evil and realize that in Spirit there is no injustice, but only perfect poise, balance, order, harmony; in other words, truth and justice. We can do this by meditating upon Absolute Justice, and also by affirming the Truth. Such state-ments as the following may be used:

'I deny that injustice can have dominion over Spirit. Because I am a child of God (or in Christ), I am in Spirit, and no injustice can have dominion over me.'
or:

'Because I am a child of God, one with Christ (or in the Spirit) only justice can manifest in my life and all my affairs.'

Establishing ourselves in Truth in this way, we have only to wait and see bow the Lord will deliver us. Principle never errs and never fails us.

Desiring for you an ever-widening conception of Truth,
Yours in the One Service,
HENRY THOMAS HAMBLIN

ADDITIONAL NOTE

There is a healing and restoring principle always at work, and this is termed Divine Grace. God gives always justice and a square deal (a thing that we can seldom get from man), but when we violate the law of justice, Divine Grace steps in and heals the matter to the extent that we repent and turn to the Lord. What we are apt to think of as retribution is simply a remedial experience. Instead of our actions bringing retribution, Divine Grace turns it into an experience which, if met with cooperation and love, and with repentance and a sincere desire to live wholly in harmony with God's will, becomes a stepping-stone to higher and better things. Everything that happens is designed to bring us nearer to God and to our highest good and eternal joy, if we will but co-operate with it, and bless it, and love it.

INSTRUCTIONS IN PROGRESSIVE REFLECTIVE MEDITATION

We meditate as before, realizing our at-one-ment with God, in Christ.
One with Thee, the Infinite Good.
One with Thee, the Infinite Wholeness.
One with Thee, the One.
There is only the One, and I am one with Thee.
Now I thank Thee that Thou art the Principle of Absolute Justice. The Scales of Justice are delicately and accurately balanced. I am at the point of balance, swinging neither up nor down, neither to the right nor to the left—one with Thee.
Identified with Thee, Perfect Principle of Absolute Justice.
Because I am one with Thee, the Principle of Absolute Justice dominates my life, and regulates my thoughts and actions, so

that integrity, probity, righteousness, straightness, square ness, honesty of thought and purpose are expressed in all that I do.

When this meditation has been thoroughly absorbed, Good will always be associated in consciousness with absolute Justice, with which we are one. Justice, absolute and complete, becomes part of our life.

LESSON XV

Dear Fellow Student of Truth,

Absolute Justice includes in itself Divine Mercy, for it takes account of and makes allowances for all our weaknesses, and the special difficulties of our life.

Not only is God Absolute Justice, so that we always receive a square deal from Heaven, but He is also Infinite Mercy. As soon as we confess our fault to God and turn to the Light, we are freed from our sin, and filled instead with Divine Life and power.

Instead of fighting life and our fellows, we learn to co-operate with them. By refusing to retaliate, we give life no opportunity of hitting us back. Also, the more we give in love and service the more we receive back from life, and the more blessed do we become. Harmony, peace and joy are present, where before was disorder, friction and unhappiness.

How glorious is the new life of the Spirit!

Yours in Unity and Service,

HENRY THOMAS HAMBLIN

LESSON XV

INFINITE JUSTICE AND DIVINE PRINCIPLE

God being Absolute Truth, there can be no injustice in life or in the Cosmic Scheme. Inasmuch as God and His Idea are infinitely Perfect, life is absolutely just. There are no favouritisms,

likes or dislikes either in God or the Laws which govern His universe: all is justice. Man reaps with mathematical exactness the
result of that which he sows. He cannot think an evil thought or
do an evil deed, without receiving it, with absolute impartiality,
back again, sometime, somewhere, through the ages. Neither
can he think a noble thought, or do a kindly deed, without receiving it back again with unerring precision. Eternal justice is
referred to in the words of Jesus, 'For with what measure ye mete,
it shall be measured to you again'. We are spiritual and immortal beings, living an endless life, of which this fleeting existence is
but a day. What we do here will, in addition to having its effect
today, bear fruit in other 'days' as well. The apparent injustices
of this life are seen, when viewed in the light of Eternity, to be
but the sure workings of Infinite Justice. We reap now as we have
sown. We have it, then, in our power, not only to improve this
life by thinking and living in harmony with Principle and Divine
Law, but also to build up for the future which is without end.

Life is eternal and universal: it can be understood only when
viewed from a universal standpoint and looked at in the light of
eternity. At close quarters, we see apparent injustices, but the
wider and more universal the point of view, the more we realize
the absolute justice of life and the Divine Plan. All the apparent
injustices which are manifested in inequalities of birth, education, inherited ill-health or disease, good traits or bad, good looks
or plainness, are all dissolved when we realize that life is endless
and that the law of cause and effect, of sowing and reaping, is
constantly at work. Nothing that is not for our highest good, that
is not absolutely just, can come into your life or mine. We can
make but little progress in the Path until we accept this truth,
and acknowledge the absolute justice of life. I do not mean that,
in this relative existence, we cannot see around us many injustices. What I do mean is that the laws of life are so infinitely just,
that what is unjust is so only in a local sense; and is not so, in
reality, and when looked at from the standpoint of a long period
of time. For every effect there is a cause and, if we could go back

far enough, a cause could be found for every apparent injustice. If God is the very Principle of Justice and all Divine Law is absolutely just, then there can be no injustice throughout the whole of our life.

Some time ago, certain things came to pass in my life which looked like gross injustice. At first I thought in the usual finite way that I was very unjustly treated. At that time, however, I was just awakening to the truth, and was reaching out after God. Suddenly I realized that God is Infinite justice, and, therefore, as He is my life, there could be no injustice in my life. Immediately I was relieved of a great load, and I made a big step forward in the new life. If I had not been able to believe in the Principle of Universal Justice, my life would have been embittered and robbed of all fruitfulness. It would have become joyless, useless and full of discord. Instead, through this belief in Justice, and through surrender to It, my life has become sweetened and more useful than formerly: it is a continual joy and thanksgiving. By accepting the Principle of Infinite Justice and surrendering our life to It; by refusing to believe that apparent injustices are injustices in reality, we enter into harmonious relationship with God and the scheme of things: we make a big step forward in the Path of Attainment. In addition, we come to a realization of the Truth, so that, instead of merely believing, we know.

Not only is it necessary to know God as Truth itself and the Infinite Principle of Justice: we must also live every detail of our life in harmony with that Principle. To deviate ever so slightly from God's standard of Truth and Justice is to create discord in the life and bring disaster with unerring precision upon our own heads. The slightest deviation from absolute justice in our dealings with others immediately destroys the Divine Harmony and sets in motion forces which must sooner or later react upon us. Also, it makes further progress in the Path impossible. Life is like a perfectly-tuned harp; if you play upon it according to the laws of harmony, you produce delightful music. Strike, however, but one wrong note, and you get a jangling discord which jars upon the ear. If you play upon the harp of life according to God's laws of equity and justice, your life becomes a harmonious and beautiful thing; but allow only a slight lack of principle to enter, such as imputing wrong motives to others or judging them harshly or unfairly, and discord is set up which brings into the life unhappiness and unnecessary suffering.

Gaze with universal eye over God's beautiful universe, and you will see the principle of the 'square deal' running through everything. There is no cheating or chicanery in all the Cosmic Scheme, and until man learns this and brings his life into correspondence with it, he will be out of harmony and full of trouble. What is needed in business and professional life is the 'square deal'. It is the man of probity and honesty who wins in the long run. Honesty of purpose and integrity of character are of greater value than mere brilliance: the cleverest of men and women often fail to succeed because no-one can trust them. It is the same in the home and social life. To be just and honest and straightforward in all one's affairs is to bring blessing, and joy, and true, lasting success into the life. Lack of principle and justice produces chaos, and there is no room for such in the whole of this perfectly-tuned and adjusted Universe. Those who violate the eternal law of justice and equity are subject to remedial forces and influences which are exceedingly painful in character. Those who fail to learn this lesson willingly are taught it through suffering. 'God is not mocked: whatsoever a man soweth, that shall he also reap'. It may seem strange to you that I should point out such obvious truths in a course of this description, but, believe me, it is necessary. People think, in a general way, that they ought to do the right thing, but they do not understand how absolutely just is the Law, and how the slightest infraction sets up serious disharmonies which react disastrously upon the life, and, what is of far greater importance, have a stunting, dwarfing effect upon the soul.

One of the illusions of the senses is that one's life cannot be lived to a principle. Such illusion would have us believe that, in business, probity, justice, and absolute honesty do not pay; that in politics they are impossible; and that in the life of nations, double-dealing and deceit are even necessary. There is no greater illusion than this. This suffering world is crying out for men and women of principle and integrity, for men and women who are sincere. It is tired of shams and hypocrisies, and longs to honour someone, who in addition to possessing ability, is sincere and honest and 'square'.

One who lives his life to a principle is doubly blessed. He reaps the truest success in this life, builds up character, and 'lays up treasure in Heaven': i.e., he harvests in the future the fruit of his sowing here. In addition to this, he has an infallible guide in life. The man or the woman who lives his or her life to a principle need never be perplexed or worried as to which course to pursue. He or she simply chooses the path of justice, probity and perfectly straight dealing. All the perplexities of expediency are swept away. The issue is clean-cut and clear. 'Which is right?', 'Which is just?', are the only questions asked. Such a one does not have to scheme and worry. The course lies straight ahead and is unmistakable; what he or she has to do is simply to choose the right, and trust in the Divine Principle of Justice to work everything together for good. To some, this may seem a hard road, but it is the road to true success, of harmony and lasting satisfaction. It is also the carefree life, for one need never worry or plan: one simply acts in harmony with Principle and leaves all the details to be worked out by the Immutable Laws of Justice and Compensation.

*

The great lesson that we have to learn is to resist not evil. If an injustice is done to us we must not resist it. This does not mean, I think, that in the ordinary way we are not to explain that we are innocent. In spiritual things, however, we have even to refrain from making any protest or explanation.

Every experience that comes to us, no matter how cruel or unjust it may appear to be, is good—that is, if we resist not, but meet it with good. Love is the magic Key. When people slander us or inflict any injustice upon us, if we resist not, but actively love them in return, the experience is blessed to us, and we become all the better for it. When assailed in this way, we should sit down quietly and say of the one who has injured us, 'Brother so-and-so, or Sister so-and-so: I love you even as Christ loves me. I forgive you freely, and desire for you all blessing, peace, happiness, joy, and every possible form of good'.

When life itself seems to be unjust to us, when we have done our best and all that we appear to receive in return is loss and suffering, we should then take ourselves to prayer, saying, *'Father, Thy wisdom is infinite, Thy love immeasurable, and Thy justice absolute. I trust Thee. Do Thou Thy Will in me; lead me in Thine own way, for Thou canst guide me only to my highest good'.*

Life consists of one experience after another, all of which become blessings if we meet them in the right way: that is, with love, co-operation, non-resistance of evil, and with trust in God's Goodness,

Gradually, if we live our life according to Divine Law and Principle—forgiving, loving, allowing God to load us where He will—the highest good manifests in our lives. Not wealth and its cares; not material success and its strain; but harmony and peace. Instead of being tossed this way and that by forces we do not understand, we live in quietness and peace.

Our faith, however, is generally tested before we reach the calm waters. Storms may rage before we find entrance to the quiet harbour. But if, having put ourselves right with God, and our life right with Life, we are patient, allowing Divine Principle to work itself out, all must be well. Divine Order is inherent, and when we come into harmony with Truth, we allow it to escape, so to speak, and thus to permeate our whole life and affairs.

Faith, patience, trust. God does the work.

WEEK SIXTEEN :
MANIFESTING HEALTH

AS WE HAVE already seen, evil is not a principle, or reality, or anything in itself, but is a falling away from God, or a falling short of God's Perfection. Jacob Boehme explains evil as a power of God, let loose and brought into a state of disorder which is due to our contrary will and false imagination.

Sin is a falling short. 'For we have all sinned and come short of God's glory (perfection)'. 'Sin' may manifest in the form of disease, sickness, ill-health. 'Sin' may be anything almost, for without God man falls into every kind of 'evil', but the sense in which we are now using it is the falling short in consciousness of God's Perfection.

Disease, or ill-health, is not a punishment, but the result of a falling short, in consciousness, of God's Perfect Reality which is Wholeness. This produces a strained attitude of mind based upon error, this, in turn, producing 'evil' and 'disease' (dis-ease). The reality is ease, but our mental distortion produces, out of the perfectly good life-force, dis-ease.

This strained or distorted state of mind misdirects the imagination. The imagination is creative, and, because it falls short of the Ideal of the perfect All-Wise Imagination, creates or produces that which is false—namely imperfection or lack of wholeness. Imagination directs the life-forces. In the ordinary way it creates after the ideas of mortal mind, instead of after the ideas of Divine Perfection.

Disease is due to a falling short in consciousness of God's Wholeness. In wholeness there is no disease.

What is the difference between suggestion and true prayer? Suggestion is a direction given to the subconscious to behave itself and produce good health instead of bad. Prayer is the raising of the heart and mind to God, surrendering everything to God, so that He can bring our creative imagination into harmony with His Own All-Wise Imagination. Our creative imagination—which produces such things as our health or ill-health and our circumstances, either harmonious or otherwise—has to be born again. After being born again, it creates after the Divine Pattern of Perfection, Order, Harmony, Beauty, Wholeness and Abundance.

In prayer we endeavour to realize the perfection of the Divine Order, the wholeness, completeness, beauty and joy of the Perfect World of Order which is God's Idea in harmonious expression; in other words, the Reality, from which we have fallen short. This is the Kingdom of the Spirit or Christ, to which we ally ourselves and with which we become identified through aspiration and meditation.

Secondly, we realize the perfection of Christ, the Archetypal Man, the Divine Pattern, the Only Son of God. Perfect, whole, complete, without blemish, He is the real Son as created in the likeness of God. In other words, He is God expressed in beauty, wholeness, perfection, love. Next we realize that we are in Christ and one with Him so that all our imperfection is swallowed up in His Perfection, and God sees us, not as we see ourselves, full of limitations, disease and unwholesomeness, but as Christ, beautiful, complete and whole. God sees only Christ, and us as perfect in Him.

By realizing the perfection of the true world of Spirit and by realizing our oneness with the Spirit (Christ), giving up ourselves and surrendering our will to the Divine Will, and our imagination to the Divine Imagination, allowing God to create us anew according to His infinite wisdom, after the Divine pattern, and by continually affirming our oneness with the One (through surrender to the Love Principle): through all this, we become changed, not according to our own ideas, but according to infinite wisdom.

In order to become healed, it is necessary for us to realize God's Perfection more particularly as regards life, health, wholeness, eternal youthfulness, and so on; then to affirm and realize our oneness with God's Life, Health, Wholeness, Eternal Youthfulness, and so on, in or through Christ. Christ is the connecting link. Christ in us heals us by enabling us to become one in consciousness with God and His Perfection.

Therefore, while in one sense there is nothing to heal, yet in another sense, Christ heals us by raising our consciousness to the Truth, so that we become free from all error, or falling short, or mis-imagining. In other words, we realize the truth that in Christ, or in Spirit, there is no disorder, but only perfect Divine Order, Wholeness, and so on: that in Christ we are one with the One, and therefore all the perfection, wholeness and completeness of the One are ours now. Knowing it intellectually, or merely believing it, does not deliver us, but realization does. What realization is cannot be described. It differs with various individuals, but each one knows when he enters this higher state, although he cannot describe it.

Denials are most helpful in raising the mind from wallowing in error. We can say: *'I deny that error can have any dominion over Spirit'*; or, *'I deny that there is any disease, or disorder, in Spirit; therefore, because I am in Spirit, it can have no dominion over me'*. The denial reveals to our consciousness how utterly impossible it is for disease or any form of disorder to have any power over, or place in, Spirit. Then by identifying ourselves with Spirit, we enter into Truth.

On the one side is human disorder, evil, disease, misery, sin, bondage to the things of the flesh. On the other side is the Spirit, in which are Divine Order, Harmony, Wholeness and Perfection. It is by realizing our unity with the latter that we become saved, in mind, body and estate.

By declaring our unity with Spirit, i.e., God, Christ, we identify ourselves with the real eternal. We cannot serve two masters.

We must choose this day whom we will serve.

The secret of healing is persistently to declare our oneness with the Christ Spirit. The subconscious thinking is that of separateness and disease, limitation and evil. This is the thinking that has to be changed. By continually affirming our oneness with Spirit (or, at any rate, as often as we think about our health, and whenever evil suggestions of ill-health meet us), and by declaring the Spirit's wholeness and perfection, and also by realizing that all imperfection is not a thing in itself, but is a falling short of that which *is*, the subconscious habit of thought becomes changed. It revolves around a new centre—around an idea of God and Perfection, Oneness and Wholeness, instead of an idea of separateness and imperfection. True healing is not accomplished by driving finite ideas down into the subconscious, but by lifting up the mind and affirming oneness with the Infinite Life, Health, Wholeness and Oneness of God (and by 'letting go').

Persistence is necessary because the subconscious mind will still go on its old erroneous way of thinking, as soon as our back is turned, so to speak. It is only by persistently and perseveringly allying ourselves with Truth that the required change can be brought about.

We must, however, get away from the idea that we can heal ourselves. All that we can do is to ally ourselves with Truth. God, or rather the creative life-force, does the rest. The more we think that we are doing something, the worse we become. The mental strain and care that this entails makes us worse instead of better. It is when we give up straining and striving that healing comes.

'In quietness and in confidence shall be your strength.' Strain and struggle, using willpower and domination, only produce a state of reversed suggestion. That is, the subconscious mind does just the reverse of that which you want it to. Therefore, all 'treatment' must be done in quietness and confidence. Just a quiet faith and trust are what is required. A quiet turning to God and identifying ourselves with Him, claiming His perfection because of our oneness with Him. We know that there is no disease or imperfection in God or Spirit, Who is perfect Life, Health and Wholeness and Who can know nothing of disease or imperfection, any more than we are conscious of the limited two dimensional world sensed by a dog.

Healing is accomplished not by effort or by doing anything (another paradox), but by 'letting go'. We do not have to create good health, in reality, but only have to 'let go' and allow the Divine Wholeness to appear. All sick people are in a state of strain. It is a strained condition of mind based on error that produces disorder, for it will not allow the Divine Order to manifest. When we let go and leave the matter to God, the Divine Order appears. The object of 'treatment' and statements of Truth is simply to enable us to realize the Truth so that we can 'let go', give up our strained attitude of mind, and allow the Divine Perfection to appear.

Health is not something that has to be manufactured, but is inherent. It already *is*, and will manifest itself as soon as our strained attitude of mind (based on error) is abandoned, rest in the Truth taking its place.

The subconscious mind does not really have to be impressed with Truth so much as that the wrong impress has to be removed. We are all of us apt to think that wrong has to be put right, much of our teaching being in this strain, but the deeper truth is that nothing has to be put right, for all that is necessary is that the Divine, inherent Perfection and Wholeness should be allowed to manifest itself.

Therefore healing is accomplished not by 'working against' this evil or that, but by allying ourselves with God through Christ, and 'letting go' so as to allow the Divine Order to appear.

You can distort a ball of solid rubber by force. You can press or strain it so that it is no longer a sphere for a short period of time. In order to restore the ball to its true spherical form, we do not have to alter it in any way, or to improve upon it, or to press it into a fresh form; but all that we have to do is to 'let go', whereupon the ball resumes its spherical shape. The true spherical form is inherent, it is our strain and compression that distort it, therefore all that we have to do is to 'let go'.

It is the same with health. All that we have to do is to 'let go', and allow Divine Wholeness to become manifest. Jesus healed instantaneously, because those whom he healed had such faith in Him, they could let go. Therefore, when declaring our unity with the Indwelling Christ Spirit, we must do so in rest, confidence and relaxation. We must leave off straining and striving, and just 'let go', so that God's perfection can appear. We must acknowledge and realize that good in the form of health is always trying to manifest itself in us, because it is inherent—just in the same way as that rubber ball, when pinched and distorted, is all the time trying to resume its true spherical form. By realizing our oneness with the Spirit of Christ we are able to take courage and 'let go', in much the same way that a boy learning to swim has more courage to lean and rest on the water when his father is near, than when he is alone.

Remember that health depends upon rest, peace of mind, relaxation and so on. If you find that attempting a 'treatment' induces a feeling of strain instead of rest, cease attempting it and repeat the Twenty-Third Psalm, or something of a similar restful character, instead. Do this very quietly, until you become rested and relaxed. Then remain in this state for a time, breathing deeply, yet easily. Then forget all about it.

Whenever, during the day, you are reminded of ill-health, just repeat over some words that will recall the restful state you have experienced. Any words will do so long as they recall the truth to your remembrance. '*The Good is seeking me*', might be sufficient, but it is better for each student to use the words that appeal to him or her most. Involved or lengthy sentences should be avoided; just a word or two is better. They should be repeated at once, before the negative suggestion can find a lodging place in the mind. In cases of setback or powerful suggestion of disease or evil, the denial already given can be advantageously used, namely '*I deny that sickness (or disease, etc.) can have any dominion over*

Spirit'. This can be followed by: *'The Spirit in me is the Spirit of Health, Wholeness and Joy'*.

Remember that health is inherent, it is part of the Eternal Wholeness. Because it is inherent it is seeking you. 'Behold I stand at the door and knock. If any man hear my voice, and open the door, I will come into him and will sup with him, and he with me.' Quietness, rest, relaxation, trust, acknowledging that health is inherent and therefore is seeking to escape and find expression: this is the great secret.

Finally, let it be said that the best 'treatment' of all for every disharmony, although much more advanced, is to meditate upon our oneness, or at-one-ment with our Divine Centre. When we truly realize our oneness with the One, all strain ceases. We enter the quiet stillness which is the Kingdom of Heaven, after which everything falls into its proper place, Divine Order taking the place of human disorder, just as Jesus said it would.

Yours in the Knowledge of Health,

HENRY THOMAS HAMBLIN

INSTRUCTIONS IN PROGRESSIVE REFLECTIVE MEDITATION

We now meditate upon God as Love. We have not done so before, for it was first necessary to establish in our minds the truth that God is Good, is One, is Whole, is Justice. The majority of us—in a sickly, sentimental sort of way—have some idea of the Deity being Love, but very imperfect ideas of God as Justice. Both are intertwined and mingled together. Indeed they are one. Love is not perfect if it is not allied with Justice.

So now we meditate upon God as LOVE.

Love draws us to our Divine Centre: Wisdom guides us. Love is integrating. It holds the Universe together. If we obey Its dictates we become drawn to the Heart of God.

It is only Love that can 'soften' us and make us pliable or

plastic enough to be recast in the Divine Mould, refashioned in the Divine likeness, becoming completely one with the ONE.

By obeying Love's call, by surrendering to its claims, by obeying its laws, we enter the Kingdom of Heaven. The Lord of Love takes us and plants us in His Garden of Love.

'Behold, what manner of love the Father hath bestowed upon us, that we should be called the sons of God!'.

So through Love we become sons of God.

When once by meditation the truth of God as Love has become absorbed into our very being, then ever afterwards meditating upon God as Good and the One with whom we are one will call up this truth of God's Love.

Already, if we have mastered what has been taught in these letters, meditating upon our oneness with the One will call up to our unconscious mind the truth that God is Good, the truth that God is Wholeness, the truth that God is One, the truth that God is Justice. Now we add to it

GOD IS LOVE.

*

Slowly, we are building up our beautiful Palace of Truth.

When starting our meditation at this stage it is necessary for us to touch briefly upon the various points which we have mastered.

God as Good, beyond all pairs of opposites.
God as Wholeness.
God as One.
Surrender to the One.
God as Justice.

What has been learnt and realized by the soul through meditation upon these aspects of Truth will be recalled at once and flood the consciousness. Later, they will all be recalled automatically as soon as we turn to God and meditate upon Him and our oneness with Him.

LESSON XVI

Dear Fellow Student of Truth,

It is a great day when we wake up to the truth that God wants us to be well and happy. In our real and higher selves we are health, wholeness, beauty, perfection, happiness and joy. In us God has implanted His Divine Ideal of perfect wholeness, even as the perfect oak tree is hidden in the acorn. God wants this heavenly ideal in us to come forth into manifestation, even as a lovely flower grows and unfolds from a lowly seed.

The highest ideal of health and wholeness that we can hold in our mind is the truth about our real selves. Therefore, when we hold a Divine ideal in our mind, Divine states of consciousness and Divine achievements become possible in our experience. As we meditate upon Divine Wholeness and Health, then we know that God wants these glorious states to manifest in us. It is God's will that we should be whole, healthy, happy and carefree.

Therefore, let this glorious truth sing in your heart. Let it colour all your thoughts. *God wants you to be happy and well, and any present ill-health is passing away, to make room for Divine wholeness to be manifested in you.*

Joy, joy, all is joy and gladness. The whole universe is packed with joy. Divine good is seeking to manifest. We have only to hold it in our mind, joyfully, and affirm it, for it to come forth, like Lazarus from the tomb.

Yours in the Great Adventure,

HENRY THOMAS HAMBLIN

LESSON XVI

HOW TO MANIFEST HEALTH

It is the Divine intention that we should be whole and well, and that we should live harmonious lives. Intuition tells us that God is not the author of disease. There is nothing more foreign to the

Divine Idea than disease in its various forms. The Divine Idea is beauty, harmony, order, health, wholeness, and all that is good and lovely. When we get this idea really into our minds it makes a great difference to our health; indeed, if it is accepted by the inner mind then it may make all the difference in the world to us. We can help to bring this about by repeating and reflecting upon this truth, that

'God's intention and desire are that we should be perfectly whole.'

Or, the whole truth that God is not the author of disease— that it is revolting to Him, and that He does not want us to suffer from it, but that God is the Author of wholeness, health, beauty and joy, and desires greatly that we should enjoy these things— can all be summed up in a short statement, such as the following:

'God wants me to be well.'

Now say this over to yourself. Do you not feel a thrill as you do so? *'God does not want me to be ill or diseased, but to be well, joyous and happy!'* The joy of it, when we realize this great truth! It comes rushing into our consciousness like a flood of light when we open the shutters to let in the sunshine. All our life we have had the mistaken idea, somehow, that God wanted us to be diseased, or that disease might come at any time, and if so it was His will, or that it was inevitable. But God does not want us to be ill, but desires very much indeed that we should be well and happy. This word 'happy' is a good one to add to our statement of Truth, because happiness and health are linked together, so we will do so. It now will read:

'God wants me to be well amd happy.'

By cultivating happiness and a sunshiny disposition, and by being sweet instead of sour, or 'snappy', and by being kind, forgiving, loving, and generous, and helpful in our thoughts for others, we hasten the coming of health. We prepare, as it were, the way of the Lord. Health cannot grow in a bad soil. It cannot grow in the soil of bitterness, fault-finding, self-pity, condemnation of others, unforgiveness, hardness, and irritability. But when our nature becomes sweetened and happy, then it also becomes possible for health to take root and grow.

So just let your thoughts rest upon this truth, and caress it, so to speak, and play around it, in a quiet, happy restful way:

'God wants me to be well amd happy.'

When we realize this great truth it is as though a dark cloud had been rolled away, or that a great, crushing burden had been removed.

Very simple, you say. Yes, very simple. Simple methods are always the best. Jesus, the Great Healer, was simple in His methods. He did not wade through a maze of metaphysics, He simply spoke the word, and the patient was healed according to his or her faith. Wherever people were willing for Him to heal them, and had faith in his *power* to do so, Jesus healed them, without complication, but simply and directly. Our Lord knew that the Father wanted those poor people to be whole, so He healed them. He did not tell them to bear their disease patiently because it was the Lord's will, or because it was good for them spiritually and morally; but He simply healed them, and they became whole, and remained whole, from that moment.

Simple methods are always best; the simpler they are, the better, because they are more direct. They are also more effective, for the reason that the human mind, whose continuous and unresting activity prevents healing, is not allowed to become excited, but becomes rested instead. It is when the finite mind ceases its activities, and allows itself to become still for a moment, that God's beautiful life of wholeness can enter, thus making all things new.

But it is very unwise to make the mind merely blank and receptive, for then it is possible for error of a very serious kind to enter. Especially is this true of those who are of a passive, psychic, or mediumistic type. But all is well, if we quieten the surface mind by filling it with a restful statement of Truth. When we quieten ourselves, relaxing all tension, loosening the muscles, smoothing out our nerves, letting go our fears and anxieties, also breathing deeply and naturally instead of in shallow gasps, and at the same time whisper softly to our inner self,

'God want me to be well amd happy.'

then the good news is accepted. As soon as the good news that God wants us to be well and happy is accepted, we wake up as from a frightful dream. We look back on the past nightmare of disease, ill-health, misery and suffering as an incredible thralldom and slavery, and we wonder why we were ever in bondage to it. But this is not all; the subconscious mind accepts the idea, and afterwards produces health, order and perfection, in place of disease, sickness, and disorder.

We repudiate the thought that God's idea concerning us can be other than that of a Heavenly nature. Intuition tells us that Heaven is peopled with those who are deathless and diseaseless, and who are in a state of prime, a prime that includes health, strength, beauty and vigour. Any other idea revolts us. God's idea expressed in the conditions of Heaven, is God's idea concerning us.

'God want me to be well amd happy.'

God wants us to be whole, every whit. It is the Divine idea and intention that the wholeness and completeness of His own life should be enjoyed by His own sons and daughters. 'Beloved, now are we the sons of God', enjoying all a son's powers and privileges, nothing less. When we realize this great truth, old things pass away, and all things become new.

Healing, and entering into a larger, saner and more wholesome life of health, happiness and joy, is not a result of strain and effort, but of quiet realization of the great truth that we are God's children and that our Father wants us to be healthy and happy just as much as we desire our own children to be well and happy—indeed infinitely more so. Arguing and thinking about it will not help matters, but a state of quietness can be achieved through filling the mind with this truth, and whispering it to ourselves until a beautiful sense of peace and joy comes to us. This is called 'realization'.

Here follows what I term the Threefold Path of Liberation. It does not matter what our trouble may be, God is able to deliver us, and to bring about a Divine adjustment; and also wants to do so. God does not want us to remain in any difficulty or unhappy situation a moment longer than the, present moment. He is able and willing and wants to deliver us, *now*, if we will only quietly enter into liberation.

Here it is.

(1) God is the only One Who can liberate us.
(2) God is able to deliver us and set us completely free.
(3) God is willing to do for us abundantly beyond our hopes and desires.

This threefold path, to me, is the secret of all deliverance. To me, it is the golden key to all liberation and freedom. It has been worked out through much tribulation and trial. I pass it on to you, so that you may know the way, which was something that was denied me, but which I had to work out, so to speak, with blood and tears. It is the only way I know: it is the only way that has been revealed to me: it is the only method that has proved effective. It is equally effective when applied to financial difficulties as it is when used for health or healing, or for getting other people out of trouble, or for restoring harmony in the home, when such a thing appears to be an impossibility. It does not matter what the trouble may be, God is the only One Who can deliver, God is able to deliver, and God wants to deliver us. After these three realizations, when we know the truth of them, we can exercise faith by thanking and praising God for the blessing and deliverance which we know is already ours, although outwardly everything may appear to be the same as before.

In this lesson, I have given you the greatest thing that has come to me in this life. You may wonder why I was compelled to work this thing out through experience with blood and tears. I think it is that all who are called to teach have to work out the Truth stop by step alone, not only for themselves, but also for the sake of those souls who have been given them. Just as our Lord and the saints and martyrs of the past have worked out the Truth through blood and tears for us, so also do we, in our much smaller way, have to work out, through our own experience, that aspect or ray of Truth which it is our privilege to pass on to you and others, and those who shall come after us.

In closing, I want to point out that the principal lesson for you to learn now is this:

'God wants me to be well amd happy.'

The other parts of the threefold path of Realization will be dealt with more fully in our next lesson.

WEEK SEVENTEEN :
HOW TO HELP OTHERS

EVERY DISCORDANT condition can be healed by a right understanding and realization of Truth. God is not limited to the healing of the body, for to find and know Him results in the healing of the whole life, right from the centre to the circumference, thus including mind, body and estate. No matter how complicated and tangled up our life may have become, God—Who is Infinite Life, Health, Wholeness, Order, Harmony, Power, Might, Wisdom, Knowledge, Intelligence, and LOVE—is able to untangle it, and bring it into a state of order, beauty, harmony and good.

God does not have to be changed. God's mind does not have to be altered. God's will does not have to be made different. God is Love that is infinite, Wholeness that is infinite, Life that is infinite. His Love is such that He desires nothing better than that we should be changed into the Divine Image and Likeness, which is God's true thought and idea concerning us.

God has only one idea or thought concerning us, and this is perfect, whole, complete. This image of man and woman in the Mind of God is termed the Archetype. The Archetype or Christ is the true creation. He who contemplates the Archetype, with unveiled face, becomes changed into the same image, from glory to glory, as by the Spirit of the Lord, to quote St Paul.

St Paul tells us that when our hearts are turned to the Lord then the veil which keeps us from seeing the Archetype (God's true Idea concerning man) is taken away, so that we can then, with unveiled face, contemplate the Divine Perfection, and thus become changed into Its likeness, and also substance, as by the Spirit of the Lord.

He also said: 'Now the Lord is that Spirit'. The Lord, Who is infinite life, health, wholeness, perfection, good, order, beauty, harmony and peace, is Spirit. Our Lord said to the woman of Samaria, at the well, that God was not a local presence Who could be worshipped only in the Temple at Jerusalem, but that He is Spirit. The correct translation, we are told, is not 'God is a spirit', but that 'God is Spirit'. The Lord, then, is the One Universal, Indwelling Spirit; and He is Life, Health, Wholeness, Perfection, Beauty, Order and Harmony. All this is within us. The Lord, Who is this Spirit, indwells us, making it possible for us to contemplate the Archetype. Through this contemplation, we become transformed into the Image of His Son, the Archetype. In other words, we correspond to God's Idea concerning us, which He forever holds in His Mind, and which, really, all the time, has been the only thing that has been true about us.

'Creation', it has been said, 'is the result of Spirit contemplating Itself'. In the same way, we contemplate God's Idea, the true Self, and then a true creation follows. God contemplates Himself in all His Divine Perfection, and a true Creation is the result. Thus the true Creation is always perfect. The imperfect creation that we see with mortal eyes is the result of our contemplating our imperfect lower selves. This all becomes changed through contemplating our true self, the One Self, or Archetypal Man, or Christ.

This is beautifully and perfectly stated by the Divine Pymander (or, more accurately, 'Poemandres'). This is the name given by Hermes Trismegistus to the Supreme Archetype. It corresponds to our term, 'Christ'. Here is what Hermes says:

'Contemplate through Me the Cosmos now subject to thy vision; regard carefully its beauty, a Body in pure perfection, though one than which there is none more ancient, ever in the prime of Life, and ever young, nay, rather in ever fuller and yet fuller prime'.

This ancient teaching, which was regarded by the early Church Fathers as authoritative and authentic, and was quoted by St Augustine and many others, confirms what I have so often said: namely that if we were to see with the eyes of Christ, we should see everything and everybody in absolute perfection. No wonder our Lord tells us to take the beam out of our own eye, before attempting to remove the mote from our brother's. When our eye is single, our whole body is full of light.

In order to find perfection in the Cosmos, and also in our brother, it is necessary that we should be changed. The Cosmos does not have to be altered, and neither, strange to say, does our brother: it is we who have to be changed. We have to see with spiritual eyes; we have to see that which is invisible.

This brings me to the pith of this lesson—how to help others. Before dealing with this, however, I want to touch on another important point.

I said, just now, that the Lord is the One Indwelling Spirit; therefore the Lord is in everyone, and when we are dealing with people, we are really dealing with the Lord. The realization of this truth should make our conduct towards others more kindly and considerate.

But there is another aspect of this truth of God being the One Universal Spirit. St Paul says that there is 'one God and Father of all, Who is above all, and through all, and in you all'. We see from this that the Divine Spirit, Who is God, is indwelling us, and also that we dwell in God. This explains our Lord's cryptic saying: 'Except ye abide in Me and I in you'. It is obvious that we cannot dwell in the human, physical Jesus, neither can the human, physical Jesus dwell in us. Our Lord was speaking as the One Universal, Indwelling and Enfolding Spirit, which he knew Himself to be. When we realize this, we are able to understand His sayings, but not otherwise.

Perfection, in the form of the One Divine Spirit, indwells us. Perfection, in the form of the One Divine Spirit, unfolds us. Realizing and acknowledging the Perfection within, and the Perfection without, we are brought the more completely into conformity with the Divine. 'For without Me ye can do nothing', but 'with God all things are possible'.

When we realize that we are indwelt by the one eternal Spirit of Wholeness, Perfection, Harmony, Order and Good, and that we are enfolded by the same, we may become conscious that we are being worked upon in two directions at once—from within and from without. The Indwelling Spirit enable us to realize that 'This is none other but the House of God, and this is the gate of Heaven'.

Probably the greatest discovery that we can make in this life is that we are Divine children, living in Heaven now. The uninitiated say, in reply to this, 'How can this be true, when there is so much disorder around us, and not only around us, but even in our own life?' The disorder, of course, is due to our lack of correspondence with the harmony of Heaven. The same power that produces order, when the laws of Divine Harmony are observed, will also produce disorder if the laws of Divine Harmony are not observed. Heaven is here, and we are living in it. Its harmony and order enter our consciousness to the extent that we come into correspondence with it.

We enter into Heaven, or the Heavenly consciousness, when we acknowledge and realize that we are children of God, that we are thoughts or ideas of God, forever held in the Divine Mind as whole, perfect, and good, and that other people are in the same relationship, and that we are all subject to the laws of Heaven, which are love, co-operation, and service.

How different life becomes when we cease to scramble and grab for self, and instead live for others, seeking to serve the Whole! We discover joy in life, whereas before we could not even find ordinary happiness. So long as we act from self-interest, we keep ourselves in a state of separateness from God and our environment. We remain out of correspondence with the Internal Harmony. As soon, however, as we follow the teaching of our Lord, Who tells us to love God with all our heart, mind and strength, and our neighbour as ourself, we enter into unity with the Whole, and become an integral part of the Internal Harmony.

To realize this great Truth, and to live in the consciousness of it, together produce a complete change in our thought and action; and also our attitude towards life becomes entirely different. Instead of being the companions of evil powers, we become the companions of Angelic beings, and are encompassed about by Heavenly influences. So long as we maintain this attitude, and live in harmony with Heaven, we are looked upon by Heaven as Heaven's child, and every possible aid is given to us, so that we grow in grace and knowledge, and increase in spiritual growth.

The question naturally arises, 'How can we help others?' The way by which we can help others most is by seeing them as they are held in the Mind of God. That is to say, we try not to see the imperfect human manifestation, but rather the Ideal, or the true Archetype, the idea or thought of them, as it has been created in Divine Mind, and which is forever perfect, whole, lovely, complete. God is unable to think less than this about any one of us; and God's idea about us is the only thing that is really true about us.

Consequently, when we try to see those whom we desire to help as God sees them, we come into alignment with Truth. By Truth I mean that which is eternally true about God and equally true about God's creation, which is forever perfect, because Creation is God contemplating Himself.

This is indeed a great mystery, hid from before the foundation of the world. Yet it is revealed to all true, seekers, while it is withheld from the learned. 'I thank Thee, O Father, Lord of Heaven and earth, because Thou hast hid these things from the wise and prudent, and hast revealed them unto babes. Even so, Father: for so it seemed good in Thy sight', said Jesus.

This is indeed a great and wondrous mystery, that God should contemplate Himself, and that Creation should be the result; and that we too can contemplate the Archetype, and through so doing find our true Self. But it is so, and by applying this same process to others, we help them to attain also.

When we turn to God, on behalf of others, attempting to see

only the Christ or Archetype, in place of their failings, imperfec-tions or difficulties, we help to set them free from their bondage, and to liberate the true Self so that Christ can be seen instead of the imperfect self.

Immediately we do this, all the old thoughts about the one for whom we are praying come surging into our mind—thoughts of his or her sickness, sin, troubles, the danger he or she is in— and so on. But we must refuse to accept such thoughts, at all costs. Instead, we must think no evil, accept no evil, entertain no evil concerning the one whom we are trying to help, but perse-vere in seeing only Christ, that is, the Archetype, or God's Per-fect Idea concerning him.

If we persevere in this way we discover, to our amazement, that that which makes the one for whom we pray imperfect to out-ward sense is our own wrong thought, and that when this is re-placed by thoughts of Truth the one for whom we pray is set free.

Yours in the One Service,

HENRY THOMAS HAMBLIN

FURTHER INSTRUCTIONS IN MEDITATION

In course of time, by simply meditating upon our oneness with the One we are put 'in contact' with all the Divine Ideas, or Qualities, upon which we have previously meditated, so that eve-rything that we need is poured into us, as we quietly rest in the truth of our at-one-ment with our Divine Source.

We will now meditate upon WISDOM. Love and Wisdom form the stem of the Divine Logos, our Father–Mother God. Father, Love—Mother, Wisdom. Love is the masculine aspect of God; Wisdom, the feminine.

We reflect upon Wisdom that is infinite. Only wisdom that is infinite could have planned this universe, foreseen all, and ar-ranged for everything to happen just in the right way and at the right moment, in spite of man's freewill.

We worship and adore the Wisdom that makes no mistakes,

encounters no difficulties, and which has foreseen every problem with which we are faced, or may be faced, and provided a
way of escape.

We cannot, however, with our finite minds, understand or
grasp what INFINITE Wisdom means. Therefore we hold the
thought or idea of infinite Wisdom at the top of our mind, keeping all other thoughts away from it, thus allowing the Light of
the Spirit of Truth to beat upon it, to bring illumination and
understanding to the soul.

When we have meditated for some time in this way, with the
idea of Divine Wisdom in our mind for the Spirit to illumine, we
can say: 'Infinite Wisdom is now guiding in all my affairs; therefore all my decisions are wise decisions, and I am led to do just
the right thing at the right moment, so that the whole of my
work and activities is brought into harmony with the Divine Will
and Purpose, thus allowing the Divine Order to manifest itself,
without effort and without strain'.

LESSON XVII

Dear Fellow Student of Truth,

In this lesson you have explained to you the threefold way of
effectual prayer. God is the *only* One Who can deliver you out of
any and every trouble. God also is *able* to do this, even though a
miracle is necessary. God also is *willing* to deliver you and longs
to do so. When I have been in a state of extremity this method
of prayer has been the only method that has proved effective. It
is when we acknowledge and realize that God alone can deliver,
that we surrender ourselves utterly and completely to Him, so
that miracles become possible, through the unimpeded action
of Divine grace.

This is rather advanced, spiritually, and it was only through
passing through great and deep experiences that I was able to
work it out. Therefore, if you find it too advanced for you at
present you can rely on other methods.

For your own health and healing, you can say: 'In my real spiritual self, I am a child of God. In me the Divine life is now present in perfect health, wholeness, beauty and joy.' Because what you state is Truth, what you declare will manifest. You can condense this truth into simpler language by saying, 'I am a child of God, and I am filled with Divine health, wholeness, and power.'

Then, when helping others, you can say: 'I see you as a child of God, with the gift of God's perfect life and wholeness already yours. Your trouble is passing, making way for God's wholeness and health to be expressed in you.'

Whichever, or whatever, method you adopt, God is the only healer, and the patient is healed because he, or she, is a child of God, a spiritual being capable of receiving and expressing the life of God.

Yours in the Sure Knowledge,

HENRY THOMAS HAMBLIN

LESSON XVII

HEALING

In our last lesson, although the three steps of effectual prayer were given and explained, yet the truth that was emphasized most was that God wants us to be well and happy—that it is God's desire, the longing of His heart of love, that we should be whole, healthy and happy, and our life filled with every good thing.

Each child of God belongs to the Kingdom of God or Heaven, and shares in its blessings, and forms part of its Divine order. It is therefore the privilege of each child of God to manifest the Divine order, wholeness and perfection of the Heavenly state, which is the Reality. Because Divine order is the Reality it forever *is*, and is therefore always present. It is our privilege to discover this Divine order, present with us here and always, and to bring ourselves and our life in accord with it.

It is, then, the desire of God's heart that we should be well and happy. It is one thing, however, to read about this great and transforming truth, or even to accept it and believe it, and quite another for this same truth to enter the inner mind, so that it is worked out in our body and life. It is because of this that you were taught in our preceding lesson to whisper quietly to yourself the glad tidings, *'God wants me to be well and happy'*.

Have you ever realized that the Lord's Prayer refers to the same thing? 'Thy Kingdom come, Thy will be done on earth as it is in Heaven.' This is an invocation that the Divine order of Reality should manifest in this earthly life of ours; that the health and wholeness of the spiritual or heavenly Man should find expression in the material man.

We are, as it were, encased in a hard shell of material thought that is of the earth, earthy. Underneath this shell, the subconscious mind works to an untrue pattern, a pattern that is not true of Reality, but is a product of the Race Mind.* The whispering of a statement of Truth quietly and restfully to ourselves gets the truth through to something within, which, when it accepts the message, is able to act on it in a wonderful manner. When the inner self, or whatever it is, or whatever it might be termed, accepts Truth, then Truth becomes manifested in the form of health, wholeness, beauty, and order. Because of this you were taught to relax and say quietly to yourself the statement of Truth:

'God wants me to be well amd happy.'

Now, as you were told in the previous lesson, No. XVI, there are three steps to a complete 'treatment' or effectual prayer. The first stage is to acknowledge and realize that God alone can heal and deliver. So long as we have the slightest dependence either upon others or upon our finite self, we cannot pray effectively. The prayers that we make may be good for our soul, because all turning to God is good for the soul, but it will not bring results,

---

*I.e., what other teachers might call the instinctive, or the animal or elemental mind or being.

either in healing or in causing a Divine adjustment of one's life and affairs. The man who trusts ever so little in 'the arm of flesh', puts himself outside the sphere of Divine blessing. But the one who puts his whole trust in 'the Arm of the Lord' is like a tree planted by the waters. Therefore, what we have to do, when starting effective prayer, or 'treatment', is to acknowledge that God is the only One Who can heal, and deliver. All that we need is God. When we possess God, or when God really possesses us, then all our needs are supplied, and a perfect Divine adjustment of our life, body and affairs follows.

'God alone can heal.'

All good comes from the Lord. At first we think that we can create our own good, but a time comes when we have to acknowledge that we can do no good of ourselves, and that God alone can bring good into our life. If we trust God, entirely, acknowledging that He alone can save, bless and keep, and we, of ourselves, can do nothing good, and that no human being can help us, then God is able to heal us, protect us, guide us, and supply abundantly all our needs. Through this acknowledgment and surrender to God we enter into a realization in which we *know* that God is indeed the only One Who can save, deliver, protect, heal, guide, instruct and keep us. This realization is the end of the first stage, which is summed up in the statement:

'God alone can heal.'

The second stage is: That God is *able* to do for us exceeding abundantly above all that we can ask or think. In other words: That God is able to do the (humanly) impossible, and thus bring about that which is termed 'the miraculous'.

When we open our mind to the Truth that God is able to do the impossible, then what are termed miracles become possible in our experience. Even Jesus could not heal those who had no faith, and who, therefore, did not believe He could heal them. But as soon as they acknowledged that He was able to heal them, and when they exhibited even a little faith, then He was able to heal them. God is not bound or limited by the physical laws of the material plane. There are higher powers than those of Nature, and there are higher laws than those known by Physical Scientists. 'The Lord is mighty'. 'Not by might, nor by power, but by my Spirit, saith the Lord.' The Spirit is all-powerful. 'Nothing is too hard for God.' The things impossible with man are possible with God. This world, so solid to us, is to God like a vapour, which can be altered instantaneously, if only our faith is able to proclaim that all things are possible.

The second truth, then, that we have to acknowledge and affirm and realize is:

'God alone can heal.'

The third stage in our threefold effectual prayer is that God is willing to heal, and greatly desirous of healing us (and our whole life), and maintaining us in a state of health, wholeness and happiness. This stage was taught and explained in Lesson XVI, because I wanted you to have it first—because of the change that a realization of this truth has upon the outlook and upon the health. It is also most necessary for our personal health and healing that we should enter into this truth, and, frequently, it is all that is necessary. In this lesson we state the same truth in these words:

'God is willing to heal.'

God wants to heal all who are sick, diseased, or afflicted. Healing awaits all. God does not want any one to suffer, or to manifest disease. It is necessary, then, when we are helping others to realize this great truth that God is more anxious than we are that one who is diseased or ill should be made well and happy. We state and realize then that

'God is willing to heal.'

Now, by putting all that has been said into the form of thanksgiving, the whole treatment is made positive and dynamic: it opens

the consciousness for the Truth to enter. We therefore turn to
the Lord and say:

> 'I thank Thee because Thou art the only One Who can heal.
> 'I thank Thee because Thou art able to heal.
> 'I thank Thee because Thou art willing to heal.'

*

If we persevere with the use of this threefold method of effectual
prayer we enter, sooner or later, into a state of joyful realization
in which we *know* that our prayer is answered, and that all that
we need, and far more, are already ours, in the mercy and love
of God. This understanding which comes to us fills us with such
joy that we immediately start praising and thanking God for all
His love and mercy, not from a sense of duty, but for the sheer
love of it. This praise and thanksgiving, accompanied by ecstatic
joy, should be kept up as long as possible, and frequently renewed.

This should be persevered with, in spite of the fact that outwardly there may be no improvement. This is when faith comes
in. Faith is the substance of things hoped for, the evidence of things
not seen. We *know* that our prayer is answered, and we affirm
this Truth and maintain it in the face of all sense-evidence to the
contrary. Then, if we are faithful, deliverance comes, in God's
own way, which is always better than our way would have been.
Then we realize the truth that *'God is able to do for us exceeding
abundantly, above all that we ask or think, according to the power that
worketh in us'*.

*

When praying for others in this way, we take on as it were the
patient's condition. I do not mean his or her physical condition,
but his or her mental and spiritual darkness. Instead of obtain-
ing a clear and happy realization, we become conscious of great
darkness and oppression. Thus our prayer is really vicarious intercession—we take on ourselves the patient's mental and spir-

itual darkness in order that he or she may be prayed through it, and thus brought into the light of Truth. Through persevering in prayer, until light and realization come, we help the patient into a state of healing; but he or she must faithfully practise Truth, and make a habit of thinking Truth, otherwise the old condition will return.

Where possible, all who surround the patient—relatives and friends alike—should learn to understand the truth:

(1) God is the only One Who can heal, although, of course, such healing may possibly come through doctors and nurses. All healing comes from the Lord, and from nowhere else.

(2) God is able to heal. All things are possible with God, no matter how hopeless things may appear to be, if we will only believe that they are possible.

(3) God is willing to heal, and wants to heal, if we will let Him. They should be taught to think in this way instead of in terms of sickness and disease. Instead of dwelling on the disease or illness, they should endeavour to think of the patient as being upheld by Spiritual powers and ministered to by Heavenly beings. They must be taught that every time they brood over the illness and think of the patient as sick and ill, they make it very difficult for him or her to recover, for they hold the patient in bondage by so doing, and attract to him or her undesirable influences.

Let them, when tempted to think of the patient in the old way as being ill, or diseased, say and declare: 'I refuse to think of ———— in the old way, but I think of him or her as ministered to by Divine Powers, that are healing and blessing him or her.'

Help of this kind from the friends and relatives of the patient is a great assistance and should be encouraged as much as possible.

The patient, if able to think clearly himself, may also be taught to say: '*I see myself as gloriously healed by Divine love and ministered to by Heavenly powers*'.

INTERLUDE:
THREEFOLD BEING

THE HERMETIC Philosophy postulates a threefold aspect of
Deity, namely
   God Abiding.
   God Proceeding.
   God Returning.
These correspond to St Paul's teaching of the Christian Trinity:
   God the Father,
   God the Son, proceeding from the Father.
   God the Holy Spirit, helping us back to the Father.
   Thank God, we are returning. Not only are we returning, we
also are conscious of the glorious fact, and also that we are nearly
Home. At Home, when in our meditations—but, alas, liable to
forget all about it during our everyday life!
   But, blessed fact, we *are* returning, and the Spirit helps our
infirmities. We must at all times listen to the voice of the Spirit,
obeying the call to higher things, for 'My Spirit shall not always
strive with man'.
   We are sunken in a low vibration. Christ calls us to a higher
one, and the Spirit helps us to respond. From hate, revenge, resentment, illwill, we are called to love. Christ calls us to a life of
love to the uttermost; love to our fellows, love to our enemies.
Jesus Christ, the Lord of Love, has shown us how to love.
   From sensual love and the love of passion, Christ calls us to
the pure heights of universal love, of love to God and our neighbour. From purer, yet selfish love and attachment to personali-

ties, Christ calls us to exercise a love that is a universal pouring out of ourselves in blessing, benediction and service to others.

From weakness, Christ calls us to strength, and from vacillation to steadfastness. Unto him that overcometh, to him that endureth, to the one who is faithful, the reward is given. But 'the Spirit helpeth our Infirmities'.

Christ calls us from the pomp and vanity of the world, with its beat, feverish haste, self-interest, self-seeking, vainglory, and baubles and shams, to the quiet pastures and cool waters of meditation upon eternal things.

Christ calls us from poverty of soul and trust in material possessions, to the riches of the Kingdom of Heaven, which fade not away.

Christ calls us from disease and sickness to perfect ease, wholeness and delightful health.

Christ calls us from a life of privation and emptiness to one that is abundant and satisfying.

Christ calls us from misery and sadness to taste ineffable joy and delights beyond description.

Christ calls us from earth to heaven, while we are yet in the body.

Christ calls us from the negative pole to the positive; or rather, He calls us to a point of contact with That which transcends all negative and positive, all pairs of opposites, all that is relative and limited, to our One, Divine, Spiritual Imperishable Source, God.

How are we to respond? In thought. Thought is the cause: by it we rise or fall. Every time we turn to God, affirming our oneness, in Christ, with Him, our thoughts become polarized and our mind raised to a higher vibration. The more we turn to God, realizing our oneness with Him, the more we see through the eyes of Christ, the Archetypal Man. Seeing through the eyes of Christ enables us to discern the Truth: to look out over life and the Universe, realizing that all is well, a thousand times well; that God makes no mistakes, that everything is indeed working together for good.

By meditation, we become raised to supernal heights. We realize that there is only the Reality and that all else is a falling short, a privation, or absence of the Reality, Good.

The fundamental cure for all our ills is simply to get back to God. 'How many hired servants of my Father have bread enough and to spare, and I perish with hunger.' All that the poor prodigal needed was to return to his Father. There was no necessity for him to devise any wonderful scheme of food production; all that he had to do was to return to his Father who had bread enough and to spare.

In the same way, all that we need is to get back to God, our Father. We have not to deal with disease, we have not to fight poverty, we have not to wrestle with external circumstances: we have only to get back to God. Our life is perfect as imaged in Divine Mind; therefore, all that we have to do is to become one with the Perfect One.

When we are one with God, all our negative ills, no matter what they may be, must cease; for our Father is not a God of disease, or ill-health, or poverty or misery, but of wholeness, beauty and joy. All heaven is filled with laughter, the sweet laughter of ransomed souls, the laughter of bliss indescribable.

It is simply a case of returning to God. Truth is very simple in reality. It does away with all complications. If we branch off from the true Path we become lost in a maze of complications. But in the true Path all is very simple, just like a child finding its mother's arms.

We find God through meditation. When we find God, in this, way, we have found all. We are safely home at last.

We also find God, and come to know Him intimately, through meeting with great problems, perplexities and crises in both spiritual and mundane experience. While most of these experiences are due to our failure to meet smaller experiences in the right way, yet God works everything together for good, so that through trouble and disaster we learn to know God in a way we never knew Him before. By meeting with a great perplexing problem we learn to tap Infinite Wisdom. By meeting with financial crises, we learn to know God as our only Source of Supply. By meeting with illness or sickness, we get to know Christ as the only healer, and God as our Source of Life and Health. And so on.

As we look back we thank God for the trouble, and cannot, in our finite way, see how the lessons could have been learnt in any other way. But God is not a God of trouble, disaster and suffering (we are the cause of these things): and, although He overrules everything for good, there is a better way to wisdom than by calamity, loss and crisis. This is the way of meditation, and surrender to the way of the Spirit, by which we become meet for the Kingdom of God, through being changed into the Divine likeness. It is through anticipating the Divine Purpose regarding our unfoldment that needless suffering is avoided.

'And the peace of God, which passeth all understanding, shall keep your hearts and minds through Christ Jesus'.

Yours in His Service,

HENRY THOMAS HAMBLIN

INSTRUCTIONS IN PROGRESSIVE REFLECTIVE MEDITATION

The secret of meditation is this, that when we meditate, what we know God to be becomes incorporated with our own being and character. That is to say, the qualities which we have associated with God, and, through meditation, have realized to be part of God's being and character, become reflected into our character and built into the very fibre of our being.

For instance, if, in our past meditations, we have realized God as wholeness, health, completeness, etc. (which allows no room for disease, sickness or any other lack of wholeness), directly we turn to God and meditate upon Him, realizing His presence and our oneness with Him (the ONE), our consciousness becomes built up by, or impregnated with, a sense, or understandings of wholeness, health, completeness, and so on. What I want you to understand is that although we may not meditate upon God as wholeness, health, etc., but only bask in His presence, the healing process takes place.

In the same way, whatever other qualities we have associated with God, such as Oneness, Unity, Good, Love, Wisdom, Justice, and so on, become reflected into our character, being and consciousness, whenever we meditate upon God.

Thus our work in meditation, if well and soundly performed, is constructive and cumulative. First we lay the foundation, next, the ground floor, and after that, the superstructure. Our meditation is not something that has to be done all over again every day. We do not have to begin at the foundation again and again, but at where we left off. The foundation must, however, be well and truly laid. Each step must be thoroughly mastered. There is nothing to be gained and everything to be lost by attempting to go ahead too quickly, thus scamping the work.

We turn now from the ugliness and squalor of life, as man has made it, and meditate upon

BEAUTY.

Divine Beauty : The Beauty Inherent.

The reality is infinite beauty. God is not a being of ugliness or imperfection, but of beauty beyond our wildest flights of imagination.

Recall the most glorious picture of beauty that Nature has ever presented to your view, and it will lead your thoughts and imagination to some conception of the inherent beauty of God. If I had the pen of a ready writer and the tongue of an angel I might describe, in a feeble measure, something of the Beauty of God, or of God as Beauty. But whatever I might write or say would convey but little to your soul. The only way to realize God as Beauty is to hold the Idea of Beauty in the top of your mind, then think of the most beautiful manifestation of God that you can recall, and meditate upon it, allowing the Spirit of Truth,

Who alone can help us to realize the Truth, to lead us higher and higher, until we realize God as Beauty.

You will not be able to describe that which you realize, but you, yourself, will *know*.

There must be, of course, an entire absence of strain, anxiety and effort. We have to rest quietly, with our mind raised to the Divine Object of our meditation, allowing the Spirit of Truth to bring understanding to our soul, and light to our consciousness.

'In quietness and in confidence' is the great secret.

This aspect of Divine Mind should be meditated upon daily until it is thoroughly mastered, so that immediately you commence meditating upon God as Beauty you enter into a realization of this facet of Truth.

But God is beyond Beauty, or any other attribute.

LESSON XVIIa

Dear Fellow Student of Truth,

This lesson has been provided in order to give you a view of Truth from a different angle. It does not contradict previous teaching, but, rather confirms and strengthens it. No matter from what angle or point of view we approach the Truth we are led to the same conclusion, namely that only Good and Absolute Perfection exist and have any reality: all else being a NO-thing or non-entity. Let us thank God continually that evil and imperfection have no reality, for if they had we could never escape from them. That which is real is eternal and permanent and thus can never be destroyed. It is because evil has no reality that we can escape from it and rise above it. Thank God that there is only God and His Perfect Manifestation or Idea (Omnipresent Good). It is by realizing the unreality of evil and by turning to God as the only Reality, Good and Perfection inherent and present everywhere, that we learn and know the Truth which forever sets us free.

Yours in Unity and Truth,

HENRY THOMAS HAMBLIN

PREFACE

By looking at Truth from different viewpoints, inward understanding is, to a certain extent, helped. Let me state here a tremendous truth, which you will probably reject at this stage but
which you may accept later. This truth is that really our only task
is to convince the self. All the work of this Course, all its denials,
affirmations, meditations and 'treatments' are directed towards
this one end: convincing the self of Truth. This is what Jesus
meant when He said that man could remove mountains if his
faith were even as a grain of mustard seed. Faith comes through
convincing the self. The more the self 'knows' or 'realizes' the
greater the faith that becomes possible. Great faith, the faith that
works wonders, is not the blind belief in something one does not
understand, but is the outcome of *knowing inwardly*, or by the self.

I have said that these intellectual explanations from different
viewpoints are helpful. In some measure, they help to convince
the self. They are, however, incomplete. Every intellectual explanation of Truth breaks down somewhere, at some point. The
critic can always find, in any philosophy, a joint in the armour
into which he can thrust his dart. He can always ask questions
which cannot be answered in a fair and square manner. No intellectual explanation of Truth can ever be complete or entirely
true. This is because Truth is absolute and infinite: therefore it
can never be explained in human language, for this is capable
only of explaining that which is relative and finite. This aspect
of the Truth which is presented in this extra lesson breaks down
at one point, as do all explanations both in this Course and all
courses and all books. There is a point where intellect can help
us no longer. It can take us to the foot of the mountain, but, after
that, we have to proceed alone. The 'jumping-off' point in all the
explanations given in this Course is this: If God's manifestations
are all perfect and all that exists is Perfect Good, how is it that
our finite mentality is imperfect? Why is it that we cannot see
things as they really are? If we say that this life is a dream, why

the dream? If we say that life is experience by which we 'improve' and develop, then why this improving and developing, if all is perfect here and now? If we say that this mentality and this life do not exist, then why the illusion? And so we might go on. It is here that intellectual explanations fail lamentably. Finite cannot explain Infinite.

At this point, like the child learning to swim, who, for the first time, trusts the water to support him and finds that he cannot sink, we leave behind the finite intellect and, trusting our intuitions, learn the Truth through direct knowing from Spirit to Spirit. Having exhausted many intellectual avenues and finding them all incomplete, we are thrown back upon Spirit for knowledge, guidance and understanding. The great Truth is that there is nothing but Infinite Good, Love, Peace, Perfection, Beauty, Bliss; but this can be realized only within by the Spirit. The direct way to this spiritual realization is by denying that there is any principle of evil, or any evil purpose in life, supplemented by affirmations that Good is the only reality. Every night and morning this should be done in the Silence, and also at odd moments during the day. If this is persevered with, a time comes when the Truth is realized spiritually and inwardly. We *know* the Truth and intellectual discrepancies no longer trouble us. We are free. We are filled with joy unspeakable. 'Old things have passed away and all things become new.'

LESSON XVIIa

THE LAW OF VIBRATION, POLARITY AND MENTAL ALCHEMY

This extra lesson has been written and introduced in order to make this teaching still more helpful. It explains the Truth from a different standpoint than that of pure metaphysics, but even those who are at home with abstract reasoning find help in this aspect of the subject.

This teaching of vibration and polarity dates back to ancient days. Modern science accepts this theory in a material sense, and the ancient teaching is an extension of the same principle to all planes.

Briefly, everything manifested, both seen and unseen, is energy exhibited in the form of vibration. We all know that what we call sound does not really exist, but that it is a sensation in the brain caused by vibrations in the air impinging on the drum of the ear. These vibrations in turn stimulate a nerve that produces in the sensorium of the brain a sensation which we call sound. We know that there are vibrations of energy in the luminiferous ether which enter the eye and stimulate the optic nerve through the rods and cones of the retina, and this is transmitted to the brain causing a sensation that we call light. The universe is a mass of energy. Our imperfect senses enable us to 'sense' a very limited range of vibration only. This produces certain sensations in our brain, but if our senses were different, or had a wider range, that which we should then sense would be something quite different from our present idea of things. The man in the street thinks that everything is as he sees it, hears it, or otherwise senses it, yet a little thought would show him that he is only receiving sensations from 'something' which he does not understand.

As Sir W.F. Barrett pointed out in his book *Creative Thought*, what we see around us is a sort of reflection of our own mind. He says: 'The world around us is the projection of a series of phantasms from our own minds, created, it is true, by stimulus received through one or other of the organs of sense. Take the case of vision. External objects form a minute inverted image of themselves on the retina, as they do on a photographic plate in the camera. The retinal image is transmitted to the brain: a certain tract of nerve-cells is therefore stimulated: this multitude of separate stimuli our ego collects into a coherent whole, and we then mentally project outside ourselves a phantasm of the object, apparently as big and erect as the object really is. But the appearance is the creative act of our own mind, and leads us, rightly or wrongly, to think that the appearance is a real objective thing resembling the thing in itself'.

Again, as another illustration, let us take the case of water. Water, when at a low rate of vibration, freezes and becomes solid ice. As the temperature is raised its vibrations become more rapid and it becomes fluid, and, if the temperature is raised high enough it is converted into steam.

Yet again, a poker is a piece of black iron, yet if it is placed in the fire the vibrations of its particles become raised and it changes to the colour of red. If the rate is raised still higher, the poker becomes white instead of red.

These crude illustrations show us how a difference in rate of vibration affects matter, but still greater changes take place when we deal with mind.

Matter, mind and spirit are all manifestations of the one eternal Energy. Matter, in spite of the incredible speed of its vibrations, is of a low rate of vibration compared with mind. Mind, although much higher than matter, is of low vibration compared with spirit. Spirit, it is said, is of so high a vibration that it is apparently motionless, just as a wheel when revolved very rapidly appears to be at rest.

According to this teaching, then, all is vibration on all planes. So complex is the universe and all its different rates of vibrations that we can only deal with the subject in a very broad and general way.

The highest vibration of all is called the positive pole and the lower vibrations are spoken of as the negative pole. The reality is at the positive pole; all else is unreality, for the negative pole is the reality seen or 'sensed' imperfectly through varying degrees of negative or lower vibrations. This explains why in metaphysics we deny evil, as a reality, and why some even deny the existence of matter, and thereby arrive at a knowledge of the Truth.

The ancient teaching speaks of the lower vibrations and negative poles as though they had a real existence (not in an absolute sense, but purely relative). This really agrees with our own teaching. In this consciousness we see everything in the form of pairs of opposites, good and evil, light and darkness, and so on. They have no reality. They are relative, not absolute. They belong solely to this present limited consciousness. Good, or the positive pole of things, is the abiding reality. Evil is the negative of good, and absence of the reality, good. By turning always to Christ (Good) by believing only in good, by thinking only good, by believing that only good can come to us, by living always in the consciousness of good, by choosing always the good, the beautiful and the true: by so doing, our thought life becomes polarized. We become established in good, the only reality. Our vibrations become raised to a higher pitch, so that we behold the real universe, through the eyes of the Divine Man, the Eternal Son, perfect, whole, complete—beautiful beyond compare.

It is all a question of polarity and vibration. The masters have to climb patiently from low vibrations to higher, and the higher they climb, the nearer to perfection do their lives become. This upward climb is open to all. The Reality is Perfection, God's Perfect Idea, *and every soul can climb this way, by raising the rate of its vibrations, through the transmutation of its thoughts from negative to positive.*

We have already said that your life exists, as a perfect life, complete in every detail, in the mind of God. Your life in the Great Reality is perfect, in health, in love, in service, in happiness, in abundance, in peace, in harmony. All departures from this perfection are due to low vibrations: to negativity; to an absence of the reality, good. All the events in your life are perfect events: every incident is a manifestation of Divine Love.

Think of it, your life is perfect! What is necessary is to realize it and live in that realization. A difficult task, you say? Yes, but it is possible, in course of time, by training and self-discipline.

Your Real Self

Real man is not what, to these limited senses, he appears to be. The real man is spiritual, a spark from the Sacred Fire, a true son of God. Just as your life is perfect in the Divine Idea, so also is your Higher Self, or real man, eternally perfect in the mind of God. 'In heaven their angels do always behold the face of my Father which is in heaven.' This Guardian Angel or Higher or Real Self is, like our lives, a perfect creation of a perfect God. In the East, this Spiritual or Real Man is called the Self; in the West, we call it the Indwelling Christ; some call it the divinity inherent. It does not matter what term you use so long as you realize that the false, finite, material man is not the real Self; that the true Self, although it indwells us, yet exists in God's mind eternally perfect. God's manifestations are perfect, here and now; all imperfection is but the negative pole of the Reality. 'Beloved, *now* are we the sons of God, and it doth not yet appear what we shall be: but we know that, when He shall appear, we shall be like Him; for we shall see Him as He is.' In this verse is contained the great secret of Divine Union, but all we can note here is this: that *now* we are the sons of God, and that when we get away from the negative pole and see the Reality; when we behold this Perfect One, we find that we are like Him, eternally perfect in the Mind of God.

We see, therefore, that not only our life but our real Self exists here and now, as a perfect creation of a perfect God. God cannot create an imperfect self nor an imperfect life. Jesus threw light on this truth when He said: 'Be ye perfect, even as your Heavenly Father is perfect.' By this He meant us to realize the Truth that, as we exist in the Divine Mind, we are perfect. His words also were meant to inspire us to rise from the negative pole of imperfection to the positive Reality as it exists eternally in the Mind of God.

The only reality is perfection. If evil and imperfection possessed any reality, they could never be overcome, for what is real is permanent and co-exists eternally with God: neither could it be overcome by God, for it, being Real, would be *co-equal* with God. Evil and imperfection can be overcome here and now, in this life, by a process of mental alchemy. It is because the difference between good and evil, love and hate, perfection and imperfection, health and disease, happiness and misery, abundance and poverty, is purely one of vibration, that all negative evils can be overcome, here, and in this life.

We have not to create perfection. We have not to destroy evil—for the more we fight it, the more power we invest it with. We have, instead, to change ourselves from within and rise above it. In other words, we polarize our thoughts from negative to positive. By these means the vibrations of our life are raised and negative ills disappear.

To sum up:

GOD
(Good and so-called Evil)

God is Good: Infinite Perfection. God's Manifestation is Good: here and now. God is ALL in ALL, therefore ALL that really is. There is nothing outside of God and His Perfection. Evil is merely the negative pole of Good: it is the negation or absence of Good. Evil is real to the consciousness but not in reality. Because evil has no reality, it can be overcome.

LIFE
(True and False)

Our life exists in absolute perfection in the Divine Mind. There is no evil in our true life: it is a perfect creation of a Perfect God. The evil in man's environment is due to the fact that he vibrates at the negative pole of life. Disease, sickness, poverty, misery, hate, lust, have no existence in the Eternal Reality. They are the negation of God's Wholeness, abundance, joy, love, and purity. The latter are real and unchanging.

MAN
(Spiritual and Material) (Real and Unreal)

The false personality of the senses is not the true man: this is a false sense-perception of the real. The real man is spiritual, he is a son of God: he exists eternally perfect in the Divine Mind.

God cannot create or beget imperfection. Either the true man is perfect or man does not exist at all. The Spiritual Ego, the Divine Son in man is the real Man. NOW are we the sons of God.

THE WAY OUT

Man can be raised from all evils of the negative sense-life by polarizing his thoughts. He has not to alter things outside of him but to transform his mind. There must be an utter and complete change of thought. Thinking must be positive, systematic, and constructive. He must learn to see that which is invisible, and to bring the Unseen into the seen.

Thoughts of dislike and resentment must be reversed into a realization of the Perfect Love of the Divine Mind. All thoughts of poverty or restricted means must be changed into a realization of the Abundance of the Divine Provision. And so on. In this way all negative thoughts can be transmuted into their positive opposites, and this will in time transform the life, changing disease, sickness, want, sadness, unhappiness and failure into perfect health, abundance, happiness, true success and achievement.

AFFIRMATIONS FOR USE WITH THIS LESSON

'All is perfect. Nothing exists in Reality but God and Infinite Perfection.'
'My life is perfect here and now. My real self also is perfect in the Mind of God.'

In Christ we become restored to consciousness of our oneness with the Divine. In Christ God sees us as Christ, the only-begotten Son of the Father, perfect, whole, complete. By choosing the Christ way; by bringing all our thoughts into harmony with Him, we find ourselves one with Christ Who reigns in us, and is our Real Self. *'Not I but Christ liveth in me.'*

Live your life in the light of this glorious truth: *'There is nothing that really exists except God and His infinitely perfect Christ'*. Let the joy of it sing in your heart and mind. Behind the apparent imperfection, endeavour always to see the eternal Perfection of the Divine Idea. Above all, endeavour always to realize that your neighbour is perfect. See in him or her the divinity inherent, the Omnipresent Good, God's Real Perfect Man. Cease to criticize your fellows. Refuse to hear any evil about them. See their good qualities, for they truly exist. Never blame anyone else for that which is disharmonious in your own life. Look within your own mind for the cause of all outside trouble, for the outer life is a reflection of the inner mental life. Do this and your life will, in course of time, become transformed.

WEEK EIGHTEEN:
SUCCESS

GREAT AND wonderful indeed are the inner, invisible powers of Life and Spirit. For this reason, it is of the utmost importance that they should be applied both wisely and unselfishly.

One who has trained himself in meditation can enter at any time into the Secret Presence of the Most High, and set in motion Omnipotent Power. He has freewill. He can either use or misuse the Power. At the beginning, the student can set the Power in motion but, later on, it reaches such dimensions as to control him completely. Thus, a man may start forces to work on his behalf in order to achieve a personal and selfish success, only to find later on that he is the helpless, unwilling and miserable slave of a success which has become not only his master but also an iron tyrant. In the same way, by meditation of the right kind, we set Omnipotence in motion in the only right direction. The Spirit goes before us preparing the way, opening doors of opportunity, and gathering together all the required material, and also bringing to pass the necessary trend of events in order to make our success assured. It is true that this success will, in time, become our master, but not a cruel taskmaster, for it brings to us the work that we love, and places us in the only position in which we could be happy—namely that place in the scheme of things designed for us, in all perfection, in the Divine

Like our Lord, we are tempted, tested and tried. On the one hand, there is the path of service, of doing the Will of our Father, no matter where it may lead (but it will always be to our highest good). This is the way of humility, obedience, the giving of love to all, self-sacrifice—in other words, the Christ way. On the other hand is the way of personal triumph, pomp, power, wealth, fame, selfishness, self-aggrandizement, pride, and all the baubles and allurements of the world, the flesh and the devil. We have to decide which path we shall follow. God or Mammon. The Way of the Cross, or the way of the world. The way of true service, or of selfish gain. Which shall it be?

It will be seen how necessary it is to work hand in hand with Infinite Wisdom, for if we make a wrong choice the results, although they will be overruled by God for good, will yet bring so much pain, suffering, or unpleasantness that one who is wise will do everything possible to avoid them.

There is only one success possible in any life, and that is to live the life as mapped out in Divine Mind, doing the work Infinite Wisdom has designed for us to do. This implies the building-up of character. True success is a reflection of character. No success is true or real which is not an expression of character. True success, then, in any laudable branch of human endeavour, is an outward, or visible, expression of character. The good effect of winning success of this kind is obvious, for it entails the development of character. Character is the only form of riches that we can take with us when we pass on. Character is eternal and can never be effaced. The worst possible thing, apart from developing a vicious and wicked character, is to pass on with a weak, unstable and undeveloped character. The really successful man or woman is one who takes with him or her a strong, lofty, steadfast, mellowed character.

To many advanced souls, the truest success is, however, often found in humble and obscure work. Very often, many grand ideas of personal success have to be put on one side and a complete surrender made to the Divine Will, so that we do not the will of the personality, but the Will of 'our Father in Heaven'. God's ideas of success and achievement values are very often quite different from those of the finite mind. Whatever it is, however, to which we may be called, it will demand of us the greatest possible accomplishment and development of which we, under God, are capable.

A difficulty with many is to know when they are divinely guided. How, they ask, are they to know when they are on the right track or not? They can hear no voice of intuition, therefore what can they take as a sign of Divine guidance? Some people also hear all sorts of voices, certainly not those of God or of Wisdom. How can they distinguish between Astral Voices and the Voice of the Spirit? In such cases, it is better to be guided to a larger extent by the way outward events shape themselves. A door closes here and another opens there. In these events we may be able to trace the hand of the Spirit. But, failing this, it is possible, generally, to make a right decision by applying the following test to our undertaking.

(1) Is it for our *highest* good?

(2) Will it further the wellbeing of others?

(3) Is our contemplated move prompted by a desire to serve better and extend our usefulness?

(4) Is what we propose doing of such a nature that at the last day, when we meet Christ face to face (or, as some would put it, when the self meets the Self), we shall not be ashamed of it, but devoutly thankful that we ever undertook it?

If we are honest with ourselves in this analysis of self and the motives underlying our proposed undertaking, we cannot go far wrong, and we shall be prevented from embarking on many courses of action that promise well, but which would lead only to unhappiness.

While it is possible for us to set in motion forces which prepare the way for us, yet we ourselves are our success. That is to say, success of any kind is an expression of certain qualities of character and mind. As we contemplate the universe and nature, and all the wonders of creation, we realize that God is successful in all that He undertakes. Infinite Mind can know no failure and can exhibit no signs of weakness. Provided that what is attempted is attainable and along right lines, failure to achieve success is always due to weakness of character. Lack of persistence, of application, of steadfastness, of perseverance, of staying power, of patience, of endurance, of 'one-pointed' sustained effort: these are a common cause of failure.

HTH goes on to talk about apparently able people, who lose direction in their material efforts. Alongside what he says should perhaps be set the example of people who find another form of satisfaction in life, something HTH's teaching overall undoubtedly endorses. HTH speaks to those who actually believe they have failed, not to the others.

As we observe and reflect upon Nature's untiring efforts, we are overwhelmed and shamed by the patience, persistence, perseverance and adaptability displayed. God never gives up and therefore always succeeds. In Nature we see this persistence reflected, and we can by meditating upon these things absorb into our very being their quiet strength, persistent application and untiring, sustained direction of forces towards a given point, learning to be steadfast and immovable.

There are large numbers of people who ought to be very successful in life, but they fail. They have ability, foresight, vision, yet they are not successful. They build up a business or a practice, or they reach a certain standard of proficiency in their calling, and then let it slip away from them; or they get tired of their work and leave it to engage in something more congenial. They fail simply because they lack staying power, steadfastness, stability, patience, persistence and perseverance. Their weakness of character manifests itself and proves to be their undoing. With the ball at their feet, with broad fields of success bathed in golden sunlight stretched before them, they let go and retire from the scene.

Those who believe they have failed in this way can overcome by following the teaching of this letter. By developing character from within, the necessary application and staying power will be forthcoming, so as to bring them round the corner, ushering them safely into the select company of the truly successful ones of the earth.

Again, many people put invisible forces into motion by demanding material success from the Infinite, but do not build up the character, moral qualities, capacities, powers and abilities necessary to achieve and maintain (and retain) real, true and lasting success, even of a material nature. Such people are bound to come to grief. Such build their house upon the sand. There is no foundation to it. The superstructure is gathered together, but there is nothing upon which it can be placed. The consequence is failure and ruin, utter and complete. But he who develops strength of character, capacity, ability and steadfastness, builds his house upon a rock, and nothing can shift it or destroy it. Days of adversity may come, but they cannot move one who is established in this manner.

In working for success, then, we first aim at true achievement (and not its glittering counterfeit), realizing that we are at all times guided by Infinite Wisdom. By extending the boundaries of our mind, and reaching out after a fuller and richer expression of the Life within us, we set in motion forces which work upon our behalf. The Spirit goes before us preparing the way, unlocking the doors of opportunity, and gathering together the necessary material.

Most important of all, we ourselves must be prepared. We must become big enough to fill a larger position of responsibility and higher service. We can never afford to stand still. Read the parable of the talents, and you will realize why you must always be rising, expanding, developing, soaring upwards—ever becoming a more perfect instrument of expression for life to use.

But of ourselves we can do nothing. It is God Who works through us, and it is by identifying ourselves with Him that we become strong and able to develop the necessary qualities, capacity and steadfastness of character that more responsible service demands of us.

Of ourselves we can do nothing, therefore we affirm our unity with Spirit by saying,

'*Thou art in me as an infinite capacity (or, as my infinite capacity) to achieve, overcome, serve and gain life's victory.'*

'Thou art in me as infinite patience, persistence, perseverance, steadfastness, staying power, endurance.'

'Thou art in me as an infinite ability to act wisely, to work efficiently, and to bring all my activities into harmony with Thy Divine Order.'

There seems to be no limit to the development that is possible along these lines. For instance, one may be conscious of lacking a certain ability, or quality, such as good judgment. In this case one would say,

'Thou art in me as an infinite capacity to make good judgment.'

This quality, if the foregoing be persevered with, will gradually develop. In the same way, alertness, quickness, resource, presence of mind, courage, decision, or any other quality can be developed or brought out from within.

The possibilities are so vast that it is evident that we can spend all the coming years in self-development of this kind.

Having opened such a big door before you I must now bid you farewell until the next letter reaches you.

Yours for true success and achievement,

HENRY THOMAS HAMBLIN

INSTRUCTIONS IN PROGRESSIVE REFLECTIVE MEDITATION

There is no true success apart from Thee. Thou art the only success, and we can be successful only as we ally ourselves with Thee. Therefore we meditate upon

DIVINE ACHIEVEMENT.

By allying ourselves with God, and by identifying ourselves with the inherent success of the Divine Mind, we make possible the only true success. True success is not ruthless, made at the expense of other people. God does not succeed at the expense of anyone, but only by helping them and loving them. In the same way, we become successful by loving and serving others.

We identify ourselves with the One Who never becomes tired, and Who never gives up.

We identify ourselves with the One Who keeps on until everything is accomplished and all things are brought to pass.

We identify ourselves with the strong and patient One—the One Who changes not.

Through identifying ourselves with the Infinite One, our minds become expanded and capable of receiving larger ideas which come to us direct from the Universal Mind.

Through identifying ourselves with the Infinite One, the One Who knows no failure and can meet with no opposition or difficulty, our success becomes already accomplished. We have only to keep on, be patient, and never give up.

Having reached the right attitude of mind, we sit restfully in the Silence, with the thought of God's Success and Divine Achievement held quietly in the top of our mind.

Appendix

Failure is often due to an inclination to stand still, to be satisfied with present achievement, and to a desire to retire and take things easily. This is against the law of life, which is growth, expansion and progression. We must go on growing like a plant, we must expand, and become bigger, so that we can fill higher and more responsible positions, and do larger and better work. Instead of retiring from our difficulties we must work through them, and find liberty on the other side. The new life is a mounting upwards, always, to higher and better and more glorious things.

LESSON XVIII

Dear Fellow Student of Truth,

God wants us to be truly successful and happy, just as much as He wants us to be healthy and happy. Life is always trying to lead us to the highest success, and if we co-operate we become truly successful. We must remember that all true success comes from God, and we must acknowledge that without Divine help and guidance we can do nothing right. God is the *only* One Who can lead us to our highest success. Also, God is *able* to bring us to our highest success. Also, God is *willing* to do so, and wants to do so.

Success is not something that has to be won through agonizing strain and tremendous effort, but it comes to us quietly and gently like the flowing of a stream, when we fulfil the conditions.

Within *you* is the Power—the power to achieve, overcome, succeed and accomplish. Try to remember this at all times.

Yours in the One Service,

HENRY THOMAS HAMBLIN

LESSON XVIII

HOW TO BE SUCCESSFUL

First of all, what is success? It can be defined simply as the accomplishment of something worthwhile. The only thing really worthwhile is service—doing something to enrich the common life. The way of the unillumined is to endeavour to enrich the self, and to let the community benefit if it can, or even try to profit at the expense of the whole. But the unillumined never find true success. They may find a gilded counterfeit, but real success never. The illumined ones however put first things first, i.e., service to life and the world, and, in so doing, attract to themselves the truest success. This result is not seen at once. As a rule one has to suffer, apparently, for one's principles, but, over a period of years, the true results become increasingly evident.

It is only when we serve the Whole that we get into the vibration of true success. All selfish striving impoverishes the life and shrivels the soul. Gold and riches and luxury there may be, but what are these if there is an aching heart, no capacity for real enjoyment, no true happiness, no satisfaction in life? Those who 'serve' get the greatest joy out of life and the only true satisfaction. Also they attract to themselves, as far as material things are concerned, a solid success. Their character and integrity tell heavily in their favour, in the long run.

We and others are constantly teaching 'Service'. True success can come only through service. The higher the quality of our service, the greater the success that becomes possible. This is seen in the ordinary affairs of life: it is the one who is a little better than his fellows who receives the plums of his calling. One who does his work a little better every day may think that he is wasting his time, but he is, in reality, laying the foundation of a lasting success. His superior work may pass unnoticed for a time, but it wins recognition sooner or later. All true success is grounded upon merit. In spite of apparent injustices, men and women find their proper level. Over a period of years, one can see how the apparently successful fall out of the race, leaving the prizes of life to those who depend upon merit and real worth, and who give life their highest service.

How then are we to increase our usefulness and thus render higher and more valuable service to the world? By following an ideal. When we strive after an ideal, we bring the inward power into expression. We become more skilful, more competent, more efficient, more inventive, more fertile in ideas, more in earnest, more industrious, more energetic, more purposeful, more persevering, more determined, more helpful, more optimistic, more concentrated. We become a power in the world, a force (for good) to be reckoned with, because through striving after a higher ideal, we bring the greater Self into expression, and have behind us all the Power of the Infinite.

Whatever ideal you hold in your mind becomes expressed in your work. Both consciously and unconsciously (or subconsciously) you will be endeavouring to make your work more like your ideal. Thus the tendency of your work will be to grow upwards towards a higher standard of perfection.

When I started business in the West End of London, I had

hardly any money, no influence, no knowledge of West End business. I started in opposition to established firms who were wealthy and whose position apparently was impregnable. The West End of London was so conservative that, in the ordinary way, it would have taken years to gain recognition. What was to be done (for I could not afford to wait; it was necessary for me to make a living right from the start)? What I did was simple enough. I introduced a higher standard of work and a more painstaking and efficient service. The work prevailing was *good*: I determined to produce something *better*. This was done. Also I explained to all who would listen, why and in what way my work was better, and although I met with the usual British prejudice and indifference, I made an impression in some quarters which speedily led to greater recognition in others. When once the higher standard of work and improved personal service became recognized, success poured in to such an extent that in three or four years, my little business had grown to be one of the largest of its kind. By introducing a higher standard of work, I gave the public better *service*. This is the secret of success. By following my ideal, I was constantly improving and raising my standard. It was by having an ideal and following after it, that enabled me to produce work of a higher order, or, in other words, render higher service.

If I had not created a higher ideal and followed after it, thus rendering higher and more efficient service, my business could never have succeeded. Within three months it would have closed down.

This account of my personal struggles is introduced solely for the reason that practical experience is of far more value than mere theory. That which will bring success in building up a business from tiny beginnings to flourishing proportions will also bring success in other callings and in other departments of life. Have an ideal and strive after it, and success will come to you in exchange for your higher and more efficient service. The way of true success is by making yourself deserving of it. There is no other way. Success has to be achieved. It will not drop into one's lap, and it can be achieved only by ever-increasing efficiency, higher service, and by making a more valuable contribution to the work of the world.

Whatever our work in life may be, we must form an ideal of something better, and ever strive after its realization. By so doing, we make our service to life and the world of greater value. It is only by raising the value of our contribution to the work of the world that we can become deserving of greater success. It is only by meriting success that we can possibly have any right to it. We must first give before we can receive. Reciprocity is the law, and all who hope to get something for nothing are merely chasing rainbows.

Occult methods of drawing success to you by mental power are better left alone. They may draw what you want (that is if you have a hypnotic type of mind) but they will also draw to you unhappiness, and bring loss in other directions.

Up to this point, I have dealt with the practical methods which are necessary to win success, and which are absent from ordinary New Thought teaching. The rest of the lesson will be devoted to the mental and spiritual side of the subject. Strictly speaking, the practical part of the lesson should come last, but I have purposely reversed the order, because I want the spiritual part to come at the end.

Before passing on to the inner part of the lesson, let me give one more word of worldly wisdom, which is this: Do not hide your light under a bushel. Put it, instead, on a bill to be seen by all. Without indulging in vulgar self-advertising, it is still possible to draw people's attention to your work, or service, or talents. Do not retire to the background with your work which is good and honest through and through, and let a charlatan push himself forward and foist his rubbish upon the public in its stead. Let people know how good your work is. Employ all legitimate means to bring your work before the largest possible public. By so doing, you will serve more people, do more good in the world, and, incidentally, be much more successful and prosperous in consequence.

One more word of worldly wisdom, which is this. Produce

something that the world needs. You can never force the public to buy what it does not want, no matter whether it be service, art, or goods. At the same time, it is true that by following your highest ideals, unfettered by any such thought, you are more likely to produce the service that the world needs. It has been my own experience that it has always been when I pursued the highest and best that the greatest success has come to me. At the same time, it must be confessed that when in business, I was practical in my idealism. This, after all, is only commonsense, for if we desire to give a friend a present we first endeavour to find out what thing is needed.

One other word. Success in life depends largely upon love. Love combined with efficiency attracts success. It draws friends, influence, customers, clients, letters and even orders. Love is integrative, it draws together. Unconsciously, people are drawn to one who actively and positively loves. Love also expresses itself in better and more efficient service. It retains clients, friends and customers because it 'suffers fools gladly' and endeavours to please.

Have you ever realized that thoughts of hate and resentment, bad feeling or irritability do, in actual fact, keep success away? These vibrations actually drive people away. Love does tell. Goodwill, co-operation, the Golden Rule, reciprocity—without these no-one can attract success.

Having been a businessman, I naturally draw my illustrations from business life, but the same laws govern every sphere of human endeavour. A writer does not win undying fame by producing 'pot-boilers', but through putting into words the passion of his soul. The former destroys his soul, deadens his imagination, and chains him to the wheel of drudgery; the latter leads to ever-increasing power of expression. One who desires to produce his or her best must put all thought of money or payment out of his or her mind, or at any rate relegate it completely to the background. In the higher realm of Spirit, our work is perfectly expressed. Let us reach up to this Perfection, here and now and always. To do this is the only path of true success.

*

While work in the outer world of human endeavour is of great importance, and while it is also true that all success comes finally through service, yet the real *cause* of success is spiritual and can be found only in the Silence. The more we enter the Silence and treat for guidance, for direct inspiration and for original ideas, the greater our success will be. It is only in the Silence that we can find those Ideals the following of which leads to the highest success. It is only in the Silence that original ideas can come: ideas which often transform one's life with startling rapidity from poverty and disappointment to amazing prosperity and success, or from humble obscurity to undying fame. 'Vain is all human wisdom'; but in the Silence, Divine ideas rise into consciousness.

There is a work for us to do in this life, which is our own special work, and which no-one else can do for us. We become truly successful only when we find this work. We may try many things and they may retain our interest for a time, but we can never be satisfied until we find the work we have come here to do.

How are we to find our true work? By treatment: by realizing that our success is, in reality, an accomplished fact in the Divine Mind: by reliance upon Divine guidance: by knowing that our success exists here and now. While it is true that we have, in the outer life, to deserve success, to achieve success, to become more efficient, to render higher and yet higher service, yet it is in the Silence where we actually find it or, as some put it, create it.

First in the Unseen, then in the seen: this is the Law. It is a weary business working in the outer world of effect, if we have not prepared the way by work in the Unseen World of Cause. If, however, we spend the necessary amount of time in the Silence, both night and morning, work in the outer life becomes comparatively easy.

I find it the greatest possible help to realize that God is success *here and now*: that His work is not in a state of becoming, but is perfect here and now. Further, to realize that my life and my work are perfect in the Divine Mind *now*, and that my work is already accomplished, smoothes away difficulties in a wonderful manner. Although my work increases, it is dealt with far more easily than formerly.

Again, to realize that one's steps are guided every inch of the way by Divine forces, and that one is being led to higher service, greater usefulness and more enduring success, is a solid source of help.

Further, it is necessary to know that by 'treatment' we come into harmony with all the Divine Forces: that behind us we have all the power of the Infinite, and, therefore, we can never fail.

HOW TO PROCEED

We therefore have not only to work outwardly in terms of service, for without it we cannot succeed in any undertaking, but we have also to work subjectively, using our creative imagination in the causative world of ideas.

It is here that feeling comes in. By 'feeling' I do not mean emotionalism, but a feeling or thrill that would normally be experienced by one who had won a great success. In our creative mind we should see ourselves, in imagination, successful, masters of our life and circumstances, and doing the work we love best in the best possible way. We should also 'feel' the same as though our success were already achieved. We should be uplifted and filled with elation, thankfulness and joy, exactly as though we had just been told that we had won the greatest possible success and achievement.

This feeling of joy and uplift should then be intensified by praise and thanks to God, for the great success and achievement that faith tells us is already ours. This state of joy and uplift and 'feeling' should be maintained by praise and thanksgiving for as long as possible. This is the most valuable work for all. It may not bring immediate results; but it lays the foundation of a success beyond our wildest dreams. And this type of success is a manifestation of what the Psalmist described as 'the blessing of Jehovah, which maketh rich, and with which He addeth no sorrow'. No sting, or catch, or curse, is attached to success of this character, because we acknowledge that it is from the Lord, and that the Divine blessing must therefore rest upon it. It is the only royal road to success. Through subjective work of this kind, and the use of the Creative Imagination, opportunities are brought to us (they even seem to be hurled at our head); and all that we need for our highest and greatest success is drawn to us. We find that there is a Power for good working on our behalf, and that a Divine blessing rests upon all our affairs. So long as we live a 'godly, righteous and sober' life, and continue our subjective work, the blessing remains with us, enriching our lives, bringing to us other blessings also. Not only are we successful, but blessing, harmony, peace, order, plenty and freedom from care attend our way. Success that is won by human effort is often a curse instead of a blessing, or it may be achieved at too great a price. But the success that comes to one as a result of realizing it subjectively, feeling it, and praising God for it in advance, brings a Divine blessing with it, and joy, harmony, and happiness.

One of the greatest difficulties that we can experience is opposition or competition. Almost as soon as we get going nicely, someone else comes along to divide things up. How shall we meet such a challenge? Shall we resent it and mentally oppose it? No. The first thing to do is to apply love to the situation, and pray that our competitor be blest in every possible way. This may seem crazy advice, but it is the highest wisdom in Heaven and earth. To practise it, and persevere with our praying, is the secret path to a Divine adjustment of the whole situation. Love is the key, and praying for the good of those who apparently are trying to destroy us is the secret of true success. However, we must be sincere and genuine in our prayers. We must not be double-minded, praying that our competitors may be blessed, in order that by some mysterious means we can thus get the better of them. No, we must be sincere, and pray for them genuinely that they may be blessed and prospered and that their lives may become better and better. This may seem like praying for our own destruction, but we can safely leave the adjustment with God. Such action brings to us the blessing of Jehovah, which maketh rich, and with which He addeth no sorrow.

*

It is helpful to enter the Silence with the idea of success, achievement, higher service, overcoming, victory, steadfastness, guidance
in affairs, and so on. Then when you realize that the Spirit is all
these things to an infinite degree, realize also your oneness with
it all. Feel, if you can, yourself being carried along by all the
power of the Spirit, to the highest achievement through service.
Also, during the day, repeatedly recall these words to your mind:
success, achievement, overcoming, victory. Endeavour to live in
a thought–atmosphere of true success. Also, try to realize that
you form part of the Divine order in which 'Man is always in his
right place, at the right time, doing his right work, and doing it
perfectly'. You will then find that this is the case with you.

Always remember that in order to be successful you must live
in the atmosphere or vibration of success. No-one can succeed
who lives in the low vibration of failure or mediocrity. It is utterly impossible, no matter how clever or gifted one may be. The
words success, achievement, overcoming and victory possess the
vibratory power of success, overcoming and victory. By repeating these words to oneself, one is lifted up and becomes attuned
to their vibration, so that all that is necessary for our success is
attracted to us: and, in addition, we are inspired to make fresh
efforts, and to work more intelligently and forcefully. When ready
to give up, or to relax effort, or to give way to depression, just
repeating the words 'success', etc., at the same time taking a deep
breath, will carry one round the corner to overcoming and victory. Most people who give up, do so just when they are nearly
round the corner. The use of constructive, positive words would
have helped them round to glorious achievement. Still better is it
if we affirm that God is our Success, and that God is the Infinite
Spirit indwelling us. *'God is able to do for us exceeding abundantly above
all we ask or think according to the power that worketh in us'.*

Only live in this high vibration and you cannot fail to succeed.

WEEK NINETEEN:
ABUNDANCE

HTH continues to talk about poverty in in causal terms. It may be unneces-
sary to stress that the poverty he means is an uncomfortable insufficiency, not
a contentment with little, or that he is addressing hmself to readers in a
Western society, where there is an overall plenty.

MORE CONVINCED am I than ever that poverty is due to
wrong thinking. Just as morbid subconscious thinking produces
disease and ill-health, so also does poverty-thinking produce poverty, financial stringency and every kind of money difficulty.

How can you and I, and others who seek to help the poverty-
type of person, get rid of the fixed idea of lack and limitation
which is the central point around which his or her thoughts revolve? I confess that it is not an easy task. It is much easier to get
a person with a fixed idea of disease to relinquish it, than it is to
get him or her to give up a fixed idea of poverty.

Of ourselves we cannot cast the devil of the fixed poverty
idea out of people, it is only the Spirit of Truth Who can do this;
but we may be used as instruments through which a glimpse of
Truth may come. The task before us is to get these poor souls to
cease brooding over their apparent lack and limitation, and instead to meditate upon God as abundance. They may promise
to do this, and may mean to keep their promise, but they will
quickly go back to their old habit of thinking around a centre of
a fixed poverty-idea, and brooding over their poor circumstances
and limitations. They must therefore be encouraged to spend a
certain amount of time each day in meditating upon God as

abundance, say from ten to twenty minutes. Also, during the day, all thoughts and suggestions of poverty or lack must be met by statements of Truth. All such statements should be brief, to the point, and should connect the student up to God as the one source of all supply. It would be unwise for him to say, 'I am abundance, or abundant supply', for this would merely antagonize the subconscious mind. He should therefore be taught to say, 'God is my abundant Supply'. This truth should be boldly declared, quickly, without hesitation, when faced by suggestions of poverty and appearance of lack and limitation. Even if the bailiffs are in, the statement should be made and boldly and perseveringly clung to.

By making use of this statement of Truth, the student connects himself up with Omnipotence. God, maker of heaven and earth, cannot fail to deliver when this affirmation is made and adhered to. Omnipotence is invoked, and Omnipotence, faithful always, responds.

It is a crude way of presenting the Truth, but an effective one, to teach the student that he lives in an ocean of Spirit Substance. God is universal, omnipresent Spirit, or Substance, from which, by the formative power of thought, all things are made. God thinks, and out of His Spirit Substance universes are formed. Man thinks and, according to his thoughts, he creates for himself either abundance or poverty. If his thoughts are in line with God's thoughts, abundance is created. If they are not in line with God's thoughts, but are cramped and limited by human ideas of lack and limitations, poverty is produced.

No matter how hopeless the case may apparently be, if the student can only be persuaded to cease brooding over limitation and, instead, to meditate upon Divine Abundance and Bounty, his or her circumstances must change for the better. We are really our own circumstances and the latter alter only when we become changed. By meditation we become changed into the likeness of that upon which we meditate. God is a God of infinite, inexhaustible abundances, and therefore, by meditating upon God as Abundance we become changed into creatures of abundance.

Be it noticed that we do not have to meditate upon material wealth or possessions, but upon God as eternal and inexhaustible supply.

By meditating upon God, the dominant thought of the sub-conscious becomes shifted. Instead of our thoughts revolving around a fixed idea of poverty and lack, they learn to circle round the Divine idea of inexhaustible and eternal supply.

Abundance is inherent. Like health and success, it is the normal state of things for man. Sickness and failure are abnormal, so also is poverty. Poverty is as much an ailment as any disease of the body. What is required is not to create abundance by mental power, or visualization and willed suggestion, but simply to get into harmony with Truth, so as to allow the Divine Order to appear, in the form of abundant and adequate supply.

This is possible if we meditate upon God as Infinite Supply and realize that God is Spiritual Substance. All exterior, or material, wealth is merely a reflection of the real spiritual substance. By realizing our at-one-ment with Spirit, we become possessed of the real riches which fade not away; which thieves cannot steal, which adversity cannot destroy. One who possesses these spiritual riches can never lack any necessary good thing.

It is not sufficient for the student to dismiss his financial worries and, maybe, coming liabilities, from his mind, thus letting things drift, to take care of themselves. He should not worry over his troubles, but he certainly must not run away from them. They must be dragged into the Light of Truth and spread out before the Divine Mind, so that Infinite Wisdom can solve his problem and provide a way of escape. He must also reverse all his ideas of lack and poverty into ideas of Divine Abundance. He must learn to lift up all his troubles and poverty and limitation above the material level and resolve them into Spirit, in which there is no such thing as lack and limitation, and where there is an infinitude of supply and plenty.

Niether must the student think that being negatively good must, or ought to, bring abundance. People often make the mistake of thinking that just because they are negatively good, or moral, they ought to prosper, and that those who are not 'good' in the same way ought not to flourish. It is true that repeatedly in the Bible prosperity is promised the righteous. But there is a great difference between negative goodness and positive righteousness. Certain people believe that they are good, godly, righteous and better than people who do not profess to be so negatively good. As a matter of fact, there is a great deal more real, positive righteousness amongst businessmen and others, who do not profess to be 'good' in this sense, than there is among those who are sanctimonious. A Christian man who used to collect money from, and do business with 'good' people of this kind as well as those of a more worldly type, told me that he would far rather do business with the man-of-the-world type than the sanctimonious or negatively 'good' type, because the former was a straighter person to deal with. In other words the more worldly type was positively righteous and could be depended upon, whereas the negatively 'good' type had no righteousness in him or her.

HTH also deals with the problem of envy, which he sees as a trap. It may be helpful to pray 'with real thankfulness of heart, and true thanksgiving, somewhat as follows',

'I thank Thee, Father, for all the wealth of the world, and all the riches and prosperity of those who are well-to-do. I thank Thee for their castles, mansions, fine houses, beautiful gardens, grounds, parks and lands; for their abundance of money, for their motor cars, horses, yachts, beautiful furniture, dresses, clothes, refinement and culture. I thank Thee for their foreign travel, for the beautiful scenery they enjoy, for the fullness and richness of their lives. I thank Thee for these from the depths of my heart, and adore Thee for Thy infinite bounty and inexhaustible abundance and profusion of riches and beauty.'

The object of this prayer is not to ally ourselves with, or to condone the vulgarity of excessive riches, or the senseless and enervating love of luxury and ease, for, knowing these things to be evil and unnecessary, we have no room for them in our life, but we pray in this way in order to banish every trace of envy, covet-ousness, and resentment from our hearts, and to come into har-mony with God's divine law of abundant provision for mankind.

When praying, or 'treating' for, one with a poverty-mind it is useless, of course, to pray that he or she should receive abun-dance, for this could never deliver him or her from bondage. As soon as you left off praying the person would become as badly off as ever. The only way in which we can help others by prayer, is by supplementing our teaching with prayers that they may be so changed by the Spirit of Truth as to think in line with Truth and from the standpoint of Truth: that they may persevere in meditating upon God, as a God of abundance, instead of brood-ing over their poverty, and so on. The individual must be changed within. There is no other way of cure.

The only remedy for poverty is a spiritual one. It is only the Spirit of Truth which can change the heart of man so that he thinks of God in a more generous fashion. We are, however, al-lowed to help in the work of the Spirit. Let us start helping now.

Yours in the One Service,

HENRY THOMAS HAMBLIN

INSTRUCTIONS IN PROGRESSIVE REFLECTIVE MEDITATION

So we come again to the quiet place and meditate calmly and peacefully upon God as ABUNDANCE.

PRAYER

We meditate not upon transient material wealth but upon Thee, the one unchanging Source of all things.

God, the One, Unchanging, Unfailing Source of all things, we meditate upon Thee.

THOU canst never fail, Heaven and earth may pass away, but Thou art the same eternal Unfailing Source of Supply.

We brush everything else on one side and recognize our unity with Thee:

the Centre, the Source, the Fountain of Inexhaustible Supply.

Because we are in a state of oneness with Thee, Who art unchanging, we can never be moved.

Because we are in unity with Thee Who can never lack anything, we also can never lack.

Because we are eternally in Thy care, all our needs are abundantly met.

We envy no-one their wealth, but we desire that all may know Thee Who art the Centre and Source of all true wealth, for Thou art the one and only Substance.

We recognize that all things are Thine and Thine alone, but Thou dost share them with Thy children, therefore we desire to hold, or possess, nothing, but simply to use Thy riches in Thy service, for the extension of Thy Kingdom.

There is a point in consciousness which, in course of time, we discover, or which is revealed to us, through patient practice of meditation. This is the Inner Holy of Holies, the Heart of God, the Centre of the Universe, the Fount from which all manifestation springs. This Point, or Centre, is changeless and eternal. It transcends all pairs of opposites: It is deathless and diseaseless: It is unaffected by change and decay: It is the very Life of Life Itself. By entering into unity with this Centre, with the thought of Abundant Supply in our mind, a God-sense of wholeness, as related to supply, in which there is neither lack nor limitation, is added to our consciousness. When we become God-conscious of abundance, we think as God thinks on this matter, so that poverty can never have any place in our life.

So we come to this secret, holy spot, making contact with this inner Centre of centres, with the thought of
GOD AS MAN'S ABUNDANT SUPPLY
in our mind. Keeping our mind fixed on this point of contact, we say:

'Thou art in me, my Source of Abundant Supply.'

Now 'rest in the Lord'. Keep in contact with your centre and keep also the sentence just given, in the top of your mind, and remain so for several minutes. Those who find supply a difficulty should meditate in this way for about twenty minutes a day *always*. It is their chief problem, and through overcoming it by meditation they will find the Kingdom of God. It is useless to do this meditation for a time and then to get slack and neglect it. It is useless to follow it by fits and starts. It must be done perseveringly and persistently, always. When, however, the trouble has been completely overcome so that prosperity and abundance become a habit, or automatic, this meditation can be added to those previously given, so as to form part of the mosaic which is being gradually built up.

Then, whenever we meditate upon the One, and our oneness with this Divine Centre, of which we have been speaking, abundance as well as health, wholeness, wisdom, love, and so on, will be unconsciously meditated upon, much to our present well-being and eternal welfare.

LESSON XIX

Dear Fellow Student of Truth,

The supply that can never fail can come only from God. All other sources may fail at any moment, but God is able to do the impossible, for as our Lord said: 'The things that are impossible with man are possible with God'.

God, then, is the only Source, the only One Who can supply our need, even in the day of calamity and doubt. He is also able to supply all our need, even when all other sources have dried up. Also, God is desirous that we should be abundantly supplied with every good thing. God does not want us to live mean lives, but to live a more abundant life, both spiritually and materially, without worry or strain, but in joy and liberty.

'God is able to do for us exceeding abundantly, above all we ask or think, according to the power that worketh in us.' Within you is the Power—the power of God.

Yours in His Name,

HENRY THOMAS HAMBLIN

LESSON XIX

HOW TO PARTAKE OF THE INFINITE ABUNDANCE

I have never met one who I believed well advanced along the Path, who had any difficulty about supply: such a one *knows* that all necessary abundance is his and this is sufficient. Just as Hindu adepts can sit unmolested in a jungle infested with man-eating tigers, so can you and I be free from poverty and the fear of it. When we enter into the knowledge that we are indeed one with God and His Infinite Abundance; that all our wants have always been supplied, even from before the beginning of time; that they always will be abundantly supplied through all Eternity, then we step out of captivity into the liberty of true knowledge.

What is held in the mind is manifested in the life. Those who suffer from poverty think poverty, and their thoughts revolve round the thought of poverty. Moreover, in addition to this, there is deeply embedded in the subconscious mind a firm belief in lack and limitation and a dread fear of want. That people are born in poverty and inherit the poverty-type of mind cannot be denied, but this is because such experience is necessary for the development of a certain quality of soul. Those who are born without the 'poverty-ideal' have some other lesson to learn. Whatever our inherited weakness may be, *it is our duty to overcome it.* Even if we are disabled from birth or accident, we can overcome by living a life of cheerfulness and service, thus rising above our disadvantage. One who does this becomes a splendid character, and, after all, it is the one thing that matters. It is the same with poverty: one who is born into this condition or who inherits a 'poverty-type' of mind, must overcome it; for by so doing, the object of life, which is character-building, can be achieved.

We see, then, that there is no need for poverty: that it is the result of thought and a settled belief in limitation, both conscious and subconscious. It is also obvious that both poverty and the 'poverty-type' of mind must be overcome. How, it will be asked, can this last be done?

Before proceeding to answer this question, it must be pointed out that well-to-do people, if they believe in poverty and have a lurking fear in their hearts that they may, by a turn of Dame Fortune's wheel, lose all, and be reduced to beggary, are just as much in bondage as one who is in absolute want. We may be quite rich, and yet, if we fear poverty, or trust in money and its powers, we are liable at any time to be broken on the wheel of life and reduced to want. The most careful people come down in this way, and the more careful and fearful they are, the more likely are they to lose their cherished possessions. Fear and over-carefulness drive away abundance: it is faith and trust in the Law that draw to us the Infinite Supply. You are, perhaps, familiar with cases of people who have started life with ample means and who have gradually descended the scale until their means become straitened in the extreme. Such, you would find if you examined them, have the 'poverty-type' of mind. They have no faith either in God, or the Law, or the Infinite Abundance; they put their trust in money and property, thinking that these can keep them from want. All who put their trust in money instead of in God, even if they remain prosperous, are yet in captivity. They never know when their turn may come, and constantly fear that it may be next. Even if they do not fear, they will yet be in bondage, for money and possessions are terrible taskmasters. Those who are poor and those who are rich who put their trust in money, property, investments or their own cleverness, are worshippers of Mammon: they know not God: they cut themselves off from liberty and freedom which belong only to those who put their trust in the Infinite and Inexhaustible Supply. 'Choose you this day *whom* ye will serve'. If you choose Mammon you will remain in bondage: if you choose God you will enter into freedom, and hereafter never lack any good thing, although at times your faith may be tested.

Poverty and fear of it must be overcome, as must also the idea that by depending upon money, property, investments, poverty can be kept away. The object of life's experiences is the bringing of the individual into living union with God. If then he believes, not in God but in material possessions, the kindest thing that the Higher Forces can do is to knock the props from under him, thus showing him that there is no stability or safety in such things. First within and then without: this is the Divine law. Seek first the Kingdom and all these things shall be added to you.

This erroneous belief that we can ever lack any good thing, and this dependence upon material means to guard us from poverty, can be overcome by realizing that God, and God alone, is the Infinite Source of all supply, and that we, being part of the Divine, are sharers with God in His Abundance. First this great truth must be grasped intellectually, and then by constant repetition, impressed, in course of time, upon the subconscious mind. It is when head-knowledge is translated into heart-knowledge that realization comes to the soul.

Think for a moment of the Infinite Source. Think of God as the Infinite Spirit filling all space: the frictionless spiritual substance in which we 'Live and move and have our being'. The Universal Spirit's power and intelligence are Infinite. Deity thinks, and worlds are born. They are formed out of the spiritual substance of God Himself. Think of it! A thought, and lo! a world is created with all its intricate life most wonderfully co-ordinated, with all its profusion and extravagance and prodigal supply. A thought, and a world is clothed with timber and water, fertile land and abundance of food, rich minerals, and beauty indescribable. Try to visualize this. Try to 'see' this wonderful process of creation: this clothing of God's thoughts in a garment of colour and form. Having done so, endeavour to grasp the fact that *you* are a most precious thought of God, clothed in material vesture. Think of it! God has thought you into being: you are a cherished and precious thought or idea of God: you are part of Him. Therefore, how can you lack any good thing? Before the foundation of the world you were provided for in the loving thought of God. The Creator expresses abundance through all creation: it is ours to share, and if we lack, it is because we think in terms of want and limitation.

We must not imagine, however, that we can drift through life, hoping that because we 'feel good' we shall know abundance, for the reverse is the case. We must work intelligently in the external world, and humanly deserve success. (If we have 'means', then we must work for the Common Good.) Also we must ever strive after the inward realization of oneness with God and His Infinite Abundance. This is very difficult, especially for some, requiring great perseverance and persistent effort.

The Source of all Supply is Spirit. We live and move and have our being in Spirit. The Universe is Spiritual and Perfect: not as it appears to our senses, material and imperfect. If we look to material means for our supply we are in bondage, no matter whether we be rich or poor. By looking to Spirit for our supply we shall probably never become rich in a material or worldly sense but, on the other hand, we shall never lack any good thing and we shall be free from worry and care.

Until we know the Truth about supply and thus become free, we think, as material beings, in terms of limitation. We have a fixed idea in our mind that we can have only 'so much'. We also think that this 'so much' comes from a material source and that if it fails, we shall be beggared.

In place of this wrong habit of thinking, we have to reverse our thoughts and realize that our source of supply is the Infinite Abundance of Spirit. This is not easy, because our whole thought-world and our very life are interwoven with this material idea of supply and its limitation, yet it is possible. If, whenever the subject of supply comes into the mind, the mind is lifted to a realization of the Infinite Abundance as the source of all, this mode of thought will, in course of time, become a habit, with most beneficial results in the life. Those whose apparent means are limited will find their circumstances improve, while those who are well-to-do will find their cares and worries lightened.

There is a subtle source of error here. We have to affirm and 'treat' in the higher superconscious plane, but we must remember that we have still to live the material life on the material plane. Therefore, while we in Spirit affirm and enter into the Infinite Abundance, yet our material selves still have to live the life on the material, sense plane. The effect of our 'treatment' will later be seen in the form of improved circumstances; but no-one, on the strength of this, should rush into foolish expenditure or debt. We should all keep out of debt and spend money wisely.

What has to be done is to lead what, in one sense, is a double life. Outwardly, to live according to one's present means, and, yet, at the same time, to live an inward life of realization of Divine Abundance and Plenty.

In order to get rid of the erroneous idea in the subconscious mind, it is necessary to reverse one's thoughts most persistently. Every night and morning, a short time should be spent in the Unseen, denying that poverty or limitation exist in the Divine Order, and affirming the Infinite Abundance of Divine Supply. Also, it is necessary to affirm the oneness of God and man (the unity of Father and son), and that we are sharers with God and His Abundance.

Whenever you are beset by doubts and fears concerning supply, do not retire to rest until by denials and affirmations, or quiet reiteration of Truth, you have overcome them, and obtained a restful realization that all is well. It is by overcoming in this way that you gradually win your way to that higher consciousness, which, when attained, prohibits your exclusion from God's Abundance. Jesus called this higher consciousness, this union with God, the Kingdom of Heaven or God. Therefore, He said, 'Seek ye first the Kingdom of God and His righteousness, and all these things shall be added unto you'.

SUGGESTED DENIALS AND AFFIRMATIONS

'The Lord is my shepherd, I shall not want.'
'I thank Thee for abundance and prosperity beyond anything that I could ask or think.'
'Because I am established in Thee, I can never lack any good thing.'

The above can be used singly at intervals during the day, whenever faced by an appearance of lack, or when fears assail.

SUGGESTED PRAYER, OR 'TREATMENT'

'There is no poverty in Spirit, but only infinite abundance and plenty. Behind all these erroneous ideas of lack and limitation is the Infinite Abundance which can never fail. All humanity's supplies are Spiritual and its source of supply is Spirit. In Thee alone all mankind's needs are abundantly met.

'Gently and quietly I now pass into a realization that I am loved and cared for, and that my prayer is answered, and that abundance and good are coming to me beyond all I ask or think.'

*

Continue 'treating' along these lines until you get your realization clear, then bask in the sunshine of this glorious knowledge. Lean back, so to speak, on the Father's Love, in full assurance that His inexhaustible Bounty is yours.

In other words, you should endeavour to 'feel' the truth that you are delivered from all care, anxiety and fear concerning supply. You can reach a state of joy and relief such as a man with great business troubles would experience if he were told that all his debts were paid. Try to imagine what his joy and relief would be like. While you wait upon God, declaring that God's child is always in the Love and Care of his Father and that all his wants are forever supplied in rich abundance, without stint, a sense of this joy and uplift will come to you. You cannot manufacture it, but you can hold yourself receptive to it. It is a sign from Heaven that already the answer to your prayer is an accomplished fact in Spirit, although it has not yet manifested in the outward life. The realization of joy and certainty that a great blessing is on the way, and that you are already feeling its near presence, may be so strong and vivid that you expect to be able to turn round and find the blessing at your feet, so to speak. Therefore, it is disappointing to find that nothing has happened outwardly. But this must not be allowed to discourage you. Instead, you must be patient, steadfast, and persevering; keeping on with your subjective work, and continually rejoicing and giving thanks. 'Delight thyself in the Lord, and He shall give thee thy heart's desire.' To feel the joy of abundance coming to us, causes us to delight and rejoice in the Creator, and because of this the desire of our heart is satisfied. The blessing may not come in the exact form or manner in which we expect it, but in a different form or manner, which is far better than what we had hoped for. 'He is able to do for us exceeding abundantly, above all we ask or think, according to the power that worketh in us.'

*

It may take some time for the blessing to manifest, but if you keep on realizing the Truth, and feeling the joy, and continually giving thanks for a far greater blessing than you could imagine possible, the answer will come, and your life will be filled with plenty and good. Many people keep prosperity and abundance away by envying those who are better off than themselves, and resenting the fact that some people seem to have every possible good thing in life without effort. This attitude of mind effectually keeps away prosperity, abundance, and easy financial conditions, and thus make life extremely difficult and painful. If, however, they were to bless those who are better off than themselves and make a practice of it, they would become themselves prosperous, because praying for, and blessing others who are rich in this world's goods, opens the consciousness so that good may enter, and enriches the consciousness so that it becomes a prospering consciousness.

WEEK TWENTY:
LIFE IS GOOD

FROM THE CRADLE to the grave, life is friendly to us, always seeking to do us a good turn, if we will only let it. Life is a glorious privilege. It is a preparation for godhood. This is distinctly a Christian doctrine; it is the teaching of the New Testament. 'Beloved, now are we the sons of God.' If sons of the Supreme Being are not gods, or gods in the making, what are they?

Life is the great trainer. It is training us to become fit for the high position that awaits us. Looking upon life as evil, or, at best, as something to be endured while it lasts, is the cause of much unhappiness and weakness.

LIFE IS GOOD

Life is good, and all that we have to do is to meet it in the right way, to co-operate with it, instead of opposing it, in order to prove that such is the case. If we look upon every discipline and hard experience as an opportunity to overcome some hidden weakness in our character, instead of an affliction, or something due to the inherent 'cussedness' of things, we find that we go from strength to strength, life becoming increasingly satisfying and satisfactory to us.

God is not a God of trouble, difficulty, suffering, disaster, but of perfect order and harmony. We create our own troubles through weakness of character. We do things we ought not to do, or we leave undone things we ought to do, and therefore there is no health in us. We may do things which are against the Will of the Father and not in harmony with the Law of Love, or we may keep on evading our duty in a certain direction. Either of these things will produce a form of trouble in the life which, if met in the right way, will tend to correct the character, modifying or building it up, as the case may be, thus preventing a repetition of the disharmony. If, however, the trouble is met in the wrong way, either by opposition or evasion, it will result in suffering and a repetition of the disharmony—each time becoming more painful, until we are obliged, when our backs are against the wall, and we have no more fight left in us, nor is there any way of escape left, to face the trouble in the right way at last, either by submission to the Will of God, or by doing the duties, or bearing the responsibilities, we have been trying to evade.

When life seems to be restraining us from following a course of action which we love, or from asserting ourselves instead of following always the dictates of love; or when life keeps bringing us up against difficulties of a certain character, we are wise if we heed the warning and change our course of action.

It may be difficult to find out what the inward cause or weakness is, for we ourselves may be blind to defects which are apparent enough to other people. By prayerful introspection, however, the cause can be found and, when found, it must be grappled with courageously. When faced by trouble or difficulty, we should take the matter into the Silence for light and understanding to be given us. We can say: *'The Light of the Spirit now shows me where I have erred, and what is the cause of my difficulty (or trouble)'*.

If this is done sincerely and faithfully, the cause will be revealed. Then we can say, *'The Strength of the Spirit enables me to act in such and such a way'* (i.e., the opposite of the course of action that has been the cause of the trouble).

This affirmation can be used at all times when we are prompted to act in the old way. It needs perseverance, patience, persistence, but the reward is such that no trouble is too great to win it.

Of course, the very quality that we find necessary for us to cultivate must also be meditated upon daily, until it has become the strongest part of our character. For instance, our weakness may be that of doing something we should not do—say, that of retaliation, as I heard a man say recently: 'If people are nice to me, I am nice to them, but, if they try to be nasty, by Heaven, they soon find that I can be far nastier than ever they dreamed of being'. This is the old idea of returning evil for evil, and we are all prone to fall into this ancient error. If this is the case, we must meditate much upon love: love which returns good for evil never feels resentment, and which forgives to the uttermost.

Or it may be that the cause of our trouble is procrastination. If so, we must meditate upon Action, everything being done at the right time, instantly, without hesitation or delay, as obtains in the Divine Order.

Or the cause of our trouble may be a certain slovenliness or lack of clean, clear-cut precision and accuracy in our work. If this is the case, then we must meditate upon Divine Efficiency, accuracy and clear-cut precision as revealed in the Divine Order.

Whatever our weakness may be, we must meditate upon its opposite quality as it exists in the Divine character, until it becomes the strongest part of our character.

The idea of the special quality desired must be held in the top part of the mind when we are in the Silence. This should be done quite restfully, without effort. The word which describes the idea upon which we are meditating may be repeated softly at intervals, but nothing should be done to disturb the restful quietness of our meditation.

At other times, however, all that has been accomplished in the Silence must be backed up by action. If we have been meditating upon courage, we must act in a courageous way in order to let the Divine Power, which we have absorbed, find expression. If we are afraid of people looking at us, we must overcome our diffidence by taking up the most prominent position where all eyes are upon us, in order to bring the Divine Confidence into action. If we have been procrastinators in the past, we must make a hobby of doing things at once, even though this is not altogether necessary. We may offend some of our friends by answering their letters by return of post, but that is better than offending and slighting the whole of them by not answering their letter at all.

Or, if our besetting sin has been untidiness and muddle, we must not be satisfied with meditating upon Divine Order, wherein everything is in its right place at all times, but we must also set to work to tidy our desk, straighten our papers, clean up our workshop, or reorganize our business, or home, as the case may be. When this is accomplished we find that we can do more work than formerly and with less effort and worry.

Quietness and rest in the Silence and in meditation; quick, prompt, fearless action in the external life: this is the secret of progress.

We overcome circumstances, then, by overcoming ourselves. This is the only way.

Desiring for you the attainment to the full measure of the stature of Christ.

>   Yours in His Service,
>   HENRY THOMAS HAMBLIN

INSTRUCTIONS IN PROGRESSIVE
REFLECTIVE MEDITATION

By this time, you will see that by meditating upon all the qualities and excellencies of the Divine Character we build up a series of contact points between ourselves and the Eternal Father (and Mother) Spirit. Through this cumulative meditation our unconscious mind is taught to know God as One, Good, Wholeness, Health, Love, Wisdom, Justice, and so on. As soon as we meditate upon God and our oneness with our Divine Source, through all these points of contact, or recognition, Divine Life flows into us, building us up in the very qualities which we have associated with God, in our progressive meditation. We thus make use of the well-known mental law of association.

Several of the most important 'points of contact' have been given you, but it will be unnecessary to give all of the remainder in detail, for you have only to apply the teaching you have already received to the following (and also others that may occur to you) in a progressive manner in order to continue the 'building'.

It must be pointed out, however, that each quality must be meditated upon day after day, and week after week, and, if necessary, month after months until it is mastered and becomes built firmly into the consciousness. Jerry-building is worse than useless.

Also, about once a week you should refresh the memory of your unconscious by meditating briefly upon each of the main qualities upon which you have meditated in the past. This need not take very long, but should be done deliberately. All attempts at haste are fatal and defeat the object in view. As each quality is touched on, realization and understanding should come quickly, almost at once. Then, after you have rested in the realization for five seconds or so, the next quality should be dealt with in the same way.

Now the remaining subjects for meditation are these: knowledge, endurance, fortitude, long suffering, meekness, temperance (moderation, restraint), charity, joy, peace, compassion, humility, diligence and purity.

There is therefore work for years to come in meditating upon these spiritual qualities as parts of God's character, so as to make them form part of our own.

After our meditation upon a new aspect or quality of Divine Character, we should realize and affirm our oneness with the One, so that the quality becomes ours; not by nature, but by participation, through Grace.

And now may the Grace of the Lord Jesus Christ, and the Love of God and the communion of the Holy Ghost be with you. Amen.

*

In order to help you to refresh the unconscious memory by going over the ground which has been already covered, the following brief resumé is given. It may be read over quietly and slowly, each 'point of contact' being meditated upon for a few seconds in turn.

'I worship and meditate upon Thee, O Infinite Being, Who art infinite Good;
'Transcending all pairs of opposites, all relative states and conditions:
'Who art also Wholeness (Completeness)
'Who art also One.
'I thank Thee because as there is only the One, I am included in the One, therefore, I am in Thee through Christ.
'I make a glad surrender to Christ, the Lord of Love, and in Him become one with Thee, forever.
'I thank Thee also that Thou art infinite
'Justice,
'Love,
'Wisdom,
'Beauty,
'Achievement,
'Supply.
'Because of my oneness with Thee, through Christ, all these things find expression through me.'

*

Now meditate solely upon God, basking in the Light of His Presence.

LESSON XX

Dear Fellow Student of Truth,

There is an Infinite Intelligence, working through love, that is guiding us every step of our journey. We are not friendless and alone, we are 'shepherded' the whole time. David realized this when he made his great affirmation. 'The Lord is my shepherd, I shall not want'.

God wants to deliver us, and to bring us victoriously through the experience that confronts us, even more than we do ourselves. God wants to bring us to our highest happiness, and wants us to experience the joy of overcoming, even more than our heart desires them. There is a perfect Divine order everywhere present, in which are harmony and peace. It is God's desire that we should live in this Divine order and enjoy a heavenly state while still on earth.

God is able to bring us into this state, and is the only One Who can do so. If we put our whole trust in God, we become like a tree planted by the waters, drawing at all times upon inexhaustible fountains of spiritual life and power. To the extent that we live in harmony with the Divine order our outward difficulties are overcome, or they melt away.

Yours in the One Service,

HENRY THOMAS HAMBLIN

LESSON XX

HOW TO OVERCOME CIRCUMSTANCES

The outward life is a reflection of the greater life within. What we are 'in ourselves' is reflected in our outward circumstances. If there is lack of harmony within, there must be disharmony without. This lack of harmony may manifest in various ways, not necessarily meaning poor and sordid surroundings, for the lives of many well-to-do people are often far more difficult and unhappy than those of people of limited means.

The object of life is not to dry-nurse us and treat us like helpless babes, but to give us tasks which 'extend' us, thus making us stronger by degrees.

There are two erroneous ways of dealing with circumstances: first, the way of evasion, of trying to fight against circumstances and change: of resisting the experiences and discipline of life. Secondly, there is a weak acceptance of life's trials, environment and circumstances: a surrender to difficulties instead of overcoming them by learning their lesson which they came to teach.

First: the more we fight and struggle against circumstances, the more we refuse to learn life's lessons, and the more we try to dodge, or escape from, life's discipline, the greater do our troubles become. By trying to avoid life's discipline, or by fighting against change and circumstances, we fight against the Law, which is infinitely just and kind in purpose, but impartial and unfailing in action: it grinds to powder, slowly, perhaps, but surely, those who fight against it. Happy is the man who learns life's lesson willingly, for he avoids unspeakable troubles and disasters.

Most people resist change: they like to settle in a rut: they dislike very much being moved on to fresh experience. Yet life is never-ceasing change: it is the principle of life. Consequently, those who resist it are fighting against the law of life and its powers. The circumstances and changes of life should be met not with resistance but with open arms. We should seek to learn the lessons they come to teach, for when the lesson is learnt, the difficult, painful or unpleasant circumstances pass away. Unity with God's Will and Purpose is the secret of the truly successful life. In character, we must be strong and firm; while in the context of experience, change and circumstance, we should be pliable, seeking to adapt ourselves to changing circumstances, and to harmonize with the Divine Purpose that is behind them. We have come here to build up character through experience: to unfold our spiritual powers, and to bring into expression the inherent perfection of God's Idea that is within us. Thus we can harmonize with God's Will and the Purpose of our Destiny only when we meet the circumstances and experiences of life willingly, seeking to learn instead of trying to avoid the lessons which they are meant to teach.

The object of all experience is to lead us into the Path of Destiny. In ignorance, we wander away from it, and as progress

along this Path can be made only through character-building
and spiritual unfoldment, the experiences of life fulfil a twofold
purpose: they build up character and also carry us along the
path of our spiritual evolution. In other words, we are brought
into line with our glorious Destiny. No matter then what unpleasant or painful experience may be ours, we may always know
that it is necessary for our highest good: that it carries a lesson
which we must endeavour to learn: that as soon as we have mastered our lesson it will pass away.

There is no evil in the Cosmic Scheme: there is no evil either
in your life or mine. Every experience is infinitely good and kind,
and instead of resisting it, the highest wisdom is to unite with it
and to learn its lesson willingly. 'All together for good': nothing
can come into your life or mine which is not for our highest
good. There is no evil influence interfering with your life: all
circumstances and experiences are remedial, and, when they have
achieved their end, will disappear.

Until we learn the lesson which circumstances would teach
us we continue to think wrongly, thus producing the very troubles and difficulties which we desire to avoid. When the lesson
has been learnt, our character alters, our point of view becomes
changed: we think more in harmony with the Law: we bring a
little more of the perfection of the Divine Idea into expression:
the right relationship towards God and Life is established, together with its accompanying habit of harmonious thinking: the
painful or difficult circumstances, having fulfilled their purpose,
gradually fade away.

Secondly, to cultivate resignation, giving up life as a bad business and looking forward to something better in the next, or to
resign oneself weakly to circumstances, is just as harmful as fighting against them. Those who say: 'It is God's will that I should
suffer' and resign themselves to suffering, become helpless chronic
invalids. Those who think that it is God's Will that they should
be poor, remain in poverty and want. There is no more perni-
cious teaching than that which tells us that this life is hopeless

and the only thing to do is to put up with it for as long as it lasts, and then at death, by some magical process, everything will be made beautiful and perfect. 'Only a little while', they moan, 'in this dark vale of tears'. What an insult to God and Life: what a travesty of the Truth, what a waste of precious opportunities!

Circumstances, environment, painful or unpleasant or unhappy experiences must be overcome, not by weakly giving in to them, but by benefiting from their teaching; not by fighting or resisting them but by patience, unity, steadfastness, pliability, wisdom. By seeking to learn life's purpose, we enter the path of wisdom which leads to Wisdom itself.

It is a hard lesson for most people to learn that within themselves is the cause of everything that comes into their life. The majority put the blame on life, on God or on their fellows, and thus refuse to learn the lessons which love through experience would teach them. 'Pity me!', they cry, 'see how hardly I am treated, for no sooner is one affliction past than a greater trouble comes upon me'. We attract to ourselves the very experiences that we need for our spiritual unfoldment: consequently, self-pity is the most destructive habit possible, for it effectually prevents us from profiting by life's lessons. When the student acknowledges that the cause of all his troubles is within himself, and that life is absolutely just, he adapts himself to the Divine Purpose. He becomes a co-worker with God instead of being at enmity with Him.

The way, then, to overcome circumstance is to look within our own heart and find there the causes of outward disharmonies. If we can find a wrong attitude towards either man or God, or a selfish clinging to something which prevents our full surrender to the highest and best: if we find our heart encrusted with worldly ambitions and cares and filled with love of self, of earthly ties, of ease and physical enjoyment, then we can avoid unpleasant and painful experiences and circumstances by voluntarily changing within, instead of waiting for suffering to compel us to do so. It is always the dearest idol of our hearts that is taken, and when in agony and loneliness we turn and cast ourselves in utter aban-

don upon God, we do that which we might have done before of
our own freewill.

The object of all difficult experience is to bring us to God.
When we are brought to our extremity, and no-one can help us,
we throw ourselves completely upon God, and then begins the
life of faith. God does not send trouble to us 'to make us good',
but we bring trouble upon our own heads. Infinite Wisdom and
Love desire for us our highest good and allow us to attract to
ourselves those experiences which will, if met in the right spirit,
bring us to God and unite us with the Lord. We are so taken up
with the affairs of the world and its falsities, however, that if it
were not for 'trouble', and things 'going wrong', we should, I fear,
never turn to God at all. But trouble comes, and, like the Psalmist, we cry unto the Lord and He delivers us out of all our troubles. Thus do we come to know God in a new and intimate sense,
and all our thoughts, desires and aspirations are brought into
harmony with His will. Then we may forget God again, and lag
behind or stray from the Path, thus making it necessary for us to
attract further trouble, which will make us fly to God again. And
so we go on, unless we learn and practise the 'better way'.

This better way is the way of attainment. By travelling this
path, we forestall trouble by learning our lesson in advance. By
constant aspiration, meditation and contemplation we get to know
God and learn to become at one with His Will, and to surrender
our whole life to Him to such an extent as to make much of the
trouble of life unnecessary. Therefore it passes us by. If I meet
with trouble and grief, I realize at once that I have lagged behind and have not kept pace with my unfoldment. I recognize also
that if I had kept up with the unfoldment required of me, the trouble would have been unnecessary and would have passed me by.

Trouble can be avoided only by finding God. We can find
God through seeking Him. We can also find God through painful experience, if we will only take our Lord's hand and let Him
lead us through it.

The meaning of that hitherto mysterious statement of Jesus,

'Agree with thine adversary quickly, while thou art in the way with him; lest at any time the adversary deliver thee to the judge, and the judge deliver thee to the officer, and thou be cast into prison', is that we have to be flexible, and co-operate with life's experiences, and be willing to go with them, no matter where they may lead. If we do not do so, we are bound by the experience in a prison of difficult, painful and unhappy experience.

Again, the meaning of that other saying of Jesus, 'Not every one that saith unto Me, Lord, Lord, shall enter into the kingdom of heaven; but he that doeth the will of My Father which is in Heaven', is doing the thing that life wants us to do. Going forward bravely, taking up our cross of duty, doing willingly our task, this leads to liberation and freedom, and to the Kingdom of Heaven consciousness.

In other words, we have to learn to love our job, or those experiences which confront us, and which we either dread, or do not like. Many people want, or would like, to be helped. They do not like the position or situation in which they find themselves, so they want to be taken out of it, into a better job, or more harmonious circumstances. But there is no way of escape, except through loving their job, accepting it, and co-operating with it. If they leave it, they find themselves in fresh troubles, difficulties and disharmonies. Trouble follows them everywhere they go, until they turn and overcome, through accepting the situation and learning to love it and learning to do all its duties in a loving spirit. So long as we do not love our job, so long must we remain in servitude and bondage.

We have to work *through* our difficulties to freedom, peace, harmony and joy. There is no other way. While doing so we affirm the presence and power of God. We realize that Love and Blessing attend us, all the while we go forward. They only leave us when we hold back.

We not only have to bless our circumstances, but should pray for those who oppose us, even though their success and advancement may, humanly speaking, spell our own ruin. This may seem foolish, but it is not. It is the highest wisdom, It is the Royal Road to victory, harmony and peace. Jesus' words 'Bless them that curse you' are the most wonderful words ever spoken. They are the key to the greatest and truest success, and to a harmonious victory over all life's difficulties.

Appendix

At all times, of course, we should make a practice of turning to God, or our highest concept of Perfection and Good, for every time that we do so we open ourselves to receive an influx of Divine Life and Power. But when we are in trouble, this is especially necessary, for God is the only Deliverer, and we can be delivered only by looking to Him.

When faced by trouble, or difficult circumstances, we should not attempt to evade it, or them, but should go forward with confidence, affirming God's power and ability to deliver us and bring us victoriously through. Some of the Psalms provide us with exceedingly powerful affirmations or statements of Truth. The Twenty-Third Psalm provides us with several, and also the Ninety-First, and there are others. These statements consist of powerful, positive words of dynamic power. For instance, here is one: 'Jehovah, only, is my rock and my salvation (deliverance from trouble): He is my defence; I shall not be moved'. If this mighty statement is declared again and again in the face of disturbing or even terrifying circumstances, until a sense of peace and confidence comes to the soul, then the trouble or difficulty is overcome. Then what may have appeared to be evil, either melts away, or is found to be good in disguise. We have to persevere with this treatment even though our difficulty may persist. Truth is omnipotent and cannot fail, and it demonstrates itself by its own power.

WEEK TWENTY-ONE :
TRANSFORMATION

OUR LORD tells us to love the Lord our God with all our heart, soul, mind and strength and our neighbour as we do ourselves. We find no great difficulty over the first, for 'we love Him Who first loved us'; and when we reflect on the way we have been led and blest all our days, naturally our hearts bound with love, praise and thanksgiving. By thanking, praising and blessing God, and by telling Him that we love Him, we learn to love Him more.

But there is the greater problem of loving our fellow creatures as much as we do ourselves.

The magic key to the Inner Kingdom is simply Love. The extent of our love, forgiveness and compassion is the measure of our fitness for the Kingdom of Heaven. Thus it is that (as the New Testament tells us) publicans and harlots pass into the Kingdom, while the morally good, who are censorious, self-righteous, critical and unforgiving have to stay outside.

Christianity is the religion of simplicity. A child, entirely ignorant of doctrine and theology, can enter the Kingdom, while its learned elders must perforce stay outside. The latter are unwilling to become as a little child and to believe that simply by Love one can enter the Kingdom. They think that a complicated doctrine is necessary: they cannot accept the simple gospel of our Lord, which is simply that we leave all our false gods, and just love and forgive. Christianity is not a religion of the intellect, but of the heart. The advanced souls who became the disciples of Jesus were simple, unlettered fishermen. The disciple whom Jesus loved was John, who more than all the rest, was the disciple of Love. It is true that John was the most mystical disciple, yet the keynote of his writings is love.

The Kingdom of God, or Heaven, is the Kingdom of Love. It is obvious that we cannot enter this Kingdom except we conform to its Laws, surrendering ourselves entirely to love. The atmosphere of this Kingdom is the very essence of Love. How then can we enter if we still harbour resentment, or dislikes, or have not yet learnt to love unto the uttermost, in all circumstances and under all conditions?

Love is the secret power of the Universe. It is so intense, nothing can live in it that is not attuned to its vibrations. If we could penetrate the Inner Kingdom we should flee from it in pain, for it would be too much for us. But, according to the extent that we have learnt to love universally and unselfishly, we can enter the outer courts. Then as we learn to love more, and pass certain tests and initiations, we are allowed to enter more deeply and yet more deeply into the Heart of God.

Before every step forward in this wonderful life of the Spirit we are subjected to certain tests. If we conquer these tests by love we are advanced another stage and are admitted to a 'less outer' court. And so on, ever drawing nearer to, or penetrating more deeply into, the Heart of God. There is nothing mystical about these tests. They come to us in our everyday life. Somebody does us a grievous wrong. The ingratitude and injustice of it all arouses our resentment. We are tempted to resist and to think thoughts of anger instead of those of love.

Those whom we love, upon whom we have lavished our love, may desert us, or grow indifferent, or actively go against us, seeking to injure us. Others whom we have helped may prove ungrateful, take all that we have, and then leave us in the lurch. Those to whom we should naturally look for comfort and support may leave us, acting in a most heartless and cruel manner. We may be slandered. Even our purest motives and attempts at highest service and our searchings for Truth may be misrepresented.

We may be shunned or ostracized or even persecuted and humiliated in the eyes of others.

We are at first inclined to resent this treatment, to demand restitution, or justice, or to defend ourselves. But if we remember that these things are merely tests which can be successfully passed only by love and non-resistance, we can pull ourselves up before we do any harm.

Everyone who sets out on the Path of Attainment is tested in this way, and the only way these trials can be successfully met is by love and non-resistance. By non-resistance is meant no retaliation when attacked or injured, and no defence or justification when untrue charges are brought against us. This does not mean that we are to be weak and not to exercise firmness. We must still maintain discipline, but it must be exercised in love, always desiring and endeavouring to do the best possible thing for the other person, even though he or she may be working against us, or even slandering us. We must always act in love, endeavouring at all times to help and bless the one who is attacking us. For instance, if it were a case of physical violence, we might ward off our assailant's blows, or even hold him down so that he could not do any damage, but we must not hurt him or do anything but actively love him.

Then, when we are charged unjustly, and even our highest aims misrepresented so as to appear as sins, we are not to justify ourselves. 'Thou sayest it', said Jesus, Who, of course, knew this law more perfectly than any. No arguments, no justification, no explanation, but simply, 'Thou sayest it'. How unjust every accusation against our Lord.

How easy it would have been for Him to have explained that He sought no earthly kingdom, but that His was a Spiritual Kingdom. But there was no defence. This was not accomplished without a struggle. Our Lord was doubtless stung by the ingratitude, the duplicity, the injustice of the treatment that he received in return for His love; and, doubtless also, He was tempted again and again to justify Himself—'so He openeth not His mouth'.

But because our Lord overcame and was silent in face of His accusers, it is made possible for us, when, in our small way, we are tempted and tried in similar fashion to do the same as He, and make no defence. It is only in this way that we can pass the tests of initiation and enter the Kingdom of Love. Our Lord went through all that He did in order to prepare the way, so that we also might, by following in His footsteps, become fit to enter the Kingdom of Heaven. 'I go to prepare a place for you that where I am, there ye may be also'.

'A new commandment I give unto you, that ye love one another; as I have loved you. If ye keep my commandments, ye shall abide in my love.' Thus spoke our Lord. And the beloved John, who know so intimately the heart of the Master, says to us: 'He that loveth his brother abideth in the Light and there is none occasion of stumbling in Him'.

How simple! Just Love, and the law is fulfilled. 'Love is the fulfilling of the Law'. Our Lord, by His wonderful revelation of love to the uttermost, fulfilled the Law. By our loving in like manner the Law is fulfilled in our case also, and we abide in His love.

But it is not only in big affairs and crises that we have to follow the Lord of Love, but also in the small things of life. Little slights, indifferences, ingratitudes, insults, injuries, vexations, are capable of upsetting our peace, and of arousing feelings of resentment. Because of a certain little thing that may have happened, we go to considerable trouble transferring our custom from one tradesman to another, only to find that perfection is not to be found. Because somebody has slighted us, we treat him or her differently from the way we did before. There is a coldness in our heart—we are not the same. And so on. But we are in bondage so long as we allow these little things to cause us to love the less, in any one direction. If we are to follow our Lord, we must allow nothing to alter our love to others. It must shine both on the good and the evil, the kind and the unkind, the civil and the uncivil, the grateful and the ungrateful, the gracious and the ungracious, the flatterer and the too candid friend, those who bless us and those who injure us: upon all must the sun of our love shine and bless.

Not easy, you say? No, far from it. All our days must be spent in learning how to love even as Christ has loved us.

And the reward, 'If ye keep my commandments, ye shall abide in my love'. Our Lord might also have added: 'If ye love not as I have loved you, ye shall not abide in my love'. But the beloved John says, 'He that saith he is in the Light and hateth his brother is in darkness even until now'. If we do not love one another in the way Christ has loved us, we are outside Christ's love, we are in darkness and the Truth is not in us. But if we love one another in Christ's way, we *abide* in His love.

We have already spoken of God Abiding. Through the Ages, never changing, the One Abiding Principle. Deathless, diseaseless, eternal, always the same. This is what 'abiding' means. In the same manner we abide in Christ's love. There can be no falling away, no change, no breach of contract, no breaking of covenant—we *abide* forever in His love.

So here we have a simple explanation of a very complicated doctrine that puzzles many. God is Love. Therefore there is: Love Abiding (God the Father). Love Proceeding (God the Son). Love Returning (the Holy Spirit of Christ Who takes us back to the Father, because we abide in His love, if we love one another, even as he has loved us).

Every night before retiring we must love and forgive to the uttermost any who may have aroused our anger or resentment, or who have hurt us or injured us during the day. We must never let the sun go down upon our wrath. Everyone must be forgiven utterly, and blessed unreservedly. This may entail many a struggle at first but, because Christ overcame, so also can we.

We must pray for our enemies and slanderers and call down the richest Divine blessings on their heads, desiring for them all that we would desire ourselves and, more. The jilted or disappointed lover must pray for the one who has supplanted him or her. The public worker must pray for those who slander and

misrepresent him or her. And so on. There is no escape; it has to
be done by all who would enter the Kingdom of Love.

Hard, you say? Yes, but our Lord did it, and because He did
it, we can do it also by His Spirit that dwelleth in us. What said
our Lord? 'Father, forgive them for they know not what they do.'
'And now, little children, abide in Him.'

Yours in Love's Service,

HENRY THOMAS HAMBLIN

INSTRUCTIONS IN PROGRESSIVE REFLECTIVE MEDITATION

We have already used Love as our meditation, and also a list has
been given you of other qualities upon which we have to meditate in order to make our meditation complete. At the end of
this list is Purity. This is, however, of such importance that it
must be treated separately.

No-one should go ahead too quickly and attempt too much.
The great life-force cannot be transmuted all at once, but only
by degrees. If we become gradually emancipated that is all that
the Spirit expects of us.

Now I am quite sure of this that the object desired cannot be
attained by fighting against our natural feelings and desires, or
by looking upon them as evil; but only by meditating upon

DIVINE PURITY.

By thinking of chastity and continence, and so on, we produce
in the mind a feeling of repression. 'Thou shalt not' is the idea
generated. By meditating, however, upon PURITY there is no repression: there is no idea of crushing out, or smothering anything:
there is perfect freedom and harmony—but on a higher plane .

Through meditating upon Purity we become changed. Old
harmful repressions are dissolved away: lower desires are transmuted: certain emotions are transformed into pure, universal love.

Just what Purity is cannot be described; it is something far more transcendently beautiful than we can imagine, but Divine Mind knows our desire to be cleansed of all that belongs to the lower nature, from all love that is selfish. And the Holy Spirit, whose glorious function it is to pray for us, pleads for us in yearnings that can find no words, interprets our desires aright, so that our prayer, or meditation, is in harmony with the Divine Will. Through this 'intercession', or Divine prayer, on our behalf, we become changed into the image of that which we desire. In other words, we grow into the likeness of our Lord.

So then, we hold the thought of Purity in the top part of our mind, and just rest in the Divine Presence with our face turned towards the Light, with this idea uppermost. As we do this the dross and earthly desire are purged away, the lower is transmuted into the Higher, and we become changed from glory unto glory.

LESSON XXI

Dear Fellow Student of Truth,

God is Love. If we desire to attain we must love. Love is the great secret power, derided, mocked at and spurned by the world, that can bring us into conscious union with God. Love can never be defeated in reality, it can only be apparently overcome for a time.

Love is a perfect guide to conduct. In all events of life, we are divinely guided if we say: 'What would Love do?' or, 'What would Love say?' If we will ask these questions before doing anything, we shall be guided aright. If we follow Love we can never go astray. Love always leads us upward and onward—to happiness, peace and joy.

Love is the great panacea for every ill. All the trouble of mankind would vanish if Love reigned throughout the world, and all the troubles in our own life disappear in proportion to our obedience and surrender to the Law of Love.

Love is life, and hate is death. By loving all men, enemies and friends alike, we enter into life: we come into harmony with the

Eternal Purpose: we take our place in the Cosmic fellowship.
'Beloved, let us love.'

Yours in the Unity of One Service,

HENRY THOMAS HAMBLIN

LESSON XXI

HOW TO OVERCOME HATE AND TRANSFORM THE LIFE WITH LOVE

Love is the law. It controls every particle of the Universe, and the smallest detail of our life. He who breaks this law enters not into life: he knows not the light of life: he casts himself into outer darkness.

Love is of God: love is God: God is love. He who loves is of God, and the extent of his love is the measure of his oneness with God.

Hate, anger, malice, dislike, bitterness, resentment, revenge, envy, strife, unkindness, uncharitableness, criticism, the imputation of bad motives to others, quarrelling: all are destructive: all spring from one source, lack of love.

Hate, anger, malice, retaliation for injury, dislike of those who think and act differently from ourselves: these are destructive. Just as love builds up, sustains and holds together, so do these things break down and disintegrate life, health, and circumstances.

Hate and anger poison the blood and destroy health by breaking down the nervous system. Hate and malice destroy all happiness: they convert life, for him who hates, into a literal hell. One who indulges in these emotions destroys himself both body and soul.

He who hates, and who seeks to wrong others, hurts most of all himself. The more he hates and 'gets his own back' on life and his fellows, the heavier are the blows which he receives in return. Thoughts of hate are like boomerangs which come back and hit the sender: the harder the thought, the more severely is he punished. Life is like a punching-ball: the harder you hit it, the more heavy the recoil; and, in this case, it is impossible to avoid the rebound. One who hates is like a man taking a hammer and hitting himself on the head in order to revenge himself upon life or a fellow creature: the harder he hits, the greater his own injury.

One who hates can only harm himself, except in the case when the person towards whom his hatred is directed renders himself vulnerable by indulging in hate, or through weakness or ignorance, surrendering to it. He who hates or fears is at the mercy of an enemy, and the more he hates, the more susceptible does he become. Not so he who loves, and loves fearlessly, for he is protected by a garment, or aura, which hate cannot penetrate. He who loves constructively and fearlessly is in harmony with the Universe: he alone is vested with Infinite Power: all the Divine Forces hasten to minister to him.

Love is the sustaining power of the Universe. It manifests in many forms, from chemical affinity upwards, but it is love all the way. Move is the principle and purpose of life: it is the energizing power in operation through all God's beautiful Universe: it is the one cohesive, harmonious, attractive, integrating force which holds together the whole Cosmos: it is God Himself, for God is Love. The extent of the love which we manifest is the measure of our godhood. The more love we express, the more like God we become: the more godlike is our character.

One who repudiates the principle of love, fights against God and His law: he battles in vain against all the invincible forces of the Cosmos: he becomes broken on the wheel of life: he is ground to powder by the Mills of God. Love integrates: hate disintegrates: O men and women everywhere! O that you might know this, and with eyes awakened by true knowledge, enter the Path of Wisdom which leads to peace and unspeakable joy! It is by surrendering ourselves to the love principle, by loving universally, that we come into God's pre-established harmony. Love opens the door to our Glorious Destiny: it admits us to the inner fellowship of higher beings: it brings us into line with the Divine Will and Purpose.

'But', you exclaim, 'why emphasize this point so strongly? It is unlikely that your students should indulge in hate'. Do not be so sure that you or they do not hate. To deviate ever so slightly from the path of Perfect Love is to indulge in hate to some degree. Until you can love all creatures, both great and small, as yourself, you are still in bondage, still out of harmony. When you can think of everyone you know, or have known, and send out your love to them, wishing them all the joy and blessing that you desire for yourself: when you can love every section of the community in the same way: when you can extend your love to all peoples of every colour, clime and nation: when you can embrace in your love all creation and all the universe, seen and unseen: when you can love in this manner, and not before, you will enter into harmony and freedom.

Many good people think it their duty to hate. They feel that they are not good citizens if they do not hate extremists and politicians with whom they do not agree. One cannot read a religious paper without finding criticism, suggestions of motives, and other forms of hatred and intolerance. Religious people have not yet fully learnt that they can conquer only by love: that they can overcome evil only by good. The divine injunction that we should 'resist not evil' is disregarded. Well-meaning people say 'we must fight these terrible evils', and meet evil with evil and hatred with hate. Thus does human society suffer from a vicious circle of hate. Hate between politicians between capital and labour: between sections of religion: between religion and 'the World': between the poor and middle class and rich: between countries and nations. Some people are willing to love their personal enemies, but feel that they must hate extremists who are a danger to Society. By so doing, however, they create a force of evil which no human power can subdue or control: whereas by love the power for evil can be neutralized and evil effects frustrated. Organized religion has not followed the teaching of the Infinite Love, Who told us to love and do good to our enemies: therefore we have war and disease, social unrest and threatened revolution, and always shall have these things until the majority follow the teaching of love.

This tendency to hate and dislike and retaliate is innate in our false personality, our 'natural' self. It is vitally necessary that we overcome all hate, until at last we can love our enemies, even as we do our neighbour which is, as our own self.

'How, then', you say, 'can we overcome hate? It is natural to hate, and resist and seek to get even with others: how, therefore, can we help it?' Natural? Yes, but not godlike. Remember we are gods in the making, travelling towards perfection, and the weaknesses of the natural man must be overcome.

The belief that hate and resistance are necessary for our existence is deeply embedded in our subconscious mind, but it can be removed by degrees, if we follow the Lord of Love, yielding ourselves entirely to Him. We should take every opportunity of meditating upon Divine Love, especially as expressed by our Lord, and also as revealed in the way we have been led and kept all our life. In addition, we should make a point of forgiving, and expressing love towards all who have injured us, or offended us, angered us, or hurt our feelings in any way.

In the Silence, we can pronounce the name of the one who has injured us, or whom we dislike, and audibly forgive him or her, and then send that person thoughts and wishes for his or her highest wellbeing, desiring for the person the highest possible blessings of which we can possibly conceive. When we do this we enter into peace.

Further, if we practise this continually, our life in time becomes transformed. We carry with us an atmosphere of love which others can feel: we take a spirit of harmony into every place to which we go. Not only so, by the practice of love we actually enter heaven, for he who is entirely governed by love and who lives a life entirely of love and faith, has reached the end of his journey. He has become an image of God (for God is Love), and an inheritor of Heaven and Eternal Life.

Some students confuse love with passion, but this is quite a different thing. Others think that by love we mean warm human affection, but the love of which Christ speaks is an expression of 'goodwill towards men'. It means compassion, pity, forgiveness, forbearance, kindness, desire for the good of others, and expression of goodwill towards all. Expressing love universally in this way does not make us love 'our own' loss, but it makes us free from the state of isolation and separation that fills man's life with suffering and misery. Man's troubles are due to a state of separation from God, and isolation from his follow man. When we learn to love both God and our fellow man we enter into unity with the Whole. We thus see how infinitely wise was our Lord's injunction, that we should love the Lord our God with all our heart, soul, mind and strength; and our neighbour as ourself. Such teaching, if followed, brings us into unity with the Divine, so that we live our true life in God.

Our Lord, in His Sermon on the Mount, said: 'Love your enemies, bless them that curse you, do good to them that hate you, and pray for them which despitefully use you, and persecute you: that ye may be the children of your Father which is in Heaven: for He maketh His sun to rise on the evil, and on the good, and sendeth rain on the just and the unjust.

'For if ye love them which love you, what reward have ye? Do not even the tax-gatherers do as much? Be ye therefore perfect (in love) even as your Heavenly Father is perfect.'

From this we see that we have to broadcast goodwill, in the same way that the sun shines on the evil and the good, indiscriminately.

You should continue the practice described in Lesson I of sending your blessing and benediction to all men, everywhere.

It is helpful also to lift the heart at times during the day, saying, in a spirit of benediction: 'Dear everybody, I love you all, I love you; may you know God, and be filled with the same intense joy that I myself feel.'

Some students say that this is far too advanced for them: that they cannot possible forgive and hold in thoughts of goodwill those who have wronged them. It is not easy, but it is wonderful how this difficulty can be overcome through the use of the spoken word. If, through the Silence, we say to those who have wronged us: 'Dear So-and-so, I love you and forgive you, may all blessing attend you, and may you enter into perfect joy', then in time we find that we mean what we say, and that our dream has come true, and we have passed from death into life. For hate, resentment, unforgiveness are death, but love and forgiveness are life.

You may think, perhaps, that I have said very little about loving God in this lesson, and may wonder why. In the first place I take it for granted that each student either loves God, or earnestly wants to do so and therefore requires no telling. In the second place, I would ask, even as St John did, 'If a man love not his brother (neighbour) whom he hath seen, how can he love God, whom he hath not seen?'

The object of this lesson is to help you to love universally, both God and man, and to make it easier for you to do so, through explaining things somewhat.

WEEK TWENTY-TWO :
OVERCOMING FEAR

THE ONLY WAY by which we can overcome fear, I find, is by realizing that the Divine Presence is always with us, and that there is a Divine Purpose being unfolded in our life, which is always for our good.

First with regard to the Divine Presence. God is omnipresent, yet we see terrible things happening to people who are 'God-fearing': how, therefore, can this be accounted for? God is present everywhere, but it is only as we realize His Presence, acknowledge It, consciously identify ourselves with It, and live in It, that we receive Its protection, and the assurance of Its protection. When we realize that the Divine Presence is always with us, in a special and real sense, and that because of this no 'evil' can come near us and nothing can hurt us, then we not only are protected, in a special way, but the assurance we have that this is the case takes away all fear. But, here is the strange paradox, we are protected according to the extent that we overcome fear and realize the perfect protection of the Divine Presence.

This realization of being entirely cared for and protected by the Spirit is not attained by merely dismissing one's fears. This is better than dwelling upon them, but it is far from being enough. Indeed, in a sense, it is a coward's way of temporarily escaping from his or her fears; but it only puts off the evil day when fear rules, grips and dominates the person completely.

Instead of dismissing our fears, we must turn to God and affirm and realize the reality of His Presence, identifying ourselves with It.

Now there are two aspects or qualities of the Divine Presence which, if dwelt upon, realized and appropriated, bring peace to the soul and tranquillity to the mind, and they are these: Love and Order.

First, then, the Divine Presence is Love. Love cannot harm us, can never seek to harm us, and will never allow us to be harmed. All that we have to do is to keep within its protective arms, consciously. If we wander away from Love's protection, as we can do, in consciousness, negative ills may affect us. Therefore, we have to keep within the protective aura of Love by realizing, acknowledging, and identifying ourselves with the Divine Presence, always. When faced by fears, dangers and evil happenings, if we can realize that the Divine Presence is round about us like a cloud, and that this Presence is Love, our fears are dissolved (for the realization of Perfect Love casts out all fear), and we can go forward with confidence because we feel and know that Love is with us. Further, nothing can harm us if we realize Love's Presence, for Love is the only Power, and nothing can prevail against it.

But the ability to realize Love's Presence in times of stress, fear and danger is not something which one can take up and put down at one's own convenience. If we neglect the Presence when things are going smoothly, then when times of adversity arise, we cannot realize the Presence, so that we find ourselves naked and at the mercy of the elements, so to speak. This is why our Lord said that ability to control certain negative evils, or powers, is the result of prayer and fasting. We have to pray without ceasing, just as much when times are favourable and smooth, as when they are difficult and stormy; otherwise we cannot, in times of need, realize the Divine Presence of Love which can alone help us.

Negative prayers which dwell up on our troubles seem to increase our fears, for they are a suggestion, first, that danger is nigh and real; and, second, that God is afar off. Instead of imploring God to save us, or protect us, we should say: 'I thank Thee because Thy Presence is always with me'. Then an endeavour should be made to realize the Divine Presence as a cloud over-shadowing us, or as an aura which can never be pierced. Person-ally, I find that the frequent use of this prayer, at all times of the day or night, is not only a bringer of peace and quiet joy, a source of real protection, and a 'freer' from worry, but its cumulative effect is to produce an abiding sense of God's Presence, so that we can practise the Presence of God continually. This prayer can be made to become part of ourselves, so that at all times we can realize the Divine Presence as a very real thing. Then, when danger faces us, or fears assail, or unpleasant circumstances arise, or painful duties call, we can realize at once that the Divine Pres-ence, which is Love, is with us, so that we can go forward with confidence, knowing that all is well, and that Love will carry us safely through.

Secondly, the Divine Presence is Order. The Divine Pres-ence is a realm of Pure Spirit. Now, in the Spirit, there is no disorder, but only perfect Divine Order. In Spirit there can be no evil, no accident, no harmful happening, but just perfection of harmonious order.

Just as in the Cosmic Order, as distinct from Divine Order—that is, the order expressed in visible creation as distinct from the higher realm of Spirit—there has never been known a law to fail; as, for instance, even an electron has never been known to fail in its office, or to collide with another electron, so also in Spirit, to a far more perfect degree, exact order and harmony reign.

In the Divine Order, then, there is perfect harmony. In musi-cal harmony, every string or reed vibrates at the exact rate, or speed, assigned to it. In the Divine Order it is the same. Every-thing is exactly right, so that the Divine Composition is perfectly expressed.

In Divine Order, also, everything is in its right place, doing the duty assigned to it, doing it perfectly, and at the right moment.

The Divine Presence is Divine Order; therefore because the Divine Presence is always with us, Divine Order is with us too, and will find expression if we will only trust it.

As we make use of the prayer, 'I thank Thee because Thy Presence is always with me', we realize that not only is the Presence Love, but it is Order also. Therefore, everything must be right and in its right place, in reality, and if we rest calmly in this truth, all must be well.

Realizing the Divine Presence is really a complete system of metaphysics in itself. Some metaphysicians teach nothing else but Omnipresence. They affirm, declare and hold to the thought of Omnipresence, in which of course no disorder or imperfection can exist, until realization comes, and with it deliverance. If you prefer this method, you can apply it to every personal difficulty and use it successfully in the healing of others.

Not only, however, is the Divine Presence always with us, but a Divine Purpose is being unfolded in each life. This purpose is the Will of the Father, obedience to which was taught by our Lord. There is mapped out for us a life that is perfectly designed for the achievement of the purpose in view; namely, that we should become sons of God, that is, gods.

This Divine plan, being based upon infinite wisdom and love, is altogether wise, and can only desire for us our highest good. Therefore, there can be nothing so fine, or so good, or so altogether beautiful and splendid for us as the Will of God.

The Will of God desires that we should follow a certain line of spiritual unfoldment through certain experiences. These experiences are the tests of our apprenticeship. They are in no sense evil, and out of them come blessing and promotion in the spiritual life, and deeper and yet deeper insight into the things of the Spirit.

A splendid idea is being Divinely unfolded in each life, and if we will only co-operate with it, all is well indeed. Happy is the one who will each day say, in effect, if not in so many words, *'Lead me wherever Thou wouldst have me go: give me to do whatsoever Thou wouldst have me do: bring to me whatsoever experience Thou wouldst have me meet. Simply do Thy Will concerning me, dealing with me in whatsoever way Thou wilt'.*

We need to make ourselves perfectly plastic in the Divine

hands. We must be quite pliable, so that the Spirit shall have no trouble with us. We must surrender entirely to the Divine Will, and then see the eternal, all-wise purpose of God unfold.

When once this is done completely, we do not mind what comes to us in life, because we know that all is well, both now and forever. If things apparently go wrong, it is only an initiation, for we have to be tested before being advanced to higher things, allowed greater insight into the Divine Mysteries, and given greater responsibility in the Master's Service.

*

The result of realization and living in the Divine Presence, and of realizing that a splendid purpose is being worked out in our life, is the banishment of fear, care, anxiety and a host of other evils. We also develop the viewpoint of the seer, who looks upon life and its anxieties, cares, ambition and disappointments, with an indulgent smile, knowing all the time that behind it all Infinite Wisdom and Love are working out a splendid plan which has for its object our highest good.

The secret of harmonious progression is: (1) Practise the Presence of God, always. (2) Make yourself plastic and pliable, so that God's Will can be done completely and without hindrance. Further, rejoice at all times. Thank God for the privilege of meeting with the educative experiences of life and then cooperate with them instead of trying to avoid then. In other words, *learn to love the things that you fear. Do this, and fear will leave you for ever.*

All the meditation that has been taught you in past letters will help you to become free from fear by realizing the Divine Presence. Indeed, meditating upon our at-one-ment with God can only result in fearless trust, born of actual knowledge. One who realizes his oneness with his Divine Source cannot fear anything that may come to him, because he *knows* without the shadow of a doubt that all is well. But here is another paradox. Although realizing our oneness with God destroys our fears, yet by overcoming our fears we are brought nearer the Kingdom, until at last we enter once and for all, going in and out of the fold to find pasture whenever we so desire.

So we see that both methods lead to Divine Union, and therefore both should be practised perseveringly.

Desiring for you an ever-increasing understanding of Truth,
Yours in Service,

HENRY THOMAS HAMBLIN

NOTES ON THE PRACTICAL APPLICATION OF TRUTH

Having completed the instructions in Progressive Reflective Meditation, we now pass on to speak of other things that have to do with the practical application of Truth to the difficulties and problems of daily life. We will now explain how advanced workers invoke Divine Protection, not for themselves but for others. In the letter which you have just read, you have been told how to practise the Presence of God and consciously to live in it. It is a fact that one who truly realizes the reality of the Presence can meet with no harm, and no evil or accident can affect him, or if he does meet with an accident he is wonderfully preserved. This realization comes, as we have already seen, through constantly identifying ourselves with the Presence, declaring that it is with us, and thanking and praising God continually because it is with us. The more completely we can do this for ourselves, the better able are we to help others by similar means.

Now let it be said here that this power must not on any account be used (or misused) in order to avoid doing the Will of the Father. Our Lord could have prevented, quite easily, His arrest, trial and crucifixion, but He would not. But while we must not use it in this way, we may use it quite legitimately as a protection against negative ills and disorder, and also to help us through all the experiences which we are called upon to meet. So long as the Divine Presence is with us, all must be well, and the end glorious beyond expression.

It is the same with helping others. While we must not use our powers in order to cheat those whom we desire to bless of life's experiences, we can help them by keeping them safe from negative ills and disorder, and also assist them to go through the trials, tests and experiences they are destined to meet. How far you are justified, however, in helping others in this way, I must leave to your own judgment. All will not think alike on this subject, but the *modus operandi* is as follows.

Enter the Superconscious, then think of the 'patient' and commit him or her into God's care, saying, *'Now I commit —— wholly and entirely into Thy care. May Thy Presence be with him or her, enveloping him as a cloud'* (if you can, picture the patient enveloped by a luminous cloud of Spirit, Divine Presence) *'and may Thy Spirit go before him or her preparing the way. I thank Thee because in Spirit, there can be no disorder, accident or violence, but only Love, Harmony, Peace and Divine Order. I thank Thee, also, because no evil can penetrate Thy Divine Presence, in which —— is enshrouded, and therefore, nothing can hurt or destroy. I thank Thee, because Thou art the ONLY protection. There is no protection whatever apart from Thee. I thank Thee because Thou art perfect protection and nothing is difficult with Thee: it is as easy for Thee to protect—— when he or she is in fearful danger as it is when he or she is quietly at home; it makes no difference whatever to Thee. Therefore, because I have committed —— into Thy care, he or she is perfectly safe. I thank Thee because Thou art the hearer and answerer of prayer and because of this —— is absolutely safe, safe in Thee'.*

Now rest for a time in the knowledge that the one you are praying for is perfectly safe, as safe as God himself, because he or she is in God and around him or her is the Presence of God.

After resting for a time in the Truth, go about your daily duties with calm assurance that all is well.

At the close of each day, thank God fervently for answered prayer. Thanks and praise draw us nearer to God and open up the Truth to us more than anything. The more we thank and praise God, the more quickly we enter into His heart and realize our oneness with Him.

LESSON XXII

Dear Fellow Student of Truth,

We can never overcome worry, fear, anxiety and care except by knowing the Truth. It is the Truth that sets us free. The Truth is that there is nothing to fear, nothing about which to worry. All is perfect here and now. The evil that we sense is not real, and it cannot come near us if we deny it and turn to God Who is all there is—the only true Reality and Perfect Love and Peace.

God is All in All and is Infinite Love. Therefore there is nothing but Love, all sense-evidence to the contrary notwithstanding. All is Love: therefore, O fearful one, what is there to fear? Perfect Love casteth out fear.

All fear is generated in our own thought and in our own heart. Get rid of the thought; expunge the erroneous belief from the heart; and we realize the Truth, which is that there is in reality nothing to fear, neither has there ever been anything to fear. The extent of our protection is the measure of our faith and understanding. The more that we rely upon God, the greater our security becomes. There is no danger to fear: no evil of which to be afraid: there is only the Infinite Love.

Yours in the Confidence of True Knowledge,
HENRY THOMAS HAMBLIN

LESSON XXII

THE OVERCOMING OF FEAR, WORRY AND CARE

The greatest enemy of the human race, after hate, is fear: yet to the emancipated soul there is nothing to fear.

One who realizes that Christ is within him and who enters the Spiritual Consciousness, *knows* that only the highest good can come into his life. He knows that he is protected by invisible forces. With such people, 'None can pluck them out of my Father's hand'. Pitiable indeed is the state of many who fear: they dread the postman's knock, fearing that he brings bad news: they dread the future, seeing it peopled with phantoms of evil.

One of the principal objects of this life is the overcoming of fear. We are born with it in our heart, many of us, and we can know no peace until it is cast out. Worry and care are due to fear, not to circumstances. Those who think that if their circumstances improved, they would cease to worry, are far from the true wisdom, for no matter what these might be, they would still be anxious. The cause of anxiety is not in circumstances, but in the fear which haunts the subconscious mind. This fear can never be overcome until the soul enters into its right relationship with God, and knows, in a very real sense, that the Divine Presence is always with it. When this awareness of God's Presence is experienced, the soul realizes that it is continually protected and therefore only the highest good can come to it. Circumstances can never overcome one who has no fear; for one who is fearless and filled with faith in God, the All Good, possesses a Divine Power which is far greater than circumstances.

The cause of fear, then, is an inherited weakness, the overcoming of which is one of life's greatest privileges. Fear has to be overcome, for it poisons the life, robbing it of all peace and true happiness. It makes life a nightmare instead of a continual joy. It robs us of achievement: it is the cause of failure, of limited means, of illness and disease.

Many people know that fear and worry are destructive but cannot overcome them. They try not to worry, but it gets the better of them, and the first little thing that apparently goes wrong in their life will make them so anxious that they can neither rest nor sleep, nor attend properly to the duties of life. They have an intellectual knowledge of the evil and futility of worry but this knowledge is not realized inwardly.

It is not my desire to dwell upon the negative aspect of worry, but it must be pointed out that it is the cause of many negative ills. It has often been noticed that worry and anxiety are often associated with certain organic diseases. That is, the latter develop after long periods of worry, grief and anxiety. If such spells of worry, etc., could be avoided, the diseases would not develop, for the life-forces would not be depleted and would thus be able successfully to maintain a healthy tone, making a diseased condition impossible. It will thus be seen how true religion is the greatest possible preventive of organic disease. True religion is trusting and loving God to such an extent that fear and worry are impossible. If we know and realize that God is Omnipotent and that we are safe in His care; and if we know and realize also that only good can come to us and that all things work together for good, then it does not matter what 'happens': we know that all is well and that there is nothing to fear. If we have this realization, all fear, strain, anxiety and worry pass away. We simply rest in the Divine love.

Again, if we realize that God is Love and Omnipotent and that we are His, then Perfect Love casteth out fear. We *know* that we are safe in our Father's Love.

But while it is easy to have a theoretical knowledge and understanding of the safety of the soul that knows and loves God, it is quite another matter to realize the truth to such an extent as to be able to rest quietly in God, calmly and happily, although beset before and behind with trouble. The overcoming of fear is an important initiation: it is a great achievement in this spiritual life: it can be possible only as a result of much earnest seeking after God.

The 'happenings' of everyday life will provide you with all the experiences you need in order to learn your lesson of trust and rest in God. Every now and again, when a wave of fear comes upon you, or a first-class worry begins to develop, do not try to avoid it, or merely dismiss it from your mind, or try to forget it by going to some entertainment, for if you do you will find that the trouble will only get worse and will have to be faced just the same. The great secret is to face the matter boldly, retire to the secret place and overcome the worry, or fear, thus attaining to a state of peace, before retiring to rest.

You will find it a great help to keep on declaring the truth that God is Love, that you are in His care, that nothing can harm you; that you are being led by the Spirit, and that everything must, and does, work together for good. Another way is to read over and over again the Twenty-Third Psalm, 'The Lord is my Shepherd'. This is full of sublime positive affirmations which have brought peace to countless thousands. Also the Ninety-First Psalm is another series of positive assertions of eternal Truth, which if read over and over again and meditated upon, cannot fail to bring rest and peace to the soul.

The great thing, which is so vital, is to overcome the fear or worry before retiring for the night.* Just as it is necessary that you should not let the sun go down on your wrath, so also is it equally important that you should not retire to rest until you have overcome your fear, worry, or anxiety. It does not matter what means are adopted so long as you wait upon God and find rest in Him, instead of trying to find it in any human expediency or virtue of your own. Rest, peace, safety, and freedom from all anxiety can be found in God, and in God alone.

It is of the utmost importance that you should turn your thoughts away from your worry, care, or perplexity to God, and cease trying to solve it altogether. It is useless to try to enter the Silence if the mind is occupied in trying to find a solution to your problem. This is sheer waste of valuable time and opportunity. What is needed is that you should

Cease thinking of your trouble

or trying to solve it, and turn to God Who can and will put all things straight for you, and work everything together for your good.

As soon as you find yourself again thinking, planning, scheming, fearing, stop thinking in this way, and turn again to God. Keep perfectly quiet, and allow His peace and calm to flood your mind.

'Very difficult', you may say. Yes, and that is why the use of

*This implies that we should start early, since worries and other negative emotions tend to get worse as we get tired!—*Editor*

statements of Truth, and the repetition of certain Psalms are recommended. These keep the mind stayed upon God and Truth, so that it cannot wander to your worry or trouble. Remember that all that is necessary is that you keep your mind stayed on God and enter into his peace. Your difficulty, trouble, perplexity, or the cause of your fear or worry will be removed automatically. Finding God is the great thing, after which Divine Order manifests, and all things are added.

The secret of Divine Protection is simply one of consciousness. No evil can come near us if we can overcome the fear of it and trust entirely in God. No material means can protect us. Even if we surround ourselves with guns and barbed wire we cannot, by so doing, keep away evil. On the other hand, by realizing *that there is nothing to fear* and that we are actually in the Divine Presence—kept by Infinite Love and led by Infinite Wisdom to our highest good—we are safeguarded in absolute security and peace.

We have to bear in mind that fear is due to suggestion. If the suggestion is refused, the fear is overcome. If we accept the suggestion, then fear becomes our master and has a harmful effect on the life. We should look upon fear and doubt as temptations of the devil, and think of it as a sin to give way to them. As a child of God, the least that one can do is to trust God, and never doubt His ability to care for us, and deliver us. In the face of trouble and fear, we should affirm the presence and power of God. We should bless every situation, and give thanks to God for the experience that causes our fear. If we go right up to the experience, and thank God for it, bless it, and declare that there is a blessing in it, and that nothing but good can come out of it, and that only our highest good can come to us, and then ask God to lead us through it, it is revealed to us that God can lead us only to our highest good, and as soon as we realize this we enter into a state of peace and joy unspeakable.

Whichever method we employ, we must keep on working away at it until we enter into a state of peace. The Scripture says: 'Let

not the sun go down on thy wrath'. We might equally well say:
*'Let not rest come to your eyes until you have won the victory, 'and have
entered into peace.'* We should not retire until all fear, worry and
care are dissolved in a realization of God's love and care.

A very simple method that has been found very effective with
some students is to meet fear and worry with the following statement that should be repeatedly used.

*'There is nothing in all the world that can make me afraid. I am estab-
lished in God, upheld by the arms of Divine Love, and have behind me the
Supreme Power of the Universe.'*

Notes on Lesson XXII

It has to be emphasized and reiterated that waves of worry and
fear have to be dealt with most energetically. No calm or weak acceptance is of any use. Although at times I speak of non-resistance,
this does not mean that we are to accept suggestions of evil, or
make ourselves victims of negative forces, states, or conditions.
As soon as we become conscious of a sense of impending evil,
we should declare Truth and seek the secret place of the Most
High until it is overcome and we enter into peace. This is necessary, not only for our own peace of mind but equally for the sake
of those who are either consciously or unconsciously dependent
upon us. Several times when I have experienced a sense of impending evil, I have set to work to realize Truth in its place. Afterwards, I have been told that the threatened evil was safely
negotiated by the one in trouble, although at the time I did not
know who was in trouble or what the nature of it was. In each
case, the evil was either passed by altogether, or there was what
is called a miraculous deliverance and preservation.

In order to break up the impending evil, or wave of worry,
we have to get down to bedrock Truth, Divine Principle, and the
realities of Eternal Being. We have to declare what God is, and
what man truly is in God, and find rest and peace in realizing
this. We have to convince ourselves of Truth, and fill our mind

with Truth, until every suggestion of evil, and every thought of worry and care, is crowded out, so that only Truth occupies our consciousness.

First of all, then, we have to realize what God is. We have to fill our mind with the Truth about God. We can say:

'God is Love,
'God is Omnipotent,
'God is the Only Power,
'God is All Wisdom,
'God is All Intelligence,
'God is All Knowledge,
'God is All Understanding.
'God is the One Reality, and
'God is Good,'

until a certain sense of understanding comes to us.

Then we can say:

'God's love enfolds us.
'God's grace sustains us.
'God's mercy saves us.
'God's power delivers us.'

Further, we can say:

Man is a child of God, a spiritual being inhabiting Eternity. He is supported by Divine Love and Power. He is surrounded by Divine Forces. He lives always in a state of Divine order. No evil can come near him, nothing can hurt or destroy, for he is sustained by Divine grace and underneath him are the everlasting arms. Man is in Truth the beloved child of God; living in the perfect Divine order; he is always in his right place, doing his right work, at the right time and doing it perfectly.

As we persevere in this way, fear and worry and that which may be causing them are destroyed in a realization of Truth, and then we know that all is well.

WEEK TWENTY-THREE :
OVERCOMING GRIEF

IT IS OF supreme importance that we rise above grief and dis-appointment. Grief is probably the most destructive of all emotions or mental states. Also, to those who love deeply and strongly, it is the most difficult with which to deal. To lose one who is far dearer to us than life itself is a tremendous blow. His or her sufferings tear us far more than any suffering of our own could do. The more unselfish our love, the more our heart is torn because they suffer, or when we think of their sufferings before they left us. The years go by, yet when we think of what happened then, we find that the wound in our heart is still open and capable of giving us acute pain.

But calamities and griefs, losses and disappointments in life can be turned into stepping-stones to higher and better things. Instead of being beaten in life, and by life's experiences, we can become victors and conquerors. But of this, more later.

I said that grief is the most destructive of all emotional states. It is, because it not only lowers the tone of the body, laying it open to serious organic disease, but it may also disintegrate the whole life. One who gives way to grief ceases to strive. He or she drops out of things. Also, the negative state of his or her mind attracts negative ills, so that worry, care, loss, failure may become constant companions. This, in turn, adversely affects the health, so that a vicious circle is set up, the destructive effects of which can be readily imagined. Further, one absorbed in his or her griefs may repel friends. They cannot put up with the gloom, so they seek those who are more cheerful and inspiring.

HTH talks at some length about grief, not ignoring the fact that it is a
perfectly natural emotion which has to be allowed and faced.

As we have already seen, the dark and difficult times of life
are, in one sense, far more valuable and helpful than the happy,
bright, easy periods. The latter frequently draw us from God,
and lull us into the slumber of spiritual death; while the former,
if overcome, bring us nearer to the heart of God. It is falling into
the slumber of spiritual death, while passing through prosperous, happy times, that makes it necessary for us to pass through
times of loss and suffering in order that we may be awakened
and thus saved from spiritual destruction. We always attract to
us the experiences that are best for the soul. But we must overcome them or rise above them; otherwise, instead of being of
the greatest possible help, they become evil to us, although really
they are the very best thing that could come to us.

If then we rise above grief, loss and disappointment, every
possible good and advantage become ours; whereas if we do not
overcome, then every ill is intensified, and our life, both spiritual
and physical, is hindered greatly.

It is, then, the most vital necessity that we go forward, overcoming, or rising above, all our griefs and sorrows. If we do this,
life becomes a glorious victory, for we make stepping-stones to
higher attainment of those things which otherwise would sour
and embitter us, disintegrate our life, and make all spiritual
progress impossible.

How can we overcome, or rise above, our griefs and sorrows?

'Rise above' is an expressive term, for we overcome our griefs
and sorrows only by rising above them. Out of the depths of our
disappointment, grief, sorrow and heartache we can rise on the
wings of faith to the realm of Spirit, the presence of God, and
realize the truth that all is well, for all is love. We can realize, as
never before, that all life's experiences are based upon infinite
wisdom and love: that God makes no mistakes: that He overrules everything for good: that all is well and all is good: that we
can only see with finite vision a fragment of the Divine Plan and

Purpose, and therefore cannot see the Good behind the seeming evil. By our doing this with perseverance, realization comes again to our soul that all is well, a thousand times well: that we are being divinely guided: that all Heaven is helping us upward: that all the Divine Forces are ministering to us.

When overwhelmed by the first shock of a great sorrow, we may be numbed and stricken to such an extent that we cannot realize anything. The light may have gone out of our sky, the foundations may have slipped from under our feet, and we may feel utterly crushed. At such times we must look up, even if we see no light. We must act by faith in the darkness, just as we did, by sight, when we were in the light. Continually turning to God, persistently, is the great secret. If we do this perseveringly, light and consolation come to the soul, just as surely as dawn follows night. If we cannot realize that all is well, and that God is love, we can yet affirm it. If we do this, light and understanding must follow.

Then commences the second, higher stage: blessing and praising God for the experience. When we can praise God for the cause of our grief, thanking God for the painful experience itself, we have gained a great victory. Then we find and realize, in the very depths of our soul, that all is Love indeed. Then we become greatly humbled, for we realize that it has been our imperfection that has made the blow necessary. All spiritual realization or experience makes us humble in heart. If it does not, we are not meeting it in the right way. Every experience reveals to us more deeply the infinite love and tenderness of God.

Not only does praising God for the greatest sorrow and loss of our life enable us to rise above our grief, so that neither sickness, disease, nor financial ruin are induced thereby, but, which is of far greater importance, it brings us into intimate fellowship with God. When we have passed through deep waters; when all God's billows have passed over our heads, and yet we have lived through it all and learned to praise God, then we are admitted to an inner fellowship, wherein we know God as Infinite Love in a manner such as we have never known before.

It is a good plan ever afterwards to start our prayer or meditation with praise and thanksgiving for the greatest grief of our life. Most of us have experienced a great, calamitous loss that has split the heavens above us, and rent the ground under our feet—a grief so great we dare not speak of it. This is the event for which we should praise God most. As we praise Him in this way, realization of God's infinite love towards us comes to our soul, so that we know God, as Love unsearchable, in a way such as can never be described.

There are many earnest Christian people who have learnt not to rebel, and to be resigned to God's Will. But they have not really overcome. They have not risen above their grief and sorrow. They suffer in many ways from the negative effects of grief. Their face is sad. They carry the marks of their troubles in their care-lined face and bowed shoulders. But the one who has learned to praise God for the greatest sorrow of his or her life is lifted up and transformed. His or her face becomes softened and luminous with the inner joy of heaven. Those of spiritual understanding can read in such a face the story. They say, 'Here is one Who has come through deep trouble and has found peace: here is one who, while yet in the body, has entered the precincts of heaven'.

It is not sufficient, however, that we praise God in our prayers: we must also continually raise our thoughts to God during the day, thus rising above our griefs and sorrows. As soon as sad thoughts come to us, threatening to overwhelm us, a statement of Truth should be used, *quickly*. A few simple words will do, such as, *'Thou doest all things well'*, or, *'Thou dost overrule everything for good'*, or, *'All is well, all is love, Thou, O Lord, dost make no mistakes'*. Or even the single word *LOVE* repeated over and over again may prove sufficient. Whatever words may be used they should connect us up with the Supreme Love, Wisdom and Power, acknowledging His sovereignty and power to restore all things and overrule everything for Good.

Whatever is done, or whatever methods are employed, the thoughts must be raised *above* all grief, sorrow and depressed feelings. Depression is the cause of illness, ill-health, disease, sickness, loss, poverty, isolation, friendlessness, misery and spiritual darkness and impotence. If we rise above sorrow, grief and depression, then wonders and joys beyond description become ours. If we raise our thoughts Heavenwards all the Divine Forces can help us. If we allow ourselves to remain in the gloom, Heaven itself is powerless to help us. It is helpful to affirm:

'I raise my thoughts up to Thee, O Christ, and Thy Heaven, and all the Divine Forces minister to my eternal joy.'

No matter how deep the wound in our heart may be, no matter how great may be the blow that we have received, if we follow the teaching of this letter, which is the fruit of experience, we cannot fail to rise above the apparent ruins of our happiness, love and life to find, in God and His Love, peace and joy such as we never knew before. Further, the negative effects of sorrow cannot affect us, because, having risen above our grief, we have risen above its effect also. Therefore, instead of sorrow, grief and loss being a hindrance to us, they become the greatest possible help to us in our advancement, especially in spiritual things. All troubles in life are opportunities to overcome, not by rebelling against them, but by rising above them, getting nearer to the heart of God.

Desiring for you this greatest of victories,

Yours in the Service of the Spirit,

HENRY THOMAS HAMBLIN

SPECIAL INSTRUCTION

Although realizing our oneness with our Divine Source is a panacea for every ill, yet I know that it is a long time before we can realize this completely and fully. Therefore, some additional instruction is needed which will help the student to meet the problems and difficulties of life. One of the greatest problems is how to be sure of, and make use of Divine Wisdom and Guidance. Many desire to be guided by Infinite Wisdom, but can never be sure of such guidance. They pray about their problem, but no guidance seems to come. Now the secret of advanced working is this: to cease striving and struggling on the surface, fighting, attacking, resisting, and so on, and retire instead to the inner life, relying upon the Spirit to put all things right. On the outside, we carry on our usual duties without resisting or fighting, thus letting apparent evil have its way, but we commune greatly and perseveringly with the Inner Power of the Spirit. No matter how hopeless things may appear outwardly to be, the Spirit can sort them all out, unravel the tangled skein of our life, and manifest Divine Order in place of human disorder.

We retire, then, to the inner life, making contact with the Spirit, realizing that God alone can unravel the tangled skein, that God alone can bring order out of disorder, that God alone can lead us into the only path that is the right one. Having realized that God is the only One Who can deliver us, we next realize that it is perfectly easy for God to do, simply because His mind is infinite. There is no difficulty on the Divine Side: all the difficulty is on our side, because of the finiteness of our mind. It is just as easy for God to deliver us out of the most hopeless difficulty as it is for a champion chess player to solve what to a relatively poor player appears to be an unsolvable problem. It is just as easy for God to deliver us out of the most perplexing position as it is for a master mathematician to solve a problem altogether baffling to a schoolboy.

Next we praise God that He is delivering us, or guiding us, out of our difficulty *now*.

In the outward life, we resist not evil. If a way is neatly blocked, then we may know that the Spirit does not want us to travel it. If a way opens in another direction, and our inward monitor does not raise any objection, it is probably the way the Spirit would have us go. In choosing our path we must, however, be careful and must look before we leap. If the path is the path of service, if it is for our highest good, if it is for the good of others, if it is the path that we can the more readily ask God's blessing upon, if it is most in harmony with our highest intuitions, then we can be sure that it is the right way for us to choose.

The right path often looks uninviting, for it may appear to be the path of uninteresting, unpleasant duty. The wrong path may appear to be much more profitable and easy. The uninviting path of duty is, however, the right one, and is the only one that leads to happiness.

At times, however, we are faced by a decision between two courses of action which may look equally 'right'. We must then retire still more to the inner life and make our problem the principal subject of our meditations, for weeks, or even months, if need be.

Sometimes we may have to make a quick decision, the circumstances leaving us no time for meditation. Then we should declare: *'I am guided in all my decisions by Infinite Wisdom, I make this choice guided by the Spirit and all must be well.'* Then we make our decision at once. If doubt comes afterwards, it should be met with the statement: *'I am guided in all my decisions by Infinite Wisdom, therefore all my decisions are right decisions and the blessing of God rests upon them.'*

Lastly, some may develop a higher intuition which tells them immediately if they have gone astray, or taken a wrong turning. Immediately they have made a wrong decision they feel worried, nervous, irritable and restless. They then say, 'Something is the matter, let me examine my actions and see where the mistake has been.' Then as soon as the mistake is rectified, the whole troubled feeling goes, to be replaced by restfulness, peace and happiness, together with a sense of wellbeing and harmony.

LESSON XXIII

Dear Fellow Student of Truth,

It is a great event in our life when we can thank God for the loved one whom we have lost. In losing the dearest idol of our heart we have plumbed the depths of human sorrow, yet, when all earthly props have failed, we have, through being thrown entirely upon God, found the peace which passeth all understanding.

The great lesson which we have to learn is to avoid setting our affections too much on the things of this life and the human loves which are too selfish and self-centred, and to love, instead, more universally. We have to love God and our neighbour: not to love our near ones less, but to love God and His humanity more; to serve the Whole, asking for no reward.

We need a larger vision and outlook: we need to realize that we and our loved ones live in Eternity NOW; always progressing, always guided aright, always climbing to higher and better things. There is no standing still, no stagnation: only infinite life and eternal progression.

The flowers die in the autumn and the trees shed their leaves, but they come again in the spring to cheer and bless. When, after countless ages, the earth itself disintegrates, it will be born again in even greater beauty. Better still, behind the changing and impermanent is the Abiding Perfection. All is life, life, endless life, and we and our loved ones can never die. In spite of backslidings, we are always progressing. All is eternal progress—all is well.

Yours in the One Service,

HENRY THOMAS HAMBLIN

LESSON XXIII

THE OVERCOMING OF GRIEF AND SORROW

There are many sad hearts which refuse to be comforted, for every one of us has to experience the grief of parting from loved ones when they 'pass on'. This subject therefore demands a lesson to itself.

Grief and sorrow can be overcome only through a true understanding of life and its purpose, and by adopting a right attitude towards God, His Will and Purpose. Separation from our loved ones is part of the discipline of life. It depends upon how we meet the experience as to whether it shall crush us or raise us up to a richer and higher life.

Two people lose the one whom they love best. We will assume that both love to the same extent. One gives way to sorrow, feels bitter towards God and life, and life is henceforth unhappy. The other, although feeling the wrench just as much, enters into a new relationship with God and all mankind. The loss is great indeed, but the gain beyond all estimation.

One of my happiest students lost all her family to tuberculosis and, to crown all, saw her husband, to whom she was devotedly attached, killed before her eyes. We have all known people who, having come through great tribulation, have emerged purified and sweetened, with nobler aims, higher purpose and ambition. Ever afterwards they live, not for themselves, nor entirely for their family circle, nor for those within the ties of human affection: but their love and service are given freely to all mankind. By so doing they come into harmony with God, for the love of God is universal, and it is only by loving in a universal way that we can know God. One who loves universally becomes 'like unto God': he or she advances rapidly on a Path of Destiny which is towards godhood.

One lesson that we have to learn is that our loss is not the result of some evil, malicious purpose. Infinite love is at the back of it all. Love rules. Mankind by disorder and wrong thinking has produced a state of disruption. The whole planet is in a state of disorder, which is due to mankind's strife against God; and this would lead ultimately to human destruction, but for Divine love. In some wonderful way, love works everything together for good, and what seems to be evil is really, when seen from the spiritual side, very good.

The question is often asked: 'Why does God allow mankind to go wrong? Why does He not prevent man and thus avoid so much suffering?' The answer is of course that man would be a mere puppet if this were done. God's object is to create 'sons' for Himself, not automatons or puppets. In order to create 'sons' in His image, after His own likeness, freewill had to be allowed. Through selfwill, man has pulled, as it were, away from God, thus producing separateness, so that the whole balance has been upset throughout all creation. Thus there is violence, disorder, cruelty, and every possible form of disharmony on this planet. This pulling away from God has also made man subject to corruption and death. But Love is restoring things and working everything together for good. Because mankind is not yet restored to God, we are still subject to corruption and death, but Love rules, in spite of physical death; and the progress of redemption and restoration still goes on. Our loved ones are not dead—they are not even asleep. They are progressing more rapidly than we are towards complete restoration and at-one-ment with the Divine.

Many have thought that because they had realized Truth they would not see death. But they have gone the way of all flesh. Until mankind as a whole returns to God and Love and Truth we shall still be subject to corruption and death. But this is no hindrance to our spiritual life and unfoldment. In spite of death and partings, we are still being led to higher and better things. When humanity returns to God, then time will be no more, death will be overcome, and all things restored.

Another lesson is that God makes no mistakes in His beautiful universe. In our finite foolishness, we often try to teach the Infinite One how to manage the universe and the affairs of our life. Our intelligence, compared with that above us, is as the intelligence of a beetle contrasted with that of a man. Therefore, let us not think for a moment that the slightest mistake is ever made by the Governing Intelligence of the Universe. God makes no mistakes. All is well. We think that it is a terrible thing for a child to die, or for a man to be 'cut down' in his prime. Not so; God makes no mistakes and no-one can die before he or she has gained the experience which life had to teach. Some have to live a long life in order to learn their lesson: some but a short one. Some pay so brief a visit that it seems, to finite understanding, useless—but God makes no mistakes: all is well.

Yet a third lesson we have to master is that life is endless and eternal. 'In my Father's house are many mansions', said Christ, this being the Master's symbolic way of describing this glorious truth. We can never lose our life: we can lose our body but our life remains. We live through the countless ages; we are in eternity here and now: we pass through one door and out through another: all is life; all is well. Our beloved are not dead. They came and manifested in this life, and then, when the necessary experience had been gained, and their mission ended, they passed on to higher realms.

Our fourth lesson is that life being eternal, we shall again enjoy the companionship of those whom we 'have loved and lost awhile'. We shall meet again in the next life. Our loved ones can never be lost to us, for they are progressing eternally through the ages, and so also are we.

We can never lose our loved ones. We can never be separated from them. They are near us now. Our love must bring us together again. Love must *and will* bring us together again. Nothing can prevent it. They can never forget us, any more than we can forget them. All is love, and all is well.

Finally, the loss of our loved ones teaches us that our love should not be selfish. It should not be lavished on the few: it should be extended to the whole. We are part of the Whole of God: we belong to the great company which composes the Divine family, and we must not only love the Lord our God with all our heart, and with all our soul and mind, and with all our strength, but we must also love our neighbour as ourself. It is not necessary that we should love our nearest less, but that we should love humanity more.

Grief and sorrow, however, are not always caused by death. Some of my students have written to me and said, 'I could be resigned to the death of my son (or husband), but to see him 'going to the bad' is a far greater grief'. Others have said, 'My husband has left me and gone off with a girl whom I have loved and befriended: death would be far preferable'. One man wrote to say: 'I have been led to take your course through the nagging of my wife. Her rancour and bitterness are such as to be a source of grief to us all'. In all these experiences, I see the guiding hand of Wisdom and Love. These experiences are striving to lead the sufferer 'to look not on the things which are seen, but on the things which are not seen'. They endeavour to alter the viewpoint from being too personal, narrow and confined, to a larger and more universal outlook. They seek to show things in the light of eternity.

Take courage, suffering one, and search within your own heart for the meaning of these things. The son or husband can never be lost, either to God or to you. They have eternity before them, and although they will have to retrace their steps with much suffering and many tears, they will surely do so, in God's good time.

Nothing can come into the life that is not for our highest good. We attract these troubles and griefs for our own discipline: they teach us to enlarge our love that it may become as broad and deep as humanity itself. They teach us to look upon this brief existence from the standpoint of an eternal life. We take this outlook we see things as they are, and not as they falsely appear.

An attempt should be made to praise God for one who has been taken or for the one who is causing us grief. By the persistent exercise of 'praise affirmations', the most painful grief and sorrow can be overcome. Indeed, praise will deliver us from all troubles and misery if we only make use of it. We can say:

'I thank Thee for ———. *I thank Thee because he (or she) is safe in Thy Love, and is being led to higher and better things. I thank Thee because Thou art leading us all and drawing us to Thyself. I thank Thee for Thy wonderful Love. I thank Thee because it embraces us all, includes everyone, and can never leave one of us out. All are included in Thy great Love and are being drawn to Thyself.'*

Supplementary to Lesson XXIII

We must 'Trust the Current that *knows* the Way'. Our finite sight cannot see the end from the beginning but we can trust the vision of the One Who can: we can rely on the Infinite Wisdom and kindness of the Purpose of God. The Universe is not a meaningless chaos, but a true Cosmos founded upon perfect law and Order, behind which operates the Infinite Intelligence. Behind all this and interpenetrating it, is the Infinite Love.

We can trust the Infinite Love.

Knowing that there is nothing but love, we can learn patience and fortitude in the face of trouble: exhibit cheerfulness in spite of disappointment and grief: rejoice in spite of everything which would make us sad.

Beloved, let us 'Trust the Current that knows the Way'.

WEEK TWENTY-FOUR:
SPIRITUAL EXPERIENCE

THERE IS A HIGHER and a lower in everything. All things earthly have their heavenly counterpart. All earthly things, it has been said, are but symbols of spiritual things. Most probably it is all a matter of consciousness. As we rise in consciousness we see things differently. The change is in ourselves.

We possess a higher or spiritual mind; and we also possess a higher or spiritual consciousness. When we are ready for it, when we have been tested, tried, purified and prepared, we are granted the privilege of entering, at least to a certain extent, into this higher consciousness. It is only the pure in heart who shall see God; that is, enter the higher consciousness. Also, it is equally true that only the humble in spirit can safely enter the inner Holy of Holies.

By cultivating the higher mind we make it possible to enter the spiritual consciousness. By raising our thoughts to heavenly things we develop the Christ or spiritual mind. Every time that we meditate upon Truth and God we rise in consciousness and develop the Spiritual mind.

Man, as we have just said, has two consciousnesses. He has two selves, the lower and the higher, one living on earth, the other in Heaven. Heaven is not so much a place as a state of consciousness; but it is helpful, I find, to think of Heaven as a plane above us—say, a few yards above the head. Then, every time that a person raises his thoughts, his whole consciousness is lifted up to a plane above the material, enabling him to look out over life and human destiny from the universal, eternal-being standpoint. The present, everyday consciousness is not lost; he is still conscious of his surroundings and what is going on; but, concurrently with this, he also lives and has consciousness, to a certain extent, in heavenly places.

The more we practise this, the more permanent this realization of a higher and extended consciousness becomes. We are thus able to look at life and its experiences more from a detached, impersonal point of view. This does not lessen our sympathy with those who are still suffering in the mass consciousness, but we know that such suffering is not hopeless, and that all things are moving majestically along to a glorious consummation.

The lower has to be transmuted into the higher. This is the object of life, and there can be no harmony in life if we are not co-operating with this principle of transmutation, or raising, of the lower to the higher. Our teaching has always had this object in view. The raising of the thoughts, the use of statements of Truth that are true only of the higher spiritual realm, the quiet meditation, during which the consciousness is raised to the Divine, all these hasten the process of raising the lower to the higher. If these are persevered with, then the thought, the mind, the whole life, become spiritualized and raised to a higher plane. Even the body becomes changed, refined and regenerated. Exactly what changes take place in the body are of no interest to us. Sufficient to know that the body does become changed and purified, so that the lower becomes transmuted into the higher, and the life or generative forces are directed into fresh channels. All this is accomplished without any danger or disturbance, for it is perfectly natural and in harmony with the Divine Laws of Attainment. There is not the slightest repression about it: it is a gradual transmutation and re-direction. If we dam up a stream, a time must come when the water either overflows or sweeps away the dam. But if we divert the stream into a fresh channel, it will always flow through it. In the case of the body, however, we do not have anything to do in the matter. It takes place, of itself, if we only continue looking to God in the ways already described.

One of the greatest aids to attainment to spiritual conscious-ness is praise and thanksgiving. Every time we bless, magnify, praise and thank God for His most wonderful love and mercy, we advance a pace nearer, we climb a step higher. Every thought of praise and deep thankfulness unites us more firmly with the Divine.

SPIRITUAL BREATHING

With some of us, although not with all, there comes a time when, if we continue keeping our attention fixed on God and Christ, meditating and thinking quietly of Divine things, we find that our breathing falls into a natural harmonious rhythm. When-ever we start thinking of Heavenly things, at once our breathing changes, of itself, into a deep, harmonious, rhythmic flow, quite independently and out of our control. This is as it should be. Our physical breathing is simply brought into harmony with some rhythmic flow or pulsation of the Infinite Spirit. All that we have to do is to allow the breath to go just as it wants to do.

This breathing of which I speak is very deep. It does not have to be learnt, it comes naturally. Immediately we begin to think of Spiritual things, it starts, and then carries on just as long as we continue thinking of the Divine.

There comes a time, however, when this breathing, deep though it be, does not seem to satisfy our needs. There grows up a deep desire for more breath and yet more breath. Although the breathing is as deep as the lungs are capable of, yet there is a feeling of the need of yet deeper breathing and still more breath. This may lead to a feeling of slight stuffiness or suffocation. If this is so, in your case, do not worry about it, for all is well. Eve-rything is going along satisfactorily. If you do *not* experience this, then, again, do not worry, for all is well. So long as we continue to meditate and look to God, all is well; and our development is proceeding along the best lines for us, individually.

After the stuffiness, there *may* develop an interior breathing that is distinct from the physical. If this should be the case with you, again do not be alarmed, for all is well. All that you have to do is to keep on looking Godwards and meditating and praying as before. All of us can, however, realize that when we breathe we also breathe interiorly the sweet ethers of the breath of God.

By sitting quietly, raising the thoughts to God and Heaven, and by allowing the breathing to follow the rhythm of the Spirit, we can at once come into conscious union with the Divine. All that we need do, at this stage, is to *contemplate* God. No requests, no thoughts of special needs, no idea of attainment on our part, but just contemplation of the Divine. The more that we do this, provided we do not neglect our daily duties and service to others, the more progress we make in the spiritual life, in spiritual understanding, in developing the spiritual mind, in unfolding the spiritual consciousness.

So, in course of time, we pass from meditation, which is the royal road to attainment, to *contemplation*, which is, methinks, the last stage of this wonderful journey.

'Both now and always, according to grace, I am kept by the Spirit in the Presence of the Most High.'

Yours in the Fellowship of Christ,

HENRY THOMAS HAMBLIN

ADDITIONAL NOTES ON THE DEEPER SPIRITUAL EXPERIENCES OF LIFE

There is a subtle difference between the REAL spiritual life and the false. It is possible to develop spiritual powers without being in the True Path. There are two paths, apparently, and they run side by side for a considerable distance. But—to adopt the method of John Bunyan—the path on the left leads to a place outside the City of Light, but the True Path leads right into Heaven itself.

Now what is the difference between the two? Those who follow the path on the left bear no cross, neither do they make the supreme surrender. Those on the righthand path bear a cross, suffer the reproach of Christ, and surrender all to Him. Those on the left do not believe in humility, but boast that they are gods in their own right, following their self-created path. Those on the righthand path are known for their humbleness of heart, their humility, their recognition of the fact that of themselves they are nothing, and that it is Christ in them and the grace of God and the fellowship of the Spirit alone that have made them new creatures, meet for the Kingdom of Heaven, enabling them to travel the path mapped out for them by Infinite Wisdom and Love.

If we are truly in the Path there comes a time, or there come times, when we have to be utterly emptied of self, brought to our last extremity, when we have to confess that we, ourselves, can do nothing, that we are impotent, and that God alone can undertake for us. Then, when life's experiences and our own failures have flattened us out in the dust, and the Spirit has probed us to the very root, right down to the very base and beginnings of our nature, and when we have surrendered ourselves again and again to God, asking only that His Will might be done in us entirely, and that he should remake us after His own design, likeness and pattern, then, God graciously commences His work of synthesis.

The spiritual life is one long series of surrenders to God and Christ, but they all culminate in the time of utter, final and complete surrender to the Divine Will, Purpose, Guidance and Plan. 'Lead, kindly light ... Lead Thou me on' (to quote Newman's hymn) is then our only desire. If only GOD'S Will might be done is the one thing that alone can satisfy us. By surrendering in this way, through giving up all to God, we gain all, and enter into a fuller, richer and more abundant life. By losing our life, we gain it—or rather, we lose the false life, which seems so real to the unillumined, and gain the real life of the ages.

When once we have been completely emptied, then God can fill us entirely. When we become God-filled, with no opposition to the Divine Will anywhere in our being, God can then rebuild us, fashioning us wholly according to His Will. Only in this way can we become godlike and fit for the realms of Light.

Those on the lefthand path never pass through the two processes just described. They are self-sufficient. They prefer to build themselves on their own foundation. They are, so they think, gods in their own right, treading their self-created pathway, and are quite satisfied with themselves. But they never reach the City of Light. This is only for those who have been born again, who have surrendered all, yet have found all.

Narrow is the Path and few there be that find it. Man can never enter the Kingdom until Christ possesses him entirely, reigns completely in his life, and the lower nature is completely slain. Then is the Divine process completed. The lower is raised to the Higher. The Divine Union takes place. All is well.

LESSON XXIV

Dear Fellow Student of Truth,

The first part of this lesson deals with the subconscious mind. This mind is a good servant but a bad master and therefore must be kept in subjection.

The remainder of the lesson deals with the spiritual or superconscious mind which St Paul speaks of as 'that mind which was in Christ Jesus'. This mind is brought into action simply by raising our thoughts to higher things. By using this higher intuitive faculty, by which we 'talk with God', we become attuned to the Divine Wisdom: we are divinely guided: we are literally shown the path which it is to our highest advantage to tread. There is only one right path for us to take: Divine Wisdom alone can lead us to it.

This is the path of the only true success: it leads to peace, joy, happiness, and true content.

Yours in the Joy of Service,

HENRY THOMAS HAMBLIN

LESSON XXIV

USING THE INNER MIND

There are two inner minds—the subconscious and the super-conscious. The first of these can be trained to do an incredible amount of thinking for us without any fatigue or effort. It will work out logically and thoroughly problems quite beyond our ordinary intelligence. It is gifted with powers which appear to us to be omnipotent. For some wise reason, we are shut off from this mind and cannot make full use of its powers. Doubtless, the full use of this mind will come to the human race when it is ready for it. It is undesirable, however, to let this wonderful mind obtain control, for, although a splendid servant, it is a bad master. We must always be in complete command. The subconscious mind must be held in subjection, it must always be guided and controlled. Those who practise negative passivity run grave risks, because by so doing they relinquish control of their subconscious mind. One who is master of his or her own house, however, can control the subconscious mind and vastly increase his or her efficiency by so doing.

How much of our thinking is done for us by our subconscious mind is not known: it is probably far more than we are aware of. It is well-known that many great men and women either consciously or unconsciously work along these lines. When confronted by a difficult problem, they consider the whole of the ascertainable facts of the case; they examine the matter from every point of view, and then dismiss it from their thoughts. When an answer is required, it is ready waiting for them. Such people will often refuse to give a decision until they have slept on it. During the night the subconscious mind, which never sleeps, works out their problem for them and presents it, all complete, the next morning.

In order to make use of the subconscious mind in this manner, it is necessary to think over one's problem calmly and to marshal all the facts. It is necessary to gather together every possible fact and piece of information. The subconscious mind cannot manufacture facts or details, and can work out the problem only upon the evidence with which you supply it. Having marshalled all your facts, arrange them *pro* and *con*. Consider your problem from both sides and look at it from every possible angle and point of view and then dismiss it to your subconscious mind and say, 'Now, subconscious mind, work this problem out for me'.

The next day, take the problem up again; and, if it is not solved, you will find that it has changed. It must now be considered again from every point of view and, if any additional information can be found, it must be added, and the whole matter again dismissed to the subconscious mind. This process must be repeated until the subconscious mind completely solves the problem.

Many difficulties will be solved much more quickly than this— one night, as a rule, being sufficient. In course of time, it will be found that the subconscious mind will supply the answer almost immediately, without fatigue or effort.

Not only does the subconscious mind work night and day without resting, and without needing any rest, but it does our work for us far, far better than we could possibly do it ourselves, and without the slightest fatigue. It is completely effortless. Thus, one who makes use of his subconscious mind in this way is never fatigued or worried, but is fresh and ready for his work each morning. Contrast this effortless working with the methods of the ordinary man. He puzzles his mind, fretting and worrying about his problem until he is distraught. When he retires to rest, he tries to puzzle things out with his brain, with the result that he cannot sleep, so that in the morning he is fagged out, and quite unfit for the duties of life. And, in addition, his problem is still not solved.

It must be remembered that the subconscious mind works more or less like a machine. It does not supply information: it merely thinks out a logical result based upon the information with which you supply it. If your information is at fault, the result will be faulty. In spite of this drawback, the use of the subconscious mind is of the utmost value. One who learns to use the subconscious mind in this way uses in time the whole of his or her mind (less the spiritual) instead of only a small fraction.

We possess, however, a mind far more wonderful than the subconscious, namely the superconscious or spiritual mind. The subconscious is the instinctive mind, but the superconscious is the mind of intuition or direct knowing. This is the mind of inspiration: the mind through which God speaks to the human family.

It is far more difficult to get answers through this mind than from the subconscious, but instead of being merely based on material facts, such answers are direct inspiration from the Infinite Wisdom and Intelligence.

In order to receive inspiration and Divine Wisdom through superconscious, it is necessary to cultivate the habit of raising the consciousness above the sense-plane to the superconscious plane of Divine Perfection. It is also necessary to cultivate a super-sensitivity as though one were listening to the faintest whispers from the Inward Voice.

When seeking Divine Wisdom by direct knowing, the mind must be calmed and stilled. Every intruding thought must be turned away until the soul is left undisturbed with God. It is then in the Silence that thoughts and ideas come into consciousness, which are from God.

You may say that it is impossible to control the mind and thoughts in such a way as to make this desired stillness possible. It is, however, quite possible; but it is not easy. It becomes possible only as the result of steady, quiet persistence. We have to keep on quietly trying, persevering and persisting until at last we can keep our mind quite still and stayed upon God. All extraneous thoughts, all cares, all ambitions, all thoughts of our needs even, must be put on one side. They may persist in intruding, but they must be quietly, firmly, gently and persistently turned away again until at last our mind and spirit are perfectly still and calm in the Divine Presence. When once the Presence is entered in this way, all that we need do is to remain quiet, keeping all other thoughts away by an action that takes place, so to speak, at the back of the mind, through the use of the will, and then to contemplate the Divine. Even if we get no answer it does not matter, for everything must work together for good if we contemplate God in this way.

Do not listen for voices, or expect to hear voices. The 'voice of intuition' and the 'still, small voice' are mere figures of speech. What happens is that ideas rise into consciousness. Even these should, especially at first, be scrutinized very carefully, for it is only by experience that the true ideas can be separated from those which are false.

I said just now that it does not matter if we receive no answer. This is because when we contemplate God in the way described, we open ourselves to the influx of God's Harmony and Divine Order, which flows into our life, healing it all, right from the inmost core to its outmost circumference. Through contemplation, our spiritual or superconscious mind is brought into living contact with the Divine Mind. Because of this, our whole life is brought into harmony with the Life of God, everything in it being Divinely adjusted. Therefore, although Divine ideas may rise in our consciousness, it does not matter very much if they do not; but the more sensitive we are the more we can be guided in this way.

It may help you if you think of the superconscious mind as residing at the very top of the skull; and then try to 'live in the top of your mind'.

In order for us to attain to this super-sensitivity, food should be simple in character and in quantity: cleanliness of body must be observed: all excesses must be avoided, and great self-control exercised. The life must be one of love and highest service. Only those who are in entire harmony in thought, word and deed with the Divine can ever make contact with the mind of God.

Of our finite selves we can have no real wisdom. Our so-called wisdom is only foolishness. It forever leads us on with promises of happiness, yet each time we are disillusioned and mocked. The only wisdom comes from the Spirit through the Spiritual mind. It is only by following the lead of the Spirit that we can become successful in the highest and truest sense.

It is therefore of the utmost importance that we cultivate this superconscious quality.

It must be clearly understood that this has nothing to do with the subconscious mind. This is of the earth, earthy; it has no inspiration and no spiritual insight. It should be used merely for ordinary thinking to relieve the conscious mind of a great deal of work. The subconscious mind has to be employed as a servant, but the superconscious gives us 'Wisdom from on High'.

In order to receive direct inspiration from Divine sources, it is necessary to raise the consciousness to your highest conception of God transcendent and affirm gently and calmly, but with confidence and assurance, that the Infinite Mind is guiding you every inch of the way: that Divine Intelligence is giving you just the information that you seek, or that Divine Harmony is now manifesting in your life. Then wait and quietly contemplate God. During the whole time, the consciousness must be raised to God, but there must be no yielding up of the individuality. You must be in command the whole time. I mention this because there is certain teaching to the contrary and it is not wise teaching, far from it.

In seeking the stillness of the Divine Presence it is most important that the thoughts and the mind be *raised* to God and not allowed to sink down into a negative state of passivity. It is very necessary that we should be receptive to God only. At the back of the mind, so to speak, the will must be set like a flint against all influences other than the Divine. Against all lower forces, entities or so-called powers there must be set a strong positive attitude. But towards God and Divine things we open ourselves and become receptive.

After all, what we do amounts simply to this, that we pray to God and receive an answer, either as a thought in consciousness, or through the still, small voice within the soul, or through a providential ordering of circumstances, or by a harmonizing, or healing, of the whole life. It can become possible only to those who are in earnest and who will cultivate the necessary sensitiveness and the delicate, listening ear of expectant faith.

In course of time, it becomes possible to make contact with the Divine Mind at any time; and later, even to be in contact the whole time. But for most people it is better to spend two definite times each day in a quiet place, practising the Presence. The best posture for most students has been found to be sitting upright in a straight-backed chair with eyes closed. This does not mean that the body is to be rigid, but just the reverse. Every muscle should be relaxed and the whole body at rest, but the posture should be erect all the same. The mind also must relax and be easy and calm, but not negatively so. At the back of it the will must be set against all that is not God. Then the mind may be quietly and calmly raised above everything to God. In doing so, we rise above thought so that we make contact with That which is greater than thought.

WEEK TWENTY-FIVE:
THE OLD NATURE SLAIN, WE
BECOME NEW CREATURES

AFTER READING through Lesson XXV, it does not seem necessary in one sense to say anything more. Yet how much one could say! Could one ever cease? But while the temptation is to rise to supernal heights, endeavouring to voice the ecstatic joy in our heart, we must resist it and confine ourselves to practical instruction upon how to attain to a closer union with the Divine.

First of all, let me say this: do not bother or worry about any theoretical or intellectual aspect of the One and many. Many are afraid that they will lose their identity when they enter into the One Consciousness. Their fears are groundless, for such is not the case. Strange though it may seem, and impossible also, the individuality is not lost in the slightest degree. Instead of puzzling about this paradox, which never can be grasped or solved by the human mind, attention should be solely directed towards God and attaining to conscious union with Him. When God-consciousness is attained, then the mystery is solved, or rather, there is found to be no mystery to solve at all.

What has to take place is that our individual centre should be shifted so as to coincide with the One Divine Centre. The great surrender spoken of in the Additional Notes to Letter XXIV is the greatest step of all in this direction. It is impossible for our centre to unite and become one with the Divine Centre if there is a shred of selfwill left in us. Such a union cannot take place:

there can be no amalgamation until we are entirely free from all the lower desires and thoughts that are not entirely in harmony with the Divine.

But until realization of oneness comes, there is still a sense of separateness. We feel that our centre is one thing and the Divine Centre another. We and our centre are here, so to speak, while God and His Centre are somewhere else. Hence the separateness. How can this be overcome?

God is the Centre of the Universe, and we are each individual centers: how can we become consciously one? Within each one of us is a centre, or nodal point. All our various centres amalgamate, so to speak, and form a nodal point or plane which is our true individual centre. When we become one with other children of God through love, our various nodal points, or centres, become one with the One Nodal Point, or Centre, and so we are all one. Yet we still retain our own individual centre. We are a centre within *the* Centre. Now, as we meditate upon oneness, we can mentally shift our centre, and with it ourselves, to God's Centre, so that we become one. Then we look out upon the Universe from God's Centre: we see life from the universal and eternal standpoint; we find that we *are* the things for which formerly we prayed. Then is realized how true is the teaching that we do not have to ask God for things, we have only *to be*.

And so we enter into the consciousness of our true being. The old nature is slain and we become new creatures. We become wedded to, or amalgamated with, Christ Who is God. Christ in us, our true and real self, unites us with the Eternal Christ Who is God. And so we become one. He who meditates upon Christ becomes Christ. Christ is the Way, the Truth and the, Life. By Him we come to the Father; that is, attain to Universal Consciousness and Oneness with the Whole. By Him, we attain unto the full measure of the stature of the fullness of Christ.

But I have not emphasized enough the tremendous help that praise, rejoicing and thanksgiving are to one seeking conscious oneness with the Divine. Praise and thanksgiving must be genuine, however. They must not be imitations of the real thing, worked up in order that we may get something in return. They must be real and sincere. Every time that we lift up our hearts to God and thank Him for His love and mercy, we are brought nearer to Him, and this to a wonderful degree. I thank Thee, I thank Thee, I thank Thee. 'For Thou hast delivered my soul from death, mine eyes from tears, and my feet from falling.' I thank Thee, I thank Thee, I thank Thee.

By prayer and praise and constant thankfulness, our life becomes filled with blessings. There is no doubt about that. The more we praise and thank God, the more we find there is for which to thank Him. Many who are sunk in the depths of misery would be lifted right out of it, if only they praised God, instead of allowing themselves to slip down into a chronic state of depression. Those who praise God continually become raised to a better life entirely, attracting all the good things of life to themselves including friends of like happy condition of mind.

Just praise and thanksgiving. That is all.

*

But this is only part of the story. Raising the heart continually to God, in genuine praise and thankfulness, induces a state of quiet, deep joy, such as cannot be described. Nothing, of course, that the world can give can compare in any way with this. It is the joy that only the freed and emancipated soul can experience. It is the joy of Heaven. We find that all the Universe is saturated and packed full of joy unspeakable. That we have not experienced it before is because we have been shut out from it by separateness.

And this brings us to our main point. Praise and thankfulness continually expressed bring us nearer to the heart of God. The more we praise and thank God, the more at-one we become. When we were children in spiritual things, we were told that we should praise God because He liked it. Now we know that WE are the ones who benefit by it. God can do very well without our praise and thankfulness, but *we* cannot. Without them, we cannot attain. If we are not constantly praising God with hearts bursting with thankfulness, then the sooner we start doing so the better it will be for us.

We should start by praising God systematically for obvious blessings. A fine day, the beauties of Nature, a night's rest, food provided, clothes to wear, ability to work, for work itself, for friends, loved ones, and so on. Then for health, strength, money, and for the new pair of boots we bought last Saturday. No matter how simple or childish a thing may be, we should thank God for it. And so we can go on praising God for visible blessings. Every time we receive money we should thank and praise God for it, lifting up the heart, while so doing, acknowledging to God that He is the only source of our supply. Every time we pay money away we should thank God that we are able to do so, that we have the money for the purpose, and that our financial freedom comes from Him.

Praise and thankfulness should become a habit, so that we are constantly raising our hearts to God, all day long. It is then no effort, although at first a certain amount of attention and perseverance is necessary.

But we must not only praise and thank God for obvious blessings, but also for those which intuition, abstract reasoning and faith tell us we possess, but which are not yet manifest. By praising God for the blessings not yet visible, they are brought into sight. If we are, apparently, not well, the best thing to do is to praise God for omnipresent health. If we are, apparently, poor, the quickest way to affluence is by praising and thanking God for His abundance. If our life is, apparently, all jumbled up and filled with difficulty and disorder, the wisest course for us to pursue is to praise God that he is unravelling the tangled skein and bringing Divine Order into manifestation.

It follows also that all our prayers should be in the form of praise and thanks. If we want the Holy Spirit, then we thank and praise God for this wonderful gift. If we need greater wisdom, then we thank and praise God because it is ours now. So we go, on and on; all the time fresh blessings and Divine gifts are being brought into manifestation.

And, concurrently with this, we are daily being brought into closer union with the Divine. It is not a question of hoping that this is so, for there is no doubt at all about it.

In conclusion, let me remind you that attainment is purely the work of the Holy Spirit. Of ourselves we can do nothing. It is only the Spirit of Truth Who can lead us into Truth. All that we can do is to co-operate with the Spirit. The less we rely upon ourselves and the more we depend on the Holy Spirit, the greater the progress that is made. It is only God Who can bring us to God. 'God Returning', bringing or taking us back to 'God Abiding'.

And *'now unto Him that is able to keep you from falling, and to present you faultless before the presence of His glory with exceeding joy, to the only wise God our Saviour, be glory and majesty, dominion and power, both now and ever. Amen.'*

Yours in the Fellowship of the Mystical Body of Christ,
HENRY THOMAS HAMBLIN

ADDITIONAL NOTES ON THE
DEEPER SPIRITUAL EXPERIENCES OF LIFE

Now we come to a very important subject indeed. It is a source of grief and regret for many on the Path that though 'they have received mercy of the Lord' and the past is remembered against them no more, yet there is the evil they have wrought in days gone by. What of this? they think.

Human reasoning would tell us that the wrongs we have done in days gone by have set in motion forces of divergence which must ever widen as the centuries roll on. But this is not so. Thank God for this. God heals and restores each life, overruling everything for good.

Oh, wonderful, wonderful, are the love, mercy and wisdom of God. He is the *restoring* God. Immediately we turn to God, completely and utterly repenting of the past, and desiring only that God's will should done, the healing, restoring process commences. The great secret is this: if we continually turn to God, desiring only that His will may be done in us and through us, utterly and completely, then everything works together for good, and *must* ever do so. It was this discovery that made the apostle exclaim: 'Everything works together for good, to them that love God, and are the called according to His purpose'. The last part of this quotation need neither worry us nor puzzle us. God calls all, but can only make use of those who respond.

Let the thought that God has called us and, because of our responsiveness, has fitted us into His wonderful scheme of redemption and restoration, fill us, not only with joy, but with great humbleness. How wonderful it is, that God should make use of us, in this way! What a privilege!

And so by the approach of the great and utter surrender, we, the sons of men, are privileged to become, actually, sons of God. We, 'who sometimes were afar off, are made nigh by the blood of Christ.'

The peace, which passeth all knowledge and understanding, be yours.

LESSON XXV

Dear Fellow Student of Truth,

This lesson describes the greatest experience which can come to man. The process of involution and evolution occupies countless ages, but at last consciousness comes to the soul of man; he wakes up and realizes the Truth.

There is no separateness; there is only the One, and we are part of the Complete Whole. There is only the one I AM, and the 'I am' in you is part of the great I AM. The difference is not one of kind but of degree. Beloved, *now* are we the sons of God. Not in some future state, but *now* we are of the same nature and substance, having potentially within us the Infinite Perfection, just in the same way that an acorn carries within it potentially the future oak tree that is to be.

Our life and consciousness are expanding. 'It doth not yet appear what we shall be, but we know that when He shall appear *we* shall be like Him'. There is no limit to this expansion. The Christ-consciousness is Infinite: within us is the grain of mustard seed which shall grow and grow until it becomes a mighty tree. We therefore look forward with glowing anticipation to an everlasting life of infinite expansion.

Beloved, *now* are we the Sons of God.

Yours in this wonderful Realization,

HENRY THOMAS HAMBLIN

LESSON XXV

FINDING THE TRUE SELF

One who follows this new way of life, transmuting all negative thoughts into positive ones and living continually in the knowledge and understanding of Truth, undergoes a process of transformation. Apparently our personality is multiple. There are, at first, devils down below, and angels above, and which is our real self is difficult to tell. By losing our temper we become transformed into a devil, but by loving we become a 'perfect angel'. As one dear old lady once said to me: 'There seem so many of us, it is quite confusing'. In course of time, however, a change becomes apparent, the devils die a natural death and a new and higher Self begins to take control of our life. It does not matter what we call this radiant divine Self, so long as we realize that we are one with It. Indeed the truth is that we, in reality, are merged into this radiant Self so that we become one. We do not lose our individuality, but our consciousness expands until it becomes universal. This is the heart of the Inner Teaching. It has been taught to all advanced students throughout the ages. The laws of initiation have never altered. The prince and the beggar have to go through exactly the same process of inward change, and this is just the same today as it was in ancient times. Jesus taught this, no doubt in plain language to his disciples, but to the ordinary people in parables. This was done so that only those who possessed spiritual insight and understanding should have the truth revealed to them. This truth would do actual harm if it were imparted to those not yet ready for it, therefore it has always been veiled and made difficult to find, so that only those who are earnest seekers should find it.

This change, which is the greatest which can come to many, has aptly been called the spiritual marriage. 'Behold the Bridegroom cometh'. The Celestial Bridegroom is the Higher or True Self, or Christ, and the Divine Union is said to take place when we realize this startling fact. When we enter into this consciousness of the true Self, the Divine Union is complete. 'Old things have passed away and all things have become new'. To some this change takes place suddenly and is generally preceded by great depression and darkness of soul. To others the change is gradual, and, in some cases, may extend over a period of years. At first the truth comes in flashes. There is a flash of understanding and then it disappears, and cannot, by any effort or striving, be brought back. Other flashes follow until at last comes full understanding.

This great change cannot be forced and those who are wise will not attempt to do so. Not one moment too soon, nor one moment too late, you will enter into knowledge. 'Seek, and ye shall find', said our Lord, and this is all that you have to do together with the living of a blameless life, fully surrendered to the Law of Love and the Will of God. No special exercises should be used, and no attempts made to enter this consciousness, through surrendering the 'control of the Ship', or by cultivating a negative passivity, or by special breathing. It is necessary to be the captain of your soul at all times.

The next step is Spiritual Consciousness, when we become

universal in understanding and consciousness. We realize that
we are one with the One Self manifesting in every man, woman
and child: in all animals: in trees, in flowers, in the wind that
blows: in the sun which burns our cheeks. When we can see and
feel universally, all petty dislikes, all passions, all foolish devices
are seen at their true value. The baubles of life, for which men
and women give their happiness and sell their souls, can never
attract us again, for we have seen things as they really are, not as
they falsely appear to the senses.

Spiritual Consciousness is the Christ-consciousness: it is the universal consciousness of the Universal Mind. Being the Christ-consciousness, it is God-consciousness. It is the One Universal
Consciousness of the Whole. One who enters this higher realm
realizes that he is deathless, diseaseless, eternal. He knows that he is
not his body, nor his mind, nor his personality, but that his is the
One Conscious Life manifesting all through the Universe. This cannot be explained—it can only be experienced. The late Edward
Carpenter, a great but unrecognized seer and poet, born many years
before his time, reached this consciousness when he said, 'there comes
to him a sense of absolute repose, a consciousness of immense and
universal power, such as completely transforms the world for him.
All life is changed; he becomes master of his fate; he perceives that
all things are hurrying to perform his will; and whatever in that
region of inner life he may condescend to desire, that already is
shaping itself to utterance and expression in the outer world around
him. *"The winds are his messengers over all the world, and flames of fire
his servants; and the clouds float over the half-concealed, dappled, and shaded
Earth—to fulfil his will, to fulfil his eternal joy".*'

'Or again a strange sense of Extension comes on me—and
of presence in distant space and time. Mine is an endless Life,
unconquerable, limitless in subtlety and expanse; and strange
intimations that it is so come to me even in my tiny earth-cell—
intimations of power inexhaustible, of knowledge mysterious and
unbounded, and of far prescience through all forms and ranges
of being'. (*Art of Creation*)

This change of consciousness is the greatest event in the long history of man. From simple consciousness to God-consciousness— what a journey! Treat it with reverence, O student mine, for it is the passing from the limited human and intellectual conscious-ness to that of the Divine: it is the culmination of ages of progress.

Do not seek to hurry it. All the time that you try to force it, you will keep it away; but if you will rest in the Eternal Love and lean back, so to speak, in the Everlasting Arms, you will in time be able to find the pearl of great price, that hidden treasure, the kingdom of heaven, which was the burden of Christ's teaching. This is the heart of the Inner Teaching—the Divine Union, or Heavenly Marriage. After this, everything fades into nothing-ness. Read the whole teaching of Jesus in the light of this, and it becomes as clear as the day. Jesus taught the Inner Teaching and spoke from the standpoint of the Universal Consciousness. When we understand His teaching, it is seen to be the very heart and centre of Truth and Wisdom.

When we arrive at this stage, the Light of the Logos appears. The Light which blinded Saul shines round about us, and ever after life is transfigured. This light is not the light of the sun but of the Sun behind the sun. It is the Illumination of Spirit, which, flooding our consciousness, gives us the assurance that we are the sons of God. In thought we can resolve matter into ether, ether into Mind and Mind into Spirit. When we reach this, we transcend time and space: we rest in the Eternal Now.

In conclusion, Universal Consciousness or Divine Union does not come through doing special exercises, but simply through living a truly spiritual life, seeking the highest and best, and spend-ing as much time as possible in the Silence. Do this and in God's good time you will hear the cry: 'Behold, the Bridegroom cometh'.

Notes on the Above Lesson

Before we can enter the Higher Consciousness, a state of unity has to be brought about within. In us there are two wills:—the Divine Will and the 'creature' will. These have to be brought together and become one, something which is accomplished by surrendering our own will to the Divine Will. This has to be done again and again, through all the experiences of life, until at last the two become one. When our will is completely subservient to the Divine Will, they become one; and we find that our own will is reinforced by the Divine Will. This is a long process for most people, for the end of the journey is reached when the life is lived entirely in harmony with the Divine Will and according to the dictates of the Law of Love, and very few are anywhere near the end yet. We can, however, hold the good in view, living one day at a time, trying to do God's Will, and follow the dictates of Love. If we do this, then we become changed more and more into the Divine likeness, making what is really very rapid progress.

Also, we have within us two eyes: the Divine Eye looking heavenwards to higher and better things and Eternity, and the 'creature' eye which looks on the things of time and sense and the flesh and mortality. These two have to be merged into one. Then, when this is accomplished, our eye becomes single, and our whole body filled with light, according to our Lord's teaching. These two eyes become merged into one, or become so that they see as one: that is, become 'single', as a result of our turning constantly from evil, sin and apparent evil, to God and His Divine Perfection. This means incessant 'warfare'; but if we persist and persevere in the strength of the Spirit, a time comes when the inner eyes are one and look over upwards. Then complete unity is attained to and we are ready for the larger consciousness. As soon as we are ready, greater revelations come to us.

WEEK TWENTY-SIX:
CONCLUSION

ALL TOO SOON, we have arrived at the last letter. The journey has been a very happy and pleasant one to the writer, but, alas, we must again part for a season. But we are all one in the Spirit. In Christ we are not only made alive, but we all become one. One with Him, one in Him, and one with each other—one complete whole, the Mystical Person and Body of Christ.

It has been said that there are three steps or stages—first, the awakening, second, the finding, third, the telling to others what we have found. This is illustrated by the parable of the woman and the lost piece of silver. First, she realizes her loss, her lack, of something of great value. Second, she searches until she finds it. Third, she calls her neighbours together to tell them what a wonderful thing has happened. All three steps or stages are equally necessary. The passing of the Truth to others is just as necessary, as either conversion or finding the Christ. If we fail in this, we fail in all. We cannot live for ourselves alone, we form part of the Complete Whole.

Everything seems to be in the form of a trinity—the one in three, the three in one. For instance, there are three paths to Divine Union. There is the Path of Service and Good Works. There is the Path of Knowledge and Understanding. There is the Path of Love and Adoration. Although different, they are yet the same. Three in number, yet only one. Some follow one path, and some another, but in one sense we all have to follow the three. We must all serve: we must all understand: we must all love and adore. Each one of us finds, however, that he or she has a predilection for one path in particular. The mistake that we are liable to make is in thinking that the particular path that we are treading is the only right path for everybody. Martha thinks that Mary ought to do more practical work, while Mary thinks that Martha ought to sit at the feet of Jesus oftener than she does. And so on. But both are in their respective right paths. Why our Lord reproved Martha somewhat was simply because she criticized Mary. Our Lord did not infer that Martha was not following *her* right path. Therefore, each must follow his or her own path, allowing others the same privilege. We are each one being led by the Spirit of Truth, and to realize this is to give liberty to those whom we love and also to ourselves.

We are all of us anxious about the spiritual welfare of those whom we love. Because they do not follow us in our beliefs, or because they, apparently, have no liking at all for spiritual things, we naturally think that they are all wrong, and they must be put right and conformed to our standard. But this does not help at all. Really, it only makes matters worse. If in the Silence we 'let go' of those about whom we are anxious, realizing that God loves them just as much as He loves us, and that the Spirit is guiding them just as perfectly as it has guided and is guiding us and, therefore, that they are being led in the right path, which leads to Divine Union: if we do this, all is Well. We cannot live other people's lives for then, even though they be our sons and daughters, but we can commit them into the care of God, surrendering them to Infinite Wisdom and Love.

Intolerance and bigotry are a sign of a lack of spiritual light and understanding. We should always allow everybody else liberty to follow Truth in his own way and to tread his own particular path. An evangelical churchman is distressed because his son becomes a ritualist, and mentally opposes or coerces him. He may even pray hard and persistently that his son may be brought back to the evangelical way of belief. By so doing, he is making spiritual progress more difficult for his son, and his own life *much* more painful and thorny. A Baptist Minister, who is a spiritually-alive man and therefore gifted with spiritual insight, told me recently that he often found among those who were totally different from, and opposed to, his beliefs and tenets, spiritually-minded men, who exuded a spiritual power, which could be *felt* by those who came in contact with them.

The truth of the matter is that God has His Spirit-taught witnesses in all denominations, in all real religions, in all walks of life. Spiritual life is greater than creed and forms of belief. Here and there, scattered about the world, are to be found the true spiritual witnesses, the real sons of God—those sons of men who have been called by the Spirit to become sons of God, and who have responded, leaving all to follow our blessed Lord. These form the inner circle of spiritually-quickened men and women, who are the salt of the earth, who are the torchbearers, who form the vanguard of our all-conquering Lord of Love.

God is preparing his witnesses and torchbearers in all parts of the world. There is special service awaiting each one of us. Each one is being prepared for his or her particular work. Each one will be a centre of spiritual activity and helpfulness.

All the experiences of life, all the things that 'happen' to us each day, are a preparation. There is nothing evil or purposeless in any experience. Each day brings certain experiences, all of which are designed to prepare us for our high calling. When we realize that life consists of series of disciplinary or preparatory experiences, and nothing else, we have made, as it were, a great discovery.

This process of preparation, or training, includes a series of tests. When we have been tested, and have passed successfully, we never have to pass through the experience again. We then have a period of respite after which we pass on to the next test. And so on. After each successful passing of our test we find ourselves advanced a considerable step, and our previous stage of attainment is seen to be a long way behind.

We are all tempted or tried in every imaginable way. All the attractions of the world and the flesh are dangled before us. Every possible inducement is made to draw us back to the beggarly elements of the world. Never has sin seemed so attractive, never was evil so cunningly disguised, but if we are steadfast, all is well. The object of all trial and temptation, from the point of view of the tempter or tester, is to persuade us to take our gaze from God and Truth. If this can be accomplished, then our downfall is assured. If, however, we keep our face turned towards the Light, in spite of the fact that we fall, then we are safe, and sooner or later the test comes to an end, and the opposing forces retire beaten.

The most subtle temptation is the suggestion that because we fail, we are not fit to continue. But we should pay little or no attention to our failures, simply keeping our face turned towards the Light, no matter what happens, always resisting sin as well as we are able, but realizing all the time that God alone can save and deliver.

All that we have to do really is to keep looking up towards the Light. So long as we continue to do this we are safe, and all is well, in spite of the fact that apparently all the powers of hell and darkness are arrayed against us, or are trying to persuade us to give up the quest.

Many and various are the tests and temptations, but their object is the same in each case—to bully us, frighten us, persuade or cajole us into giving up the quest, to turn our face away from the Light, and to neglect our times of private prayer, devotion and meditation. Sometimes we are cajoled, sometimes we are intimidated, sometimes we are deceived, sometimes we, like Job, are tried by adversity. Yet all are merely tests, and if we are steadfast, looking always to God, we come safely through—very much the better for the experience.

Because we have been called to be torchbearers of the New Age, we must prove our worthiness. 'Many are called, but few are chosen' for this glorious work. God can only choose or accept for higher service those who are worthy and who have *proved* themselves to be worthy through tests and initiations.

You must not think from the foregoing that the higher life is all trial and stress. It is far from being anything of the kind; that is, if we overcome each of our tests. It is a life of great joy and happiness, and testing times are small in comparison. Also many temptations, trials and upsets are due to slips on our part. You will remember that Christian's foot slipped while he descended into the Valley of Humiliation, and, because of this, he had to have a fearful struggle with Apollyon. Later, those who came after him, whose feet did not slip as his did, had not to meet Apollyon. By keeping very close to God, and by being humble in heart, we avoid much trouble and unnecessary conflict with the enemy.

But our blessed Lord, in spite of the fact that He was victorious in all temptation, and that He always did the Father's Will, yet came to His Gethsemane. We, too, if we are faithful, come sooner or later to our Gethsemane. Then, we find that all that we can say is: *'Father not as I will, but as Thou wilt.'* When we reach this stage, we appear to have lost all; but in reality we have gained all. The great victory over self, the lower nature, sin, the flesh, the world, the devil, all have been forever slain. By non-resistance, and by obedience to the Will of the Father, the powers of darkness are vanquished. But not by fighting them. By non-resistance, they are allowed to discharge themselves and prove themselves to be impotent.

Our Lord has trodden the Path before us, opening up the Way of true attainment. He has shown us the way; all that we have to do is to follow, until the old nature is crucified and in its place there rise the resurrected sons of God. Ah yes! It sounds presumptive, but there is nothing truer than this, that we have become joint heirs with Jesus Christ and sons of the Most High. But only through great humility, along the way of the cross and by surrender. Not by vainglory, nor by self-assertiveness, nor by elevating the personal ego; but by humiliation through the eye of a needle, through the ready utterance, 'Thy Will, not mine, be done.'

Finally, through the way of surrender and humility, we glide

under ourselves, so to speak, and enter an enchanted land. A
land where we see through the eyes of Christ; and, seeing thus,
we behold things without spot or blemish. We see things as they
are and not as they falsely appear. Lo, the universe is filled with
joy unspeakable. The Divine Purpose is accomplished. All is well.

And now, beloved student, farewell.

'To him that overcometh will I grant to sit with me in my
throne, even as I also overcame, and am set down with my Father in His throne.'

'Thanks be to God which giveth us the victory, through our
Lord Jesus Christ.'

Yours in the Fellowship of Saints,
the Invisible Church of Christ,
HENRY THOMAS HAMBLIN

LESSON XXVI

CONCLUSION

The steps by which man enters the new life are three in number.
First, there is dissatisfaction with the ordinary life; a realization
of the transient, unreal nature of the world of the senses, combined with a deep desire and longing after the real and permanent, namely God. Second, there is the quest and the finding of
the Kingdom, the discovery of the true Self. There takes place
the Divine union: the expanded or Christ-consciousness is entered: old things pass away and all things become new. Third, he
descends from the mountaintop from which he has viewed the
promised land and returns to live his new life among the busy
haunts of men. Being changed himself, he finds others changed
also. In everyone he sees the divinely inherent, the Omnipresent
Good. In all the 'happenings' of life he sees the Divine Hand.
He knows that all things are working together for good. 'God's
in His Heaven, all's right with the world.' The third stage now

lies before us. No longer can we serve self, for it is dead: we can serve only the Whole. Everyone is embraced in our love and no-one is too humble for us to serve. To us is given the command 'Go ye into all the world preaching the gospel to every creature.' It is laid upon us to 'show by our love we understand'. It is for us to make known the Truth, that things are not what they seem: that all is well and all is perfect: that man is free *now* if he will only believe that it is so.

In all things, there must be that inward surrender which brings us into unity with the Father and the Divine Purpose. 'Behold I stand at the door and knock', says the Christ. To this call we must respond. By yielding to it, we enter into everlasting peace. The joyless quest of the human mind is forever ended: we rest in the Eternal love.

By living in the Spirit, and seeing in all men and women the Omnipresent Good, we help to bring It into expression. Even in the most depraved we can see the dim light burning, and by our love and sympathy help to fan the spark into a flame.

Thus, while living our life in the Infinite, we move about among the as yet unenlightened sons of men, helping them by our love and sympathy. We know the Truth: we know that things are not what they seem: we know that all is well; but we can sympathize and help those who yet believe in the reality of the unreal. Thus do we move through life inspired by this thought:

'I live my life in the Infinite, and the Infinite is in me.'

Finally, beloved, remember that 'the part' can only possess and manifest the qualities of 'The Whole' when in harmony and oneness with 'The Whole'. Of ourselves we can do nothing, but to the extent that we come into line with the Divine Will and Purpose, do we manifest God's health, life, wholeness and completeness. All things are possible to him that believeth. Beloved, *now* are we sons of God.

Remember at all times that your life is perfect as imaged in the Divine Mind. This perfect image is The Reality. Try therefore to live the real life, even in this world of unreality.

LIVE THE HIGHER LIFE

When you speak, visualize your Higher Self speaking in a higher and perfect sphere. Let this curb every hasty speech and glide your words along on the wheels of love.

When you sing, realize that the Real You is singing in the heavenly choirs. Let this inspire your song, and lift you above earthly and physical limitations.

When you work, remember that all that you have to do in this world is perfectly accomplished in the higher world of reality. Realize this and you can never fail to achieve.

In all that you do, realize that the real part of you is doing, on a higher plane, the thing that the material 'you' appears to be doing on this lower plane, and doing it perfectly. Only realize that your life is perfect in the Divine Mind; live in the consciousness of this truth, and you can never fail. Also the greatest difficulties which confront you will melt away like snow in the warm sunshine of spring.

HENCEFORWARD

no matter what may happen, nor what your circumstances may be, never allow yourself to cease for one day, either to

THINK RIGHTLY

or to

SPEND A SHORT TIME IN THE UNSEEN.

Thinking rightly is not only the reversing of every negative thought into its positive opposite but is the living of the thought-life in a new consciousness. It is living and thinking in the consciousness of perfect oneness with the Divine, of Infinite Abundance, Eternal Love, Perfect Health and Wholeness, Omnipresent Good. So long as we believe in evil, so long as we believe in lack, limitation, disease and poverty, these things will be present in some form in our life, for the outward life is but a reflection of our inward beliefs. Therefore we must live in this higher God-consciousness which realizes that love is all, that abundance is a fact, that good is all there is, and wholeness the Divine State. Living in this consciousness will transform our life and cause it to blossom like the rose.

The other vital and necessary thing to observe is to see that circumstances never deprive us of the privilege of spending a short time, both night and morning, in the Silence or Unseen. If once we allow ourselves to get out of this habit we shall find it very difficult indeed to get back. It is when we are in contact with the unseen hidden Reality that we renew our strength: we learn then to 'mount up with wings as eagles: to run and not be weary: to walk and not faint.' If I had the pen of a ready writer and the tongue of an angel, I could never tell adequately of the wonderful power of this communion with the Unseen. Prayer such as this works wonders and so-called miracles in the life. It has transformed my life, changing its unlovely desolation into beauty, harmony, happiness and peace. It has changed me from a mere encumberer of the ground into a willing worker in the great Divine Scheme for the betterment of mankind. It will do the same for all who make use of this wonderful regenerative power which comes only to those who spend some of their time in the Unseen.

PATIENCE AND PERSEVERANCE

These two qualities are essentially Godlike. Look at the persistence and patience of God's work in Nature and learn the lesson of 'keeping on'. We all feel, more, or less, the effect of the law of Rhythm. At one time we are on the mountaintop of transfiguration: at another we are in the valley of humiliation. When we are down we must raise our thoughts to the mountaintop. It is only our thoughts that have to be raised—everything else will quickly change correspondingly. One day we may feel fit for anything, and the next we may be worried, anxious and below par. When this is the case, it is of the utmost importance that we persistently raise our thoughts by treatment or true prayer from the slough of despond into which they have fallen. If this is done, we soon get over our bad time and find angels ministering to us. This fight and struggle are not against circumstances or difficulties, but against our own negative thinking. Overcome this and everything else is overcome also.

ABOVE ALL, MEDITATE UPON GOD

Although we cannot understand the Absolute, yet we can meditate upon our highest conception of God Transcendent. This we are able to do through the Christ within. Here follows a meditation which one of my students carries about with him in an ordinary notebook and reads at every available moment. When travelling by train he reads this, although to others he appears to be studying his orders and business notes. By this means his whole being becomes centred in God; and his life is demonstrating, in a wonderful way, the great truth that we become changed into the likeness of that upon which we meditate.

MEDITATION

After each statement of Truth, pause and realize the truth of the Truth. Where possible visualize what you are saying. Where actual visualizing is not possible, endeavour to *feel* the reality of the Truth.

THERE IS NO EVIL—IN THEE, OR LIFE'S PURPOSE: THERE IS ONLY INFINITE GOOD.

THOU ART THE INFINITE GOOD, THERE IS NOTHING BESIDE THEE.

THOU ART THE INFINITE PERFECTION: THOU ART ALL THERE IS.

THOU ART THE INFINITE LOVELINESS AND BEAUTY: THE INFINITE BRIGHTNESS, GLORY AND RADIANCE.

THOU ART THE INFINITE LOVE: THE INFINITE KIND PURPOSE.

THOU ART THE INFINITE JOY AND PEACE, THE QUIET HAVEN OF ALL WEARY SOULS.

THOU ART THE ROCK OF AGES, WHERE ALL WHO TRUST THEE CAN HIDE IN THE STORMS OF LIFE.

THOU ART THE ETERNAL, CHANGELESS, INFINITE, GLORIOUS REALITY. ALL THE COSMIC FELLOWSHIP OF SAINTS ADORE THEE.

THOU ART THE INFINITE ABUNDANCE AND SUPPLY: THE INEXHAUSTIBLE WEALTH AND PROFUSION.

THOU ART THE INFINITE SUCCESS, ACCOMPLISHMENT AND ACHIEVEMENT.

THOU ART THE INFINITE PERSEVERANCE, PERSISTENCE, OVERCOMING AND VICTORY.

THOU ART MAN'S PERFECT GUIDE IN LIFE, LEADING HIM EVERY STEP OF THE WAY.

THOU ART THE INFINITE WISDOM.

THOU ART THE INFINITE KNOWLEDGE.

THOU ART THE INFINITE UNDERSTANDING.

THOU ART THE ABSOLUTE TRUTH.

THOU ART THE INFINITE JUSTICE, INTEGRITY, UPRIGHTNESS, PROBITY.

THOU ART THE INFINITE LIFE AND HEALTH, WHOLENESS AND COMPLETENESS.

THOU ART THE INFINITE PROTECTION AND CARE. THOSE WHO PLACE THEIR TRUST IN THEE CAN NEVER BE BETRAYED.

Remember that the object of all this is simply to find the Secret Place of the Most High and to enter into its peace, and a realization that all is well, and that we are rooted in God and established in Eternal Life. This is the great 'treatment': to know God and to abide in His Truth. This brings about a Divine adjustment of the whole life. When we reach this consciousness, we are aware that all good is attracted to us, and is coming to us, and that all that we need is already ours, because we have entered the Stream of our true destiny.

Established in the Infinite, realizing your Eternal Nature, standing firm on the Rock, Christ, nothing can disturb you. As an eternal being, you are a Centre through which Divine Power flows, and a magnet drawing to yourself all necessary good. 'All the Divine Forces minister to you ... the winds are your messengers over all the world, and flames of fires your servants to fulfil your will, to fulfil your eternal joy.'

This brings us to the end of the Course. Before you lie infinite expansion and unfoldment. 'It doth not yet appear what we shall be, but we know that ... we shall be like Him.'

BIBLICAL REFERENCES

Hamblin's many biblical quotations, references and illusions are here listed by page. Standard abbreviations are used in the list, e.g. Ps for Psalms, Mt for St Matthew's Gospel, 1 Jn for the First Epistle of St John, and so on.

17 Hidden from the wise: Mt 11 : 25
19 When thou hast shut thy door: Mt 6 : 6
    The true vine: Jn 15 : 1
21 And the truth shall make you free: Jn 8 : 32
23 His own received him not: Jn 1 : 11
25 The Lord's Prayer: see Mt 6
27 Raised from corruption to incorruption: 1 Cor 15 : 54
33 Forgive us our trespasses: Mt 6 : 12
    All things are yours: 1 Cor 3 : 21, 23
34 He shall give thee the desires of thine heart: Ps 37 : 4
35 Thou wilt keep him in perfect peace: Isa 26 : 3
    Be still and know that I am God: Ps 46 : 10
    The Lord is my shepherd: Ps 23 : 1
    Come unto Me and I will give you rest: Mt 11 : 28
37 He doeth the works: Jn 14 : 10
43 References to the Sermon on the Mount, Mt 5–7 and Lk 11–12
45 Enter ye in at the strait gate: Mt 7 : 13–14
    Run with patience the race that is set: Heb 12 :1
    Rest in the Lord: Ps 37 : 7
    Still small voice: 1 Kings 19 : 12
51 The kingdom of God is within you: Lk 17 : 21
52 Faith is the substance of things hoped for: Heb 11 : 1

63　Christ is within you: cf Rom 8
　　Beloved, now are we sons of God: 1 Jn 3 : 2
67　Friend, go up higher: Lk 14 : 10
68　Power to become the sons of God: Jn 1 : 12–13
78　Be ye perfect: Mt 5 : 48
79　I can do all things through Christ: Phil 4 : 13
85　Choose you this day whom ye will serve: Josh 24 : 15
90　Where there is no vision the people perish: Prov 29 : 18
94　Set your affection on things above: Col 3 : 2
100　(Christ was in Hades): 1 Peter 3 : 18–20
101　God is Spirit: Jn 4 : 24
105　Cleanse thou me from secret faults: Ps 19 : 12
　　Instead of the thorn: Isa 55 : 13
106　Whatsoever things are true: Phil 4 : 8
108　I can do all things through Christ: Phil 4 : 13
　　Judge not, that ye be not judged: Mt 7 : 1
109　The mote out of our brother's eye: Mt 7 : 33
114　And the truth shall make you free: Jn 8 : 32
116　Reaping and sowing: a theme which runs through the Old
　　and New Testaments, but the direct reference is to Gal 6 : 7
118　The secret place of the most High: Ps 91 : 1
119　It shall not come nigh thee: Ps 91 : 7, 10
　　No weapon that is formed against thee: Isa 54 : 17
　　Angels shall bear thee up: Ps 91 : 11–12
121　The secret place of the most High: Ps 91 : 1
　　God is my defence, no evil can come nigh: Ps 91, Ps 31 : 3,
　　Ps 71 : 3
122　He that exalteth himself: Lk 14 : 11
132　As a man thinketh: Prov 23 : 7
136　Sell all thou hast: Mt 19 : 21
138　The pearl of great price: Mt 13 : 46
147　As a man thinketh: Prov 23 : 7
150　The face of Moses shone: Exod 34 : 29–30
151　I am the way, the truth and the life: Jn 14 : 6
　　I am the door: Jn 10 : 9

159 Transformed by the renewing of their minds: Rom 12 : 2

176 I go to prepare a place for you: Jn 14 : 2–3

177 The Lord God wipes away all tears: Isa 25 : 8

178 Our Lord tells us: the references are to the Sermon on the Mount, Mt 5–7 and Lk 11–12

180 Through Him we have access: Eph 2 : 18

184 He that seeketh, findeth: Mt 7 : 8, Lk 11 : 10

190 Give up our life to save it: Mt 10 : 39, Lk 17 : 33

191 Strait is the gate: Mt 7 : 14

192 Through a glass darkly: 1 Cor 13 : 12

194 Wait patiently; He shall give thee: Ps 37 : 7, 4

197 Seek ye first the kingdom of god: Mt 6 : 33

200 God wipes away all tears: Isa 25 : 8

203 As a man soweth: Gal 6 : 7

204 First be reconciled to thy brother: Mt 5 : 24

206 Sins of the Father: from the second commandment, and as in the book of Common Prayer

207 As a man soweth: Gal 6 : 7

212 For with what measure: Mt 7 : 2

214 As a man soweth: Gal 6 : 7

215 Resist ye not evil: Rom 12 : 21

223 Behold I stand at the door and knock: Rev 3 : 30

224 Behold, what manner of love: 1 Jn 3 : 1

228 Beloved, now are we the sons of God: 1 Jn 3 : 2

232 God is Spirit: Jn 4 : 24

233 The mote out of our brother's eye: Mt 7 : 33
If thine eye be single: Mt 6 : 22
Except ye abide in me: Jn 15 : 4

234 With God all things are possible: Mt 19 : 26
None other but the House of God: Gen 28 : 17

235 Hidden from the wise: Mt 11 : 25

239 The Lord's Prayer: see Mt 6

241 Not by might, nor by power: Zech 4 : 6

244 My Spirit shall not always strive with man: Gen 6 : 3

245 The Spirit helpeth our infirmities: Rom 8 : 26

246 How many hired servants of my Father: Lk 15 : 17
247 Peace of God, which passeth all understanding: Phil 4 : 7
250 Faith as a grain of mustard seed: Mt 17 : 20
255 In heaven the angels: Mt 18 : 10
Beloved, now are we the sons of God: 1 Jn 3 : 2
Be ye perfect: Mt 5 : 48
263 Parable of the talents: Mt 25
272 It maketh rich, and he added no sorrow: Prov 10 : 22
273 Rest in the Lord: Ps 37 : 7
283 Choose you this day whom ye will serve: Josh 24 : 15
286 Seek ye first the kingdom: Mt 6 : 33
288 Delight thyself in the Lord: Ps 37 : 4
He is able to do for us exceeding abundantly: Eph 3 : 20
289 Beloved, now are we the sons of God: 1 Jn 3 : 2
290 There is no health in us: 1 Jn 1 : 8
295 The Lord is my shepherd: Ps 23 : 1
299 Delivers us out of all our troubles: refs. to Ps 91
300 Agree with thine adversary quickly: Mt 5 : 25
He that doeth the will of my Father: Mt 7 : 21
301 Bless them that curse you: Mt 5 : 44
My rock and my salvation: Ps 62 : 6
304 Thou sayest: Mt 27 : 11
He openeth not his mouth: Prov 24 : 7
305 I go to prepare a place for you: Jn 14 : 2
A new commandment I give unto you: Jn 13 : 34
He that loveth his brother abideth in the Light: 1 Jn 2 : 10
Love is the fulfilling of the Law: Rom 13 : 10
306 If ye keep my commandments: Jn 15 : 10
He that saith he is in the Light and hateth: 1 Jn 2 : 11
307 Father, forgive them: Lk 23 : 34
309 Beloved, let us love: 1 Jn 4 : 7
311 Overcome evil with good: Rom 12 : 21
With all thy heart, with all thy soul: Mt 22 : 37
Sermon on the Mount: Mt 5–7 and Lk 11–12
314 If a man love not his brother: Jn

New Vision

is the bi-monthly magazine published by
The Hamblin Trust and started as 'The Science of
Thought Review' by HTH in October 1921.

The magazine has a broad perspective and has
a monthly theme based upon the spiritual course of
HTH. It is possible to become a member of the Trust
and receive its magazine and programme of events
free of charge. The Trust is dedicated to enriching
people's lives through positive thinking. It maintains
Hamblin's former home as a spiritual sanctuary
and welcomes spiritual pilgrims from
all over the world.

For further details contact
Bosham House
Main Road
Bosham, West Sussex, UK
PO18 8PJ
or email: office@thehamblinvision.org.uk
or go to:
www.thehamblinvision.org.uk

polair publishing

'the great little publisher for the new age'

THE WORLD IS IN MY GARDEN Chris Maser with Zane Maser
Internationally-acclaimed environmentalist Chris Maser shows
how ecological, social, personal and spiritual issues can all be
understood through the choices each one of us has to make in our
own garden. His wife, Zane, takes us further, into the world of
meditation. *Not available in the USA in this edition.*

ISBN 0-9545389-0-0 · £9.99

YOUR YOGA BODYMAP FOR VITALITY Jenny Beeken
This book has changed the way yoga postures can be taught,
because uniquely it works from each area of the body (feet and
ankles, sacrum and belly, neck and head, etc.) into a programme
of postures. It is particularly suitable for those leading an active
life. Sue Peggs' brilliant stop-action photography makes the postures unusually easy to follow.

ISBN 0-9545389-1-9 · £15.99

IGNITING SOUL FIRE Gaye Mack, MA
Spiritual dimensions of the Bach Flower Remedies. Dr Edward
Bach was a true mystic, and in this book practitioner Gaye Mack
evolves a new understanding of how the Remedies may be used
from a fuller understanding of Bach's life.

ISBN 0-9545389-2-7 · £10.99

THE SHAKESPEARE ENIGMA Peter Dawkins
Shakespeare himself let slip some words about 'both your po-
ets' which are the first clue in unravelling an extraordinary story
that puts the question 'Who wrote Shakespeare?' into a whole
new prominence. Peter's holistic approach is itself a huge contribution to enjoyment of what we call 'the Shakespeare plays'.

ISBN 0-9545389-4-3 · £16.99

www.polairpublishing.co.uk